GRANTA

12 Addison Avenue, London W11 4QR
email editorial@granta.com
To subscribe go to www.granta.com
Or call 020 8955 7011 in the United Kingdom, 845-267-3031 (toll-free 866-438-6150) in the United States

ISSUE 108

ACTING EDITOR	John Freeman
DEPUTY EDITOR	Ellah Allfrey
SENIOR EDITOR	Rosalind Porter
ONLINE EDITOR	Roy Robins
ASSOCIATE EDITORS	Helen Gordon, Liz Jobey, Simon Willis
EDITORIAL ASSISTANTS	Emily Greenhouse, Patrick Ryan
DESIGN	Lindsay Nash
FINANCE	Geoffrey Gordon, Morgan Graver
MARKETING AND SUBSCRIPTIONS	Anne Gowan, James Hollingsworth
SALES DIRECTOR	Brigid Macleod
PUBLICITY	Pru Rowlandson
VICE PRESIDENT, US OPERATIONS	Greg Lane
TO ADVERTISE IN THE UK CONTACT	Kate Rochester, krochester@granta.com
TO ADVERTISE IN THE US CONTACT	Emily Cook, ecook@granta.com
IT MANAGER	Mark Williams
PRODUCTION ASSOCIATE	Sarah Wasley
PROOFS	Lesley Levene, Jessica Rawlinson
ASSOCIATE PUBLISHER	Eric Abraham
PUBLISHER	Sigrid Rausing

In the United States, *Granta* is published in association with Grove/Atlantic Inc, 841 Broadway, 4th Floor, New York, NY 10003, and distributed by PGW. All editorial queries should be addressed to the London office.

Granta USPS 000-508 is published four times per year (March, June, September and December) by *Granta* 12 Addison Avenue, London W11 4QR, United Kingdom at the annual subscription rate of £34.95 and $45.99.

Airfreight and mailing in the USA by Agent named Air Business, C/O Worldnet Shipping USA Inc., 149-35 177th Street, Jamaica, New York, NY 11434. Periodicals postage paid at Jamaica NY 11431.

US POSTMASTER: Send address changes to *Granta*, PO Box 359 Congers, NY 10920-0359.

Granta is printed and bound in Italy by Legoprint. This magazine is printed on paper that fulfils the criteria for 'Paper for permanent document' according to ISO 9706 and the American Library Standard ANSI/NIZO Z39.48-1992 and has been certified by the Forest Stewardship Council (FSC). *Granta* is indexed in the American Humanities Index.

Granta is grateful for permission to quote four lines from 'Chicago' excerpted from *Chicago Poems* by Carl Sandburg, copyright 1916 by Holt, Rinehart and Winston and renewed 1944 by Carl Sandburg. Reprinted by permission of Houghton Mifflin Harcourt Publishing Company. All rights reserved.

ISBN 978-1-905881-12-3

ENGLISH
NATIONAL
BALLET

Christmas Magic at the Ballet

The Nutcracker
The Snow Queen
Giselle

London Coliseum
16 Dec 2009 - 23 Jan 2010
0871 911 0200
www.ballet.org.uk

National Tour Sponsor 2009

skyARTS

Supported by
ARTS COUNCIL
ENGLAND

Registered charity 214005. Photo Annabel Moeller

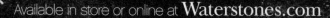

CONTENTS

Coming Night

It darkens, brother,
and your crutch-tip grinds
the gravel the deer stepped delicately along
one breakfast, you were a kid.
Mother says after thirty,
decades clip by
'and then you have the sum'
or spent it.

What was it like when the car
swerved on the ice,
what did you think of,
how long did you wait
in the wreck with the pain?

I see the sumacs by the turning space
turn their lank leaves,
the railway move to us
and the willows below us
and think of you turning nineteen,
of the deer, the sumac, trains, a wreck.

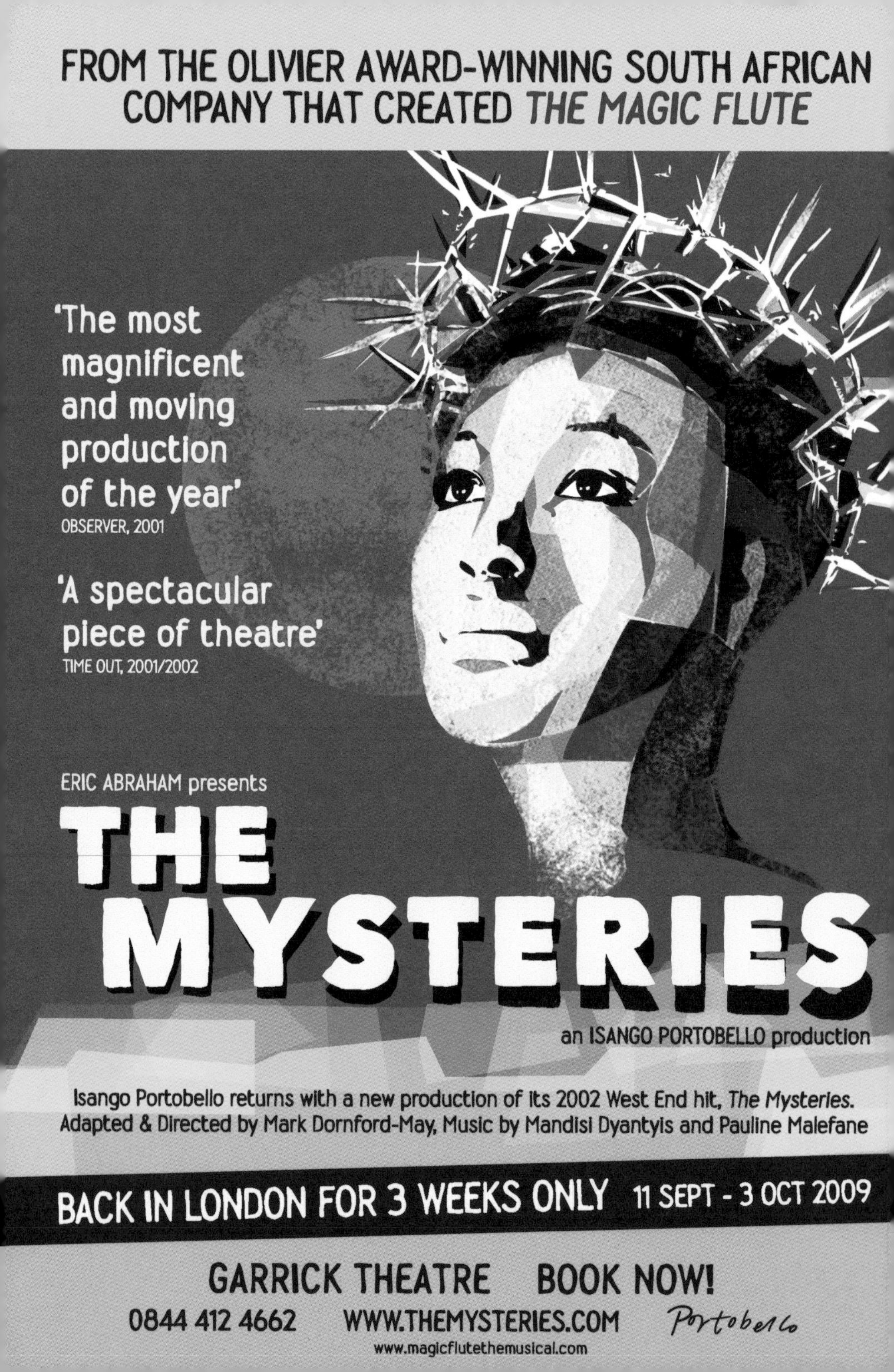
FROM THE OLIVIER AWARD-WINNING SOUTH AFRICAN COMPANY THAT CREATED *THE MAGIC FLUTE*
'The most magnificent and moving production of the year'
OBSERVER, 2001
'A spectacular piece of theatre'
TIME OUT, 2001/2002
ERIC ABRAHAM presents
THE MYSTERIES
an ISANGO PORTOBELLO production
Isango Portobello returns with a new production of its 2002 West End hit, *The Mysteries*.
Adapted & Directed by Mark Dornford-May, Music by Mandisi Dyantyis and Pauline Malefane
BACK IN LONDON FOR 3 WEEKS ONLY 11 SEPT - 3 OCT 2009
GARRICK THEATRE BOOK NOW!
0844 412 4662 WWW.THEMYSTERIES.COM
Portobello
www.magicflutethemusical.com

If God Existed, He'd be a Solid Midfielder

Aleksandar Hemon

First, a Little Bit about Me, though I am Not Important Here

I came to this fine country from Sarajevo, Bosnia-Herzegovina, in the winter of 1992, a couple of months before the war started. I did not plan to stay in the USA unless someone offered me a job, which crossed no American mind. I came to Chicago to visit my friend George and was supposed to fly back on May 1, the day the siege of Sarajevo commenced. Thus I got stuck here, no job or money, my only asset George and a couple of his friends. My life changed overnight and I became profoundly miserable: I watched CNN extensively and voyeuristically as it covered the slow killing of my hometown, and felt thoroughly disconnected from the world around me.

By Bosnian standards, I had been an athletic person. Even though I smoked two packs a day for years and enjoyed many an alcoholic potion, I had played soccer once or twice a week since time immemorial. But upon arriving in this country, I gained weight due to a diet based on Burger King and Twinkies and exacerbated by a series of tortuous attempts to quit smoking. Furthermore, I couldn't find anybody to play soccer with. Not playing soccer tormented me. It wasn't about being healthy – I was young enough not to care about my health – it was about feeling fully alive. Without soccer I was at sea, mentally and physically.

One Saturday in the summer of 1995, I was riding my bike by a lakeside field in Uptown and saw a group of people warming up and kicking the ball around. They might have been getting ready for a league game, but before I had time to consider the humiliating prospect of rejection, I asked if I could join them. 'Sure,' they said. That day I played for the first time in three years, twenty-five pounds heavier, wearing denim cut-offs and basketball shoes. I instantly pulled my groin and quickly earned blisters on my soles. I humbly played defence (although I'm a natural forward) and strictly obeyed the commands of the best player on my team – one Phillip, who had been, I learned much later, on the Nigerian 4 x 400 relay team at the Seoul Olympics. After the game, I asked Phillip if I could come back. 'Ask that guy,' Phillip said, and pointed at the ref. The ref introduced himself as 'German', and told me they played every Saturday and Sunday and I was welcome.

The Tibetan Goalie

German was not German – he was from Ecuador, but his father was born in Germany, hence the nickname. He was a UPS truck driver in his mid-forties, suntanned, wearing a moustache. Every Saturday and Sunday, he'd arrive by the lake around 2.00 p.m. in a decrepit, twenty-five-year-old van, on which a soccer ball and the words KICK ME MAKE MY DAY were painted. He'd unload goalposts and nets, bagfuls of single-colour T-shirts and balls, plus the flags of different countries – Ecuador, Colombia, Brazil, the United States, Spain, Nigeria – and he'd distribute the shirts to the guys who came to play. Most of them lived in Uptown and Edgewater and were from Mexico, Honduras, El Salvador, Peru, Chile, Colombia, Belize, Brazil, Jamaica, Nigeria, Somalia, Ethiopia, Senegal, Eritrea, Ghana, Cameroon, Morocco, Algeria, Jordan, France, Spain, Romania, Bulgaria, Bosnia, Ukraine,

Russia, Vietnam, Korea. There was even a guy from Tibet, and he was a very good goalie.

Normally, there'd be more than two teams, so the games lasted for fifteen minutes or until one team scored two goals. The games were very serious, as the winner stayed on the field, while the losing team had to wait on the sidelines. German refereed and he almost never called a foul – it seemed he needed to hear the sound of a breaking bone to use his whistle. Sometimes, if a team needed a player, he'd referee and play. He was particularly hard on himself and once he gave himself a yellow card for a brutal tackle. We – immigrants trying to stay afloat in this country – found comfort in playing by the rules we set ourselves. It made us feel that we still were part of a world much bigger than the United States.

I'd often be the first one to arrive before the games. I'd help German set up the goals and talk to him and others. In his magic van, German had photos of people who had played with him. I recognized some of the guys when they were much younger. One of them, whom everyone called Brazil since he was from Brazil, told me they had been playing for more than twenty years and German had been organizing games from the beginning, although at one point he'd had some drug and booze problems and had taken a few years off. But he came back, Brazil said. It was possible, I understood, to live in this country and still have a past shared with other people.

It wasn't clear to me why German was doing it. Even though I like to think of myself as a reasonably generous person, I could never imagine spending every single weekend putting together soccer games and refereeing, subjecting myself to verbal and other kinds of abuse, then loading up the van after everybody had left and washing a large number of T-shirts stinky with worldly sweat.

So I abused German's inexplicable generosity for years (outdoors in the summer, indoors in the winter). I'd often catch a ride in his clunky KICK ME MAKE MY DAY van, fearing for my life, as he was prone to celebrating the successful completion of a game with a few beers (he always had a well-stocked cooler in his van). He'd tell me about his favourite team (the Cameroon 1990 World Cup team) and about his search for a successor, someone who'd continue organizing the games once he retired and moved to Florida. He couldn't find the right person, he said, because people didn't have the guts to commit.

Once, during a blood-curdling ride home on the icy streets of Chicago, I asked him why he was doing it all. He was doing it for God, he said. God had instructed him to put people together, to spread His love, and it became his mission. I was uncomfortable, as I actively hate Bible toters, so I didn't ask him anything beyond that. But he never proselytized, never asked people about their religion, never flaunted his faith – people's belief in soccer was enough for him. He told me he was planning to buy a piece of land in Florida when he retired and build a church and a soccer field next to it. He'd preach and after the sermon his parishioners would play while he refereed.

German retired a few years ago at the end of the summer. One of the last weekends before he departed, we played in sweltering heat. Everybody was testy; hummingbird-sized flies were ravenous; the field was hard, humidity high, humility low; a few fights broke out. The sky was darkening over the line of skyscrapers along Lake Shore Drive, rain simmering in the clouds, close to boiling over. And then a cold front hit us, as if somebody opened a gigantic cooler, and rain arrived abruptly. I had never seen anything like it: the rain started at the other end of the field and then moved across it towards the far goal, steadily advancing, like a German World Cup team. We started running away from the rain, but it quickly caught up with us and we were soaked in no time. There was something terrifying about its blind power – its chaotic randomness. As it washed over us in waves, nothing depended on our minds or wills.

I ran towards German's van, as towards an ark, escaping the flood. There were other guys there already: German; Max from Belize; a man from Chile (consequently known as Chile); Rodrigo, German's car mechanic, who miraculously kept the van alive for more than twenty years; and Rodrigo's droopy, bare-chested buddy, who didn't seem to speak English at all, sitting on the cooler, occasionally handing out beers. We took shelter in the van; the rain clattered against the roof, as though we were in a coffin, shovelfuls of dirt dropping on us.

I asked German if he thought he'd find people to play with in Florida. He was sure he'd find somebody, he said, for if you give and ask for nothing in return there's bound to be someone to take it. Chile started saying something that you'd expect in a New Age manual – something vapid about self-actualization and unconditional surrender. 'And what if they are old and can't run?' I asked German. 'If they're old,' German said, 'they are close to entering the eternity, and they need courage. Soccer might help them get it.'

Now, I'm an atheistic man, vain and cautious. I give little, expect a lot and ask for more – what he was saying seemed far too heavy, naive and simplistic. It would have, in fact, seemed heavy, naive and simplistic if the following was not taking place.

Hakeem, the Nigerian who plays every day of his life, runs up to the van and asks us if we have seen his keys. 'Are you out of your mind?' we say, as the rain is pouring through the window. 'Can't you see it's the end of the fucking world. Look for your keys later.' '*Kids*,' he says, 'I'm looking for my *kids*.' Then we watch Hakeem running through the rain, collecting his two terrified children hiding under a tree. He moves like a shadow against the intensely grey curtain of rain, the kids hanging on his chest like little koalas. Meanwhile, on the bike path, Lalas (nicknamed after the American soccer player) stands beside his wife in a wheelchair. She has a horrific case of MS and can't move fast enough to get out of the rain. They stand together, waiting for the calamity to end, Lalas in his Uptown United T-shirt, his wife under a piece of cardboard that is slowly and irreversibly dissolving in the rain. The Tibetan goalie and his Tibetan friends, whom I had never seen before and never would after that day, are playing a game on the field completely covered with water, as if running in slow motion on the surface of a placid river. The ground is giving off vapour, the mist touching their ankles, and at moments it seems that they're levitating a few inches above the ground, untouched by the flood. Lalas and his wife are watching them with perfect calm, as if nothing could ever harm them. They see one of the Tibetans scoring a goal, the rain-heavy ball sliding between the goalie's hands. The goalie is untroubled, smiling, and from where I am, he could be the Dalai Lama himself. So this, gentlemen, is what this little narrative is about: the moment of transcendence that might be familiar to those who practise sports with other people; the moment, arising from the chaos of the game, when all your teammates occupy the ideal position on the field; the moment when the universe seems to be arranged by a meaningful will that is not yours; the moment that perishes – as moments tend to – when you complete the pass; and all you have left is a vague, physical, orgasmic memory of the instant you were completely connected with the world around you.

Michelangelo

Since German left, I've been playing in a park at Belmont, south of Uptown. It's a wholly different crowd: a lot more Europeans, thoroughly assimilated Latinos, and a few Americans. Often, when I get too excited, someone might tell me, 'Relax, it's just exercise...' whereupon I suggest that they go and run on a fucking treadmill and let me play the game the way the game's supposed to be played. No Uptown player would've ever said a thing like that, for we took our soccer seriously.

One of the Belmont people is Lido, a seventy-five-year-old Italian. Like many a man over fifty, Lido is totally delusional about his physical prowess. Topped with a lamentable toupee he never fails to wear, he's prone to discussing, after he loses the ball, all his brilliant intentions and all your obvious errors. Lido is a good, decent man.

I've retained the habit of showing up early for the game, ever tormented by the possibility of not being allowed to join in, and Lido is often there before everyone else. Sometimes he arrives flustered and annoyed, because he saw one of our American fellow players hiding in the park, staying away from us in order to avoid the uncomfortable pre-game chit-chat. 'What kind of people are they?' Lido grumbles. 'What are they afraid of? Such things would never happen in Italy.'

He's originally from Florence and proudly wears a Fiorentina jersey. In Italy, Lido says, people are always willing to talk to you and help you. If you ask them for directions, they're ready to leave their stores and houses unattended to take you where you want to go. And they talk to you, nicely, politely and not like *these* – and he points towards the trees and bushes behind which the shy Americans are cowering. When I ask him how often he goes to Italy, he says not very. He keeps a beautiful Ferrari there, he explains, and there are a lot of jealous people in Italy: they steal his wheels, smash his blinkers, scratch the doors with a nail. He doesn't like to go, he says, because people are not very nice. When I cautiously remind him that just a few moments ago he was claiming that Italians *were* incredibly nice, he exclaims, 'Yes, yes, very nice,' and I give up. It seems that Lido is able to hold two mutually exclusive thoughts without inner conflict – a quality, I realize in a flash, not uncommon among artists.

Lido came to Chicago in the Fifties. In Florence he and his brother restored Renaissance frescoes and old paintings, which are apparently a dime a dozen there, and when they arrived in Chicago, they started a business. He's been doing well since and he, as they say, loves life. He's been spotted with a young, endowed beauty or two clinging to his forearms or enjoying a ride in his American Ferrari. Besides the beauties, he seems to have had several wives and has recently married again.

Once Lido told me – after pointing at the Americans peeking from behind the trees – how dilettantes and buffoons ruined the Sistine Chapel ceiling, Michelangelo's masterpiece, under the pretence of restoring it. Despite my rich ignorance on the matter, Lido described to me all the errors they had committed. For example, they used solvent and sponge to take the patina off the frescoes. Lido insisted that I imagine *that*, and I did: assaulting the helpless Michelangelo with sponge and solvent. He got all worked up and, at that moment, cleaning up the Michelangelo verily appeared to me as a grievous act – I imagined a god far too pale to be omnipotent, or even powerful.

But those in charge of the restoration, Lido went on, realized that they had screwed up the creation of the universe according to

Michelangelo and begged him to come and fix it. Lido sent them a five-page invective, in essence suggesting that they shove the sponge and solvent up their asses. What they didn't understand, Lido said, was that the patina is the essential part of the fresco – that the world the Almighty created on the ceiling of the Sistine Chapel was *incomplete* until the mortar fully absorbed the paint, until it all became a little darker. It wasn't a sunny day when God created the world, Lido thundered. Without the patina it was all worth shit.

As he told me this, Lido was sitting on his ball (size four, overinflated) and, in his righteous ire, he made the wrong move and slid off the ball, tumbling down on the ground. I helped him get up, feeling the wrinkled, worn-out skin on his elbow, touching his human patina.

Then the sheepish Americans emerged from behind the bushes and trees, the rest of the soccer universe arrived and Lido – a man who takes any disrespect towards Michelangelo and the Creation as a personal insult – installed himself in the attack, ready to score a spectacular goal.

Whoever created Lido ought to be satisfied: Lido is perfectly complete. The rest of us must roll in the dirt, get weather-beaten, collect the patina, earn our right to simply, unconditionally be. And whenever I pass the ball to Lido – fully aware that it is going to be miskicked and wasted – I have the pleasant, tingling sensation of being connected with something bigger and better than me, the sensation wholly inaccessible to those who think soccer is about exercise. ∎

Driving with
Ed McElroy

Neil Steinberg

Ed McElroy with President Kennedy in the Oval Office, May 1963

'This is Visitation Parish,' says Ed McElroy, clear of eye, sound of mind, and eighty-three years of age, as he guides his black Cadillac down Halsted Street.

It is sunny, summer, Chicago. This South Side neighbourhood, the former epicentre of lace-curtain Irish-Catholic gentility, is quiet. The generations of politicians and businessmen who grew up and lived here have all died off or moved elsewhere, leaving behind their mansions and greystone three-flats. They radiate a certain calm and security, even now, carved up into modest apartments occupied by African-Americans whose mobility and power are not what they were for Visitation's former residents.

Ed is doing what he has always done – driving around big shots, introducing people, smoothing the grease of his charm and connections over the clanking machinery of the city. He has given lifts to cardinals, judges, police captains and baseball commissioners. He picked up John F. Kennedy at Midway Airport on several occasions, back when JFK was a senator, and squired around Barack Obama when he was coming up in the world.

I don't know where Ed's taking me now – some kind of school. I don't know why we're going, only that we've taken an unannounced detour so he can show me the neighbourhood where he grew up in the 1930s. I don't know when I met Ed – it seems I have always known him. I do know that when I got into trouble with the law a few years back it was Ed who phoned first. Ed, alone among everyone I know, found a lawyer and had him call me.

'See that vacant lot?' he says, as we cruise down Garfield Boulevard, a broad avenue with mature honey locust and American elm trees on the wide strip of green running down the middle. 'I must have played 10,000 hours of football there. I was playing football there when Gabby Hartnett hit his home run.'

That would be 'The Homer in the Gloamin'', September 28, 1938 when the Cub slugger sent a game-winning home run into the Wrigley Field stands as darkness fell.

Ed seems to have complete recall of every name, face and fact he has encountered in his lifetime. He has never had a drink, nor smoked a cigarette, tasted coffee or bet on a horse. His beverage of choice is milk or, if he's feeling festive, 7-Up. 'Your waistline is your lifeline,' Ed has told me more times than I care to hear it, since my lifeline is greater than his.

I don't know who Ed works for, at least not all of his clients. I am certain he is in the employ of the Metropolitan Water Reclamation District of Greater Chicago, which handles all the water that goes down a drain or through a sewer grate in the city and most of Cook County. I know this because twice he took me down the Deep Tunnel, the district's pharaonic, multi-billion-dollar, decades-long public works project, an enormous network of sixteen-foot-diametre storm-water conduits a hundred feet below the streets. When Ed brings the Water Reclamation District's president, Terry O'Brien, into the editorial board for a meeting at the *Chicago Sun-Times*, the newspaper I write for, and O'Brien thanks us for seeing him, I reply, 'Don't thank me – thank Ed. I have to do whatever he says.' It's a joke, sort of.

And I'm fairly certain he works for the Fraternal Order of Police. He has taken me to meet the FOP president, Mark Donahue, and invited me to FOP functions – plaque dedications, memorial services for slain cops, speeches, including one given by Obama when Ed made sure the future President and I were photographed together. The FOP banner was positioned prominently in the background of the shot, snapped by a photographer Ed had conveniently brought along. The resulting eight-by-ten photo showed up in the mail shortly thereafter, in duplicate, and is framed in my office. I'm glad to have it.

But Ed might not actually work for the cops. Given his affinity for the force, he might be volunteering. When he got married in 1955, Ed's best man was Timothy J. O'Connor, then Chicago's police commissioner. Frank Pape, acclaimed as 'the toughest cop in Chicago', was also there. He killed nine men in gunfights – they were all armed,

Pape diligently insisted – and sent another five he didn't get the chance to kill himself to the electric chair.

Ed's adventures with Frank Pape – incidents he's happy to talk about but doesn't want printed, even fifty years later – jar with the Ed before me, a lean, white-haired gentleman, not as tall as he was, with an enamelled flag pin on his lapel alongside a golden jewelled cross, the insignia of a past national commander of the Catholic War Veterans of the United States of America.

Ed's way is the old way – gifts for reporters. Bottles of bourbon at Christmas, cases of the product you are pushing, and gewgaws with your name on them. Every year Ed sends out a small, tasteful present – a clock, a business-card holder, a letter opener. The gift always features three decorative elements – his name, his phone number and an image of the American flag. Ed loves the flag. He has one flying from a fifteen-foot flagpole in his front yard, and another with a gold fringe, standing in a corner of his living room. And then there's the Fraternal Order of Police Chicago Lodge No. 7 ballpoint pens and official Chicago police card wallets he's always giving me. And the die-cast replica of a Chicago police squad car, a foot long, with doors that open and everything, which now sits on my eldest son's dresser, a present for his fifth birthday. Ed must work for the Fraternal Order of Police.

I used to introduce Ed as the father I never had, until an acquaintance said, 'Oh, I'm sorry, I didn't know your father died,' and I had to explain to him that no, my father is very much alive, doing fine, painting watercolours in the Rockies in Boulder, Colorado. It's just that he never comes around in a new Cadillac to take me to lunch the way Ed does.

It takes a long time for us to drive from my newspaper office at Wolf Point – where the Chicago river splits north and south – to wherever it is we're going. Slumped in the cool black leather seats of the Cadillac I tell Ed how tired and out of sorts I've been lately – breathing problems at night. He says he has a dentist who could help me with that. After nearly an hour of driving and sightseeing in Visitation Parish, I say, 'So this school, Ed – why are we going there?'

'Ed Carik – do you know who he is?' he replies. I shake my head no. 'Ed Carik used to work for Mike Sheehan' – the former Cook County Sheriff. 'Now he runs security for Daley Plaza. Ed Carik was a tremendous football player at Marist High School. Ed Carik's wife, Mary, is a teacher at the school.'

That answer satisfies me, and only later do I realize that Ed said nothing about the school itself or what its particular merits may be. Why should he? Ed is doing a favour for a friend and so am I. Ed McElroy is my friend. At least I think he is. No, I'm certain. Fairly certain. For a long time I didn't think so, assuming he was merely another publicist, one of an ever-dwindling band of ageing gentlemen who visited the paper to tout the glories of this or that.

They used to arrive in platoons, guys like Nate 'What'll You Have' Perlstein, who made his name ballyhooing Pabst Blue Ribbon beer at the 1933 Century of Progress Exposition. He once told me that if I wrote about a certain client of his, a plastic surgeon, I could be a guest aboard the surgeon's yacht and maybe get some free facial work. The offer seemed crass and I ignored him – you had to know how to handle these guys. They made the rounds, they bought the drinks, they pressed the flesh and fed you information. But the years passed, the media world shattered and fragmented, and the platoons turned to squads, then solitary individuals. And now it's pretty much just Ed. The idea that we were friends dawned slowly on me – he's thirty-five years older than I am, and the age difference threw me.

That changed after his eightieth birthday. His friends held a luncheon for him at the Walnut Room of the old Marshall Field's department store. Maybe twenty people were there, including a number of judges – Ed has handled many judicial campaigns. His wife was there, a trim, smiling, upbeat woman whom Ed often introduces lyrically as 'Rita Marie mother of three'. I was surprised to discover I was the only reporter, surprised to see that his son Eddie was seated at his right hand and I was seated on his left. That means something. As did his coming up with that lawyer four years ago, after an embarrassing drunken episode that made the local television news. Not all my friends stuck with me. But Ed did.

Still, it is a Chicago kind of friendship – a delicate interplay of favours given and received, of information offered and withheld. Ed is a friend who expects me to write about his clients in the newspaper, and I am a friend who expects him to pick up the lunch cheque. Though I may turn down an idea for a piece once or twice or even three times, eventually the chit becomes due and I have to yield or our relationship would begin to sour. He doesn't say this, but I sense it. If I fail to return a phone call or to pursue one of Ed's suggestions, if I ignore a judge running for election or pass on the opportunity to write about Terry O'Brien – a nice enough man but not a font of fascination – Ed will be mystified, even hurt. His voice will take on a tone of bafflement, an edge of irritation. I had to go with Ed to this school today – I had no choice, even though I was busy and didn't want to go – because I'd already cancelled on him once for this visit, and thus used up my allotment. Once is acceptable; twice would be an affront.

Ed goes to mass almost every day and never neglects – as he often reminds me – to say a prayer for my immortal soul. On Sundays he gives communion, and if someone noteworthy kneels before him – say our friend Illinois Supreme Court Justice Anne Burke or her husband, Chicago City Council powerhouse Alderman Ed Burke – Ed is not shy about sharing that fact. He carries a few spare communion wafers in a small gold box in his pocket because he visits shut-ins and the infirm so they can perform their sacred duty. He used to drive around Cardinal John Cody after His Eminence, in a fit of public poverty, renounced his car and driver. Ed stepped up at a party, and an informal relationship began, though Ed's motivation was piety leavened with more worldly concerns.

'I represented Blake-Lamb for eighteen years,' he says, referring to one of the city's premier funeral homes. 'I got the cardinal to commit to Blake-Lamb.'

Burying the cardinal is good for business. It also happened thirty-five years ago. Ed's memory is sharp, his language vivid, and sometimes it seems as if the past is ongoing, perhaps just around the corner, a few minutes ago and a few blocks away. Visitation Parish is almost entirely black now – a mile down Garfield Boulevard lies the second most dangerous neighbourhood in America. But as Ed drives down the street, it seems like his mother, his pals on the block, the five priests serving twelve masses every Sunday, the seventy Dominican nuns who lived at the Visitation nunnery, have just stepped away for a moment and will be right back. He parks next to a weedy lot and reminisces about the news-stand he ran as a boy. A pair of large men, in sideways baseball caps and enormous oversize T-shirts, amble in our direction.

'What's up guys?' Ed calls to them, in a confident tone that suggests he might leap out and toss them up against the car. They mumble something and move off.

Ed McElroy swings his Cadillac the wrong way down Sixty-third Place – a one-way street – coolly, intentionally, without so much as a flutter. A few minutes earlier he had sat at a red light for a respectful period, then, glancing to the left and right, accelerated the car through it. His licence plate is not the typical jumble of letters and numbers but '185'. He leaves his car in front of the school, in a buses-only tow zone. This is his town.

Inside the Blair Early Childhood Center, Ed doesn't so much as say hello before comparing roots.

'I'm South Side Irish Visitation Parish,' he announces.

'I was in St Dorothy's in Chatham, then I went to St Cajetan's,' replies the principal, Karen Bryar. 'I went to Longwood School.'

Ed takes a step back, eyes wide, as if thunderstruck.

'The girls from Longwood School!' he exclaims.

Blair Early Childhood Center is a school for children with disabilities – Down's syndrome, autism, birth defects. The halls are lined with a sobering train of wheelchairs, complex seating devices and heavily padded boards. We are taken to each classroom, introduced to every teacher and teacher's aide and to many of the 103 students. We see them eating, singing, being read to. Ed quizzes the teachers, even gym instructor Kathleen Houtsma, whose Dutch surname would seem to put her well beyond the charmed circle.

'A good Irish name,' Ed ventures. 'You didn't go to St Leo High School…'

'No,' she says, 'but my grandfather, Cornelius Houtsma, did.'

Ed brightens.

'He was a judge…' he says.

'Yes,' she says.

'His son was a football player…'

'My dad, Mark.'

Rosemary Cavanaugh doesn't need to wait for Ed to excavate her past. She recognizes him as soon as he walks into her first-grade classroom.

'I'm Paul Lawler's sister,' she says.

'I can see the Lawler right here,' Ed says, framing her mouth and chin with his hands.

'Your mother just died this summer,' Ed says, as if informing her of the fact. He turns to me. 'Her mother was beautiful. A beautiful woman.' Of course Ed was at the funeral – attending wakes and funerals is a duty.

'Before they closed the casket, my son Eddie kissed her,' he continues.

'My mother loved your son,' she replies, before moving on to lighter topics.

Occasionally a teacher's attention turns to me, and I have to admit that I am no one, an *auslander*. I was born in Cleveland, and came to Chicago to go to college in 1978 – thirty-one years ago, which in other communities might earn you status as an honorary resident. But not here, not in Chicago, at least not in the places that matter. Here, if you aren't from the old neighbourhood you might as well be from Mars. Nobody knows my parents, and while I am published in the newspaper four days a week, that is of little more than sporadic significance, a demi-fame that allows me to get reservations at certain booked restaurants. More than 300,000 people buy the *Sun-Times* every day, true, but Chicago has three million residents and I seldom meet anyone who knows me or cares what I do.

Nor is Ed particularly important. He is, as I said, a publicist, a driver, not an alderman, or a big campaign contributor, or a friend of Mayor Richard M. Daley, whom he calls 'Ritchie'. He has known the city's mayor since Daley was a child, but he is not close to him and hasn't gotten wealthy from him, two qualities that go together naturally – bread and butter, rod and reel, knowing the Mayor and making money.

Perhaps it is our common marginality that allowed Ed and I to become friends, to form this symbiosis, this partnership, a single strand of connection, one bond among a vast, constantly shifting network of associations, loyalties, debts and mutual dependencies that have built Chicago and allowed it to grow and prosper. It has escaped the rusty decline that wrecked other Midwestern cities – Detroit and Cleveland, Milwaukee and St Louis – and instead continues to build skyscrapers even as the recession hamstrings America, to contend with Tokyo and Rio de Janeiro for the 2016 Olympics, to be a 'world-class city', that buzz phrase that so swells the hearts of Chicago boosters.

Yet these bonds also undercut Chicago, these chains of obligation also weigh it down, hampering the efficient operation of the city and sinking it into corruption and scandal. How does new construction get city approval? A developer performs $40,000-worth of home remodelling work for an alderman, then the alderman signs off on the developer's project in his ward.

That isn't an imaginary example – it's what Alderman Isaac Carothers was charged with doing by the US Justice Deptartment this past May. (Ed of course knows Carothers and knew his dad.) A Chicago alderman is convicted of federal corruption or other criminal abuses almost every year – thirty aldermen since 1973. At one point in the mid 1990s there were four Chicago aldermen at the federal prison in Oxford, Wisconsin, quite an accomplishment for a legislative body that has only fifty members.

In our own small way, Ed and I are part of that. Ed is just doing his job, promoting his clients. But what about me? Does Ed provide my readers with a fascinating glimpse into a hidden world of Chicago cops and water reclamation projects, a view they might never otherwise get if I didn't keep his company? Not one Chicagoan in 10,000 has been down the Deep Tunnel. Or is this dull stuff, public relations pap that I occasionally buff to a shine and inflict on my tolerant audience as payment for a car ride and a steak lunch? Or is it both? Is the entire friendship just an elaborate snow job?

Corruption is a lot easier to see in others. Four of the past eight Illinois governors have gone to prison. One, George Ryan, is there now, for pocketing envelopes filled with cash, kickbacks from developer pals. Or rather, four of the past eight will have gone to prison once Ryan's successor, Rod Blagojevich, is locked away. In pure brazenness, Blago topped them all – he was the first Illinois governor to be arrested while still in office, handcuffed on the floor of his Chicago mansion by the Feds last December, taken away for trying to sell the senate seat vacated by Barack Obama. And he did so after he knew the Feds were investigating him.

'I want to make money,' Blagojevich said on tape. People were shocked in a town that does not shock easily. Just a few years earlier he had run as a reformer, a man dedicated to fixing education in Illinois. But Blagojevich should never have been governor in the first place. He got there, and quickly too, for one reason – he married the daughter of Dick Mell, a powerful Chicago alderman who gave Blago his political career as a wedding gift, the way other fathers-in-law will give their new sons-in-law a job in the family construction business.

And Illinois politics is without question a family business. Richard M. Daley, our all-powerful mayor of twenty years is the son of Richard J. Daley, the previous all-powerful mayor of twenty years. Todd Stroger, the president of the Cook County Board, is the son of John Stroger, the previous president of the Cook County Board, who contrived to hand over governance to his son with a minimum of inconvenience from the electoral process, by retiring after he had already won the primary – the true test in a predominantly Democrat county – and pressuring party leaders to slate his son as his replacement.

It goes on. Lisa Madigan, the Illinois Attorney General and governor-in-waiting, is the daughter of Michael Madigan, the mighty Speaker of the Illinois House of Representatives and Chairman of the Illinois Democratic Party. ('Mighty' is actually an understatement. Madigan is the state legislature, the other members mere puppets doing his bidding.) Chicago congressman Representative Daniel Lipinski received his congressional seat from his father, Bill, who, like Stroger, used a carefully timed retirement to spare his son a primary battle, but also recruited a sham Republican opponent for Daniel to defeat in the general election, thereby avoiding the risk of his son facing an opponent who might mount a real campaign.

We Don't Want Nobody Nobody Sent is the evocative title of Milton Rakove's oral history of the Richard J. Daley years, a line he heard a ward boss use when told there was a job applicant whom nobody had sent. That basic connection – the favour done for a relative, a friend, a classmate – is the building block of power in the city. One hand washes the other. Flip open the 1960 yearbook for De La Salle Academy, the high school from which Richard M. Daley graduated, and look at the faces – those are the movers and shakers, the builders and investors, of Chicago today, just as the 2009 De La Salle yearbook features the movers to come.

They pop up in the news with regularity. Robert Vanecko received $68 million in city pension funds to invest in risky real estate schemes. Mayor Daley is his uncle, but had nothing to do with it, Vanecko insisted. For his part the Mayor said he was shocked – shocked! – to find his nephew doing business with the city.

He said the same thing about his twenty-nine-year-old son Patrick, when the boy was found to be an investor in a sewer company suddenly awash in city cash. The Mayor – in most regards a doting and attentive father – knew nothing of his son's investments, an evasion that Daley's father would have felt was both unnecessary and beneath him.

Timothy J. O'Connor, Richard J. Daley and Ed McElroy, at Ed's wedding, 1955

'I make no apologies to anyone,' Richard J. Daley said, famously, in 1973, when it was revealed that millions of dollars in city business were being funnelled to a company employing his son John. 'If a man can't put his arms around his sons, then what kind of world are we living in?'

Can anybody rise by merit? Of course. In the majority of cases that is what happens. But the fix, the inside deal, the cut to the front of the line stands out, and a little seems like a lot – feels like the norm, even if it isn't. Ed McElroy's father was a dentist who died in 1930, when Ed was four, so Ed had to live by his wits, his boundless capacity for work and his social ease. He is a sober, churchgoing man who could be trusted, and who proved himself useful to powerful people.

He also lived in Visitation Parish. When Ed got married in 1955, two Chicago mayors attended – Martin Kennelly, the outgoing reformer, and Richard J. Daley, who had taken office the month before. Kennelly grew up on Poplar Avenue, around the corner from Elizabeth Alice Grogan, who would become Ed's mother. They knew each other all their lives. And Daley? Ed had put out campaign signs for his unsuccessful 1948 campaign for Cook County Sheriff, and was a loyal supporter. Daley – for all the criticism he received over the years – was a detail-focused politician who knew enough to take care of his people. If you wanted Daley at your wedding – and you did – Daley went to your wedding, but with the unspoken understanding that some day he would want something from you in return.

We are in Bridgeport now, historic home to the Daleys. Prim streets devoid of people. Neat blond-brick bungalows and four-flats, their only concession to the past half-century being the pairs and trios of satellite dishes perched under the eaves like resting birds, like flowers, faces tracking the sun.

'Holy Jeez, these places look good,' says Ed, as we travel down Fifty-ninth Street. 'Imagine how happy people would be if blacks moved in here?'

Ed is no racist – at the school he joyously high-fived and fist-bumped kids of all races, held their hands and danced with them. But there are facts to contend with. Race is the major consideration in Chicago – well, race and money, the twin electrical charges that hold our universe together, and Ed moves through different highly polarized worlds, from the school to the police department, where the number of black officers would need to increase fifty per cent to match the black population of the city; and the fire department, where older firefighters still insist that blacks don't belong because they're afraid of water and of heights. When firehouses were first haltingly integrated – a process that continues today – white firemen would shatter the communal coffee mugs used by new black colleagues rather than drink from them. Ed didn't invent any of this, but he has to live with it, as do we all. He is of a generation that notices differences. If a judge is Jewish, Ed will invariably point out to me that he is of my tribe. Signing off the phone, he'll often say, 'Shalom,' which at one point I found offensive and patronizing, but now just accept as Ed.

For lunch today, Ed takes me to Schaller's Pump. From the outside, it seems unremarkable – a modest two-storey brick building, a large welcome to White Sox fans painted across the wall. In the gravel parking lot, I mention that I was last here with a black columnist colleague who was hesitant to walk into Schaller's, unsure of how she would be received, though the regulars welcomed her once she went in.

'The only black you'll see here is the cook,' says Ed.

On the inside, Schaller's Pump is also unremarkable – your standard dim neighbourhood tavern that serves food, an elbow-worn wooden bar and a dozen tables. Patrons are older, all white, and Ed knows most of them. We are joined by Jackie Schaller, a tiny elderly man in a blue cardigan, less than two years older than Ed but looking far more elderly, shrunken, pale – his face seems like soft stone worn away by a river. His grandfather started the bar in 1881, and it has operated continuously ever since – all through Prohibition, which merely required installation of the peephole, still visible in the side door. Schaller calls Ed 'Eddie' and they reminisce.

'Who took you to your first World Series?' Ed says, and they both laugh. To St Louis, in 1946, to see the Cardinals beat the Red Sox.

'I drove down in my car,' says Ed. 'The Chase Hotel. A guy I knew took care of us.'

Schaller is cooler toward me. Despite Ed's company, I'm still a stranger, and a newspaperman at that.

Did Schaller know his own grandfather? I ask.

'Yes,' Schaller replies.

What was he like?

'Five foot one,' Schaller says, without a trace of warmth, and nothing more.

An older black couple arrives and is shown to a table nearby where they quietly eat. Times have changed, in some ways, and not in others. I ask Schaller how old he is.

'My birthday is January 15,' says Schaller. 'Do you know what day that is?'

I shrug – nothing pops immediately to mind.

'Martin Luther King Day,' Schaller says, with a quick flick of the thumb toward the black couple. There doesn't seem to be malice in the gesture – those days are gone – but maybe the memory of malice.

'Martin Luther King was always good to me,' Ed says. Ed was a radio announcer and newsman in the 1950s and 1960s, and attended all of King's marches in Chicago and several down south. Being good to Ed meant that King would always pause to be interviewed. Ed was probably the only marcher at Montgomery who after the demonstration had dinner with George Wallace, the segregationist governor of Alabama, whom he had befriended at the 1964 Democratic National Convention in Atlantic City, where Ed was assistant sergeant at arms.

'After dinner, Wallace had his car drive me to the airport,' says Ed. 'But I had them pull over and let me out before we got there – I didn't want King and his people to see me drive up in the governor's car.'

Jackie moves off to see after a big group of tourists arriving in the back room. Ed tells me a little about him. 'World War II guy, I think he got hit.' Schaller went from being an eighteen-year-old playing on the St Leo Light Basketball Squad and mouthing off to the priests to a solider fighting in the jungles of the Pacific. A common path for the boys of Ed's generation. They played ball, they went overseas, they fought, they got hit, they came home.

'All those guys. Overseas. Bronze stars. You couldn't get a better bunch of people,' says Ed. 'All out of Visitation Parish. In Chicago, you know, we go by parish. Especially South Side. Visitation – it's like the Pope lived there.'

Ed holds up his hands in amazement. 'Unbelievable, Visitation. So many priests came out of there. So many policemen. Commanders. Firemen. It was so friendly.'

Friendly, of course, if you belonged there. Blacks strayed south of the railroad bridge into Visitation at their peril. When a rumour ignited in 1949 that a certain homeowner in Visitation was considering selling his house to a black family, thousands of people – one estimate put the mob at 10,000 – surrounded the house for days on end. That story doesn't get told much at Schaller's Pump.

A big man with prominent ears, in khakis and a striped polo shirt, balding, sixtyish, glasses, walks over to say hello. Ed introduces me to the man, Bob Degnan.

'He's in the paper today,' Ed says, in an aside to me. Is he ever. The brother of Tim Degnan, one of the Mayor's closest friends, Bob just retired from a $116,000-a-year Chicago Transit Authority job, a position that was created especially for him, taking advantage of an early-retirement legal loophole that allows him to receive two government pensions at the same time, something, the article notes, 'particularly galling at a time when underfunded city pensions threaten to saddle future generations of Chicagoans with a debt they cannot handle.'

The newspapers create a momentary fuss, but tradition endures. Cronyism, nepotism, partisanship – they almost sound like religions, like they should be capitalized. 'I used to be a Baptist, now I practise Favouritism.' They continue because they are inherent to a society that has been based on the family unit for thousands of years and which developed a democratic government only two centuries ago and civil service a century after that. Every job that needs to be filled is power that can be used – to help a friend, to cement a relationship – or an opportunity to be squandered, picking a résumé blindly off a pile, with no guarantee that the guy best qualified on paper is any better than your wife's second cousin. I was against Lisa Madigan when she ran for attorney general – too young, too nepotistic. But you know what? She's done a good job.

'You want to hire some *stranger*?' Ed asks, after Degnan leaves, draping the final word with revulsion. 'You hire somebody you know. You come from a neighbourhood. How do you say no to people? People you played ball with?'

Another kind of system – a pure meritocracy where knowing the guy in charge eliminates you from competition – is almost unimaginable in Chicago. Here reformers are sneered at as the failures they frequently turn out to be. They are 'goo-goos' – short for 'good-government' types, but also evocative of the nursery where they belong.

Friends get friends jobs. They get their children jobs. You know someone, you go to the head of the line. Fresh from law school, Richard M. Daley flunked the bar exam twice before getting his law licence. By all accounts, he was not the sharpest tack in the box. Nevertheless, as a young attorney in private practice with his brother Michael he did extraordinarily well right away – judges fell over themselves to assign him estate cases, which generated six-figure fees. Nobody quibbled about his grades. Nor, it should be pointed out, did his father need to call the judges to wheedle or threaten. It wasn't necessary. That's just how things worked then, and how they work today. When the press caught wind of the judges steering estate cases to young Daley, and asked his father about it, the Mayor issued one of his trademark retorts: 'If they don't like it they can kiss my ass.'

Which shows you that true change has occurred in forty years. Nowadays the Mayor would never say that. Instead, he'd deny all knowledge of his son's activities. That's progress, of a sort.

Is Ed sincere? Of course, and so am I. Both of us sacrifice for our friendship. Ed has to take ribbing from cops when they ask him why he's hanging out with that drunk from the newspaper who's always writing nasty pieces about the department, how officers should obey the laws and such. He has to accept the occasional overly candid article, such as this one, difficult for a man who summed up my recent memoir by saying, 'You're telling on yourself.' And I am skewed towards subjects I would otherwise ignore, and forced to confront the guilty secret of corruption – it gets things done.

Reformers occasionally get power. Our current Governor Pat Quinn was a long-time goo-goo loose cannon who lucked into the lieutenant governor's position solely because of its complete marginality – going to pancake breakfasts and ribbon cuttings. Then Blagojevich was dragged away and, Cinderella-like, Quinn took charge. With his heart pure, his soul unstained, he wanted to do the right thing. But his call for a tax increase – the rejection of which will cause deep cuts to social services, including slashing health care for poor children

– was immediately batted away by a yawning legislature. Having never compromised himself, Quinn had no friends to help him. Ditto for his attempts at ethics legislation. If ever there were a time when tough ethics guidelines would pass, now, with one governor in prison and another on the way, would seem to be the moment. The ethics reforms went nowhere. The legislators didn't even bother with a symbolic gesture.

Being in Schaller's Pump buoys Ed – he is almost beaming. 'This is Chicago here,' he says. 'No place like it. These are neighbourhood people. It's like going to church.'

I hint that I'm ready to go back downtown. 'But I'm not done with you yet,' says Ed. We stop by his home in Beverly, where he and Rita Marie have lived for exactly forty years. In Ed's panelled basement office, I feel the heft of his collection of honorary Chicago police billy clubs. I admire photographs of Ed taken with every president from Truman to George W. Bush. I meet a pair of grandsons, helping Rita Marie with her gardening.

When Ed returns me to the paper, it is nearly four p.m. A long lunch. He is elegiac, as if sensing his extended hour on the Chicago stage is drawing to a close.

'At the funeral,' he says wearily, referring to the recent burial of a slain police officer, 'I didn't know ninety-nine per cent of the people. Captains, commanders. I used to know them all.'

'Times change,' I say, my stab at being comforting. We are in front of the newspaper now, with its view south to the river, the Sears Tower, the sensual green curve of 333 West Wacker. I thank Ed, wish him well and promise that I will see him soon.

As always, he leaves me with parting advice as I step out of the car. 'Stay sober,' he says. 'Anyone who wants you to get tight with them is not your friend.'

'Thank you for that, Ed,' I say, with less than complete sincerity. Later in the day Dr James Hogg – Ed's dentist – will call. Ed has told him I have some medical questions, and he wants to be of help. ■

Discover the
WRITER'S LIFE
In New York City

Over more than six decades of steady innovation, The New School has sustained a vital center for creative writing. Study writing and literature with The New School's renowned faculty of writers, critics, editors, and publishing professionals—in the heart of Greenwich Village.

Master of Fine Arts in Creative Writing
The New School's distinguished MFA program offers concentrations in fiction, poetry, nonfiction, and writing for children. Fellowships and financial aid are available.

Bachelor's Program in the Liberal Arts
Writing students seeking a BA may apply to the **Riggio Honors Program**. Students who are accepted into the program are eligible to receive a partial scholarship.

The Riggio Writing Honors Program is offered in conjunction with the Leonard and Louise Riggio Writing & Democracy initiative at The New School.

For more about the programs, call 212.229.5630 or visit us online.

www.newschool.edu/writing27

THE NEW SCHOOL

2008–2009

Director: Robert Polito

MFA FACULTY
Jeffery Renard Allen, Jonathan Ames, Robert Antoni, Susan Bell, Mark Bibbins, Susan Cheever, Jonathan Dee, Elaine Equi, David Gates, Jennifer Michael Hecht, Ann Hood, Shelley Jackson, Zia Jaffrey, Hettie Jones, James Lasdun, David Lehman, Suzannah Lessard, David Levithan, Phillip Lopate, Patrick McGrath, Honor Moore, Sigrid Nunez, Meghan O'Rourke, Dale Peck, Darryl Pinckney, Robert Polito, Helen Schulman, Tor Seidler, Laurie Sheck, Darcey Steinke, Benjamin Taylor, Paul Violi, Sarah Weeks, Brenda Wineapple, Stephen Wright.

Associate Director: Jackson Taylor

MFA VISITING FACULTY
Max Blagg, Deborah Brodie, Patricia Carlin, Marilyn Goldin, Vivian Gornick, Fannie Howe, Gary Indiana, Dave Johnson, Joyce Johnson, Mary Lee Kortez, Wendy Lesser, Sharon Mesmer, Marie Ponsot, David Prete, Lloyd Schwartz, Susan Shapiro, Jackson Taylor, Frederic Tuten, Susan Van Metre, Vicky Wilson.

Associate Chair: Luis Jaramillo
Associate Director: Laura Cronk

RIGGIO HONORS
PROGRAM FACULTY
Jeffery Renard Allen, Catherine Barnett, Mark Bibbins, Patricia Carlin, Elizabeth Gaffney, David Gates, Shelley Jackson, Zia Jaffrey, Suzannah Lessard, Greil Marcus, Sigrid Nunez, Honor Sachs, René Steinke, Lynne Tillman, Paul Violi.

An Affirmative Action/Equal Opportunity Institution

Seiche

Stuart Dybek

A seiche warning was in effect, prompting news accounts of the killer seiche of June 26, 1954 when a wave twenty-five miles wide and ten feet high rose from a placid Lake Michigan and swept seven fishermen from a breakwater at Montrose Harbor to their deaths. Atmospheric conditions were right for another.

Were the beaches closed? I'm no longer sure. In memory, Lake Shore Drive is empty, barred to traffic, as if awaiting a tsunami. That's how I imagined the seiche: a towering wave from a Hiroshige print, all the more menacing for its froth of moon glow, suspended for a heartbeat before dashing against the night-lit skyline. I didn't want to miss seeing it.

When I considered a vantage point, what came to mind was a single-storey utility shed in the shadow of Madonna Della Strada, the graceful art deco church on the Lake Shore campus of Loyola University. I'd attended Loyola on a track scholarship as an undergrad. Now, I was a caseworker for the Cook County Department of Public Aid. My district was Bronzeville on the South Side, not far from where I'd grown up. I lived on the North Side, in Rogers Park, the neighbourhood of the university, and I'd taken to going back to the campus on nights when I couldn't sleep. Lately, that was most nights. I'd never had insomnia before and wondered if the job was getting to me.

I'd dug out my old spiked shoes. An obsolete cinder track still circled the soccer field. I'd set up the hurdles I found toppled together in the nearly obliterated broad-jump pit, and run imaginary races until I was slick with sweat and out of breath. Then, to the tick-tock of crickets and lawn sprinklers, I'd jog from campus, along front yards, hurdling fences for two darkened, residential blocks to the deserted beach at the end of Columbia Avenue. I'd strip down to my jockstrap, drape my spikes and the T-shirt that would later serve as a towel over a crossbar of the lifeguard's chair, and wade out. A sandbar sloped down gradually and when it was finally deep enough I'd slide into the cool night water and breaststroke away from the city. I'd continue out without looking back until I'd crossed the imaginary wake left long ago by a priest I'd once watched swim.

At least people said he was a priest. I'd watched him the summer after my senior year in college, a confused, melancholy time when an exchange student whom I'd become more involved with than I'd realized returned suddenly to Beirut for the funeral of her grandfather. Her name was Nisha, which she told me meant 'dream' after I asked if it was short for Phoenicia. Her family in Lebanon were Maronite Christians. They'd cautioned her about American boys. She told me I was her first American boy and liked to ask if she was my first Phoenician girl.

I rode a cab with her to O'Hare on the day she left and took public transportation back alone. When Nisha and I checked departures for her gate, I tried to joke about not seeing any flights to Phoenicia. 'You'll have to stay,' I said, and she began to cry. We promised again to call and write. She didn't have a return ticket, but would be back in maybe a month, she said. At the international gate, while travellers hurried by, we stood kissing.

'No applause?' she asked. 'What's wrong with these people?' Then she turned and, without looking back, disappeared into the crowd.

After a week of silence, I called the numbers she'd given me, but the calls never went through, and the letters I wrote went unanswered. Each day I'd read the paper for news about the growing violence in Beirut and wait for the mail. Everything that summer seemed like waiting – I went to sleep waiting, woke waiting, read waiting, looked for a job waiting, walked waiting beside the lake.

The priest swam each morning, far out beyond the whistles of lifeguards. His arms, reflecting light, milled a steady crawl towards the distant downtown spires. Beyond him, the horizon drafted a perfectly level blue border. I assumed he launched his swim from a tiny pebble beach at Loyola. I don't know how far he swam; I never saw him returning. I wondered if swimming was for him a form of prayer, something akin to how the priests praying their breviary strolled murmuring through the lakeside park at dusk. He continued to swim after Labor Day when the lifeguards left and the beaches officially closed. He swam through autumn as the temperature fell and leaves rusted and windy days honed the waves to a metallic glint.

October mornings when the surface of the lake smouldered, I'd spot him, always at the same distance from the shore, like a man training to swim the Channel. There'd be overcast days when his arms no longer gleamed and the grey, choppy surface made him hard to see. I'd test the lake with my hand and try to imagine immersing my body into water that cold. I'd begun to wonder if, rather than prayer, it was penance or some form of mortification, not unlike a monk lashing himself in his cell, that drove him to swim. I tried to imagine his demons. He swam into November. By then, it was too blustery to walk for long beside the lake. I don't know on what day it became impossible for him to enter the water.

Now, swimming at night, years later, I consciously stroked beyond the boundary of the imagined wake he'd left in the water. Swimming would never be prayer for me, but I hoped it might serve as a kind of meditation. Instead my mind would work on what I'd seen in my South Side district. I'd think about Serena Wilson, an obese woman who'd insist on brewing a pot of coffee so we could 'visit like civilized folk'. In conversation, she seemed a caring mother, but her four-year-old, Deedee, had just had her third major 'accident' – a fall down the stairs – and I'd begun watching for and keeping a record of other signs of abuse. I thought about Mrs Hixon, a grandmother who, despite her own ailments, was raising her mentally impaired thirteen-year-old granddaughter, Alma. A year earlier, Alma had headaches so bad she was rushed screaming to the emergency room. They thought it was a brain tumour or meningitis, but it turned out to be a bean she'd inhaled months earlier into her sinus. The last time I'd visited, Alma looked pregnant. Mrs Hixon claimed it was just baby fat. She slid a butcher's knife from the knitting bag on her lap and told me that any man who laid a hand on Alma would get stuck like the pig he was, as would anyone who tried to take her away. She narrowed her eyes and added how from her windows she could see me entering 'that whorehouse hotel', as if I had clients to visit there.

'Don't think you're fooling anyone, Mr Jack,' she said.

I *was* the caseworker for the DuSable Hotel, twelve floors of disabled alcoholics, junkies and prostitutes – other names for the mostly young women addicted to crack. The cops wondered how I could go in there unarmed, and a few days earlier a package without a return address had been delivered to my mailbox. Inside was a small-calibre gun, its serial number filed off. I thought of Felicia Lavelle, an Aid to Dependent Children mother whose daughter, Dawn, had been diagnosed with leukaemia. Felicia was determined to get a college degree. Her dream was to go to law school.

I'd helped her enrol at Martin Luther King College and got her part-time secretarial work at the office of a lawyer who did pro bono work with welfare recipients, but she quit to become a cocktail waitress. She wasn't making enough yet to get off Public Aid, but she was trying. The last time I visited her apartment, the chairs and tables from ghetto resale shops had been replaced with stylish-looking furniture. The windows were opened and green silky drapes blew about the room. Dawn was in the children's wing of County Hospital, but her bedroom was waiting for her, redone in shades of pink, complete with its own TV and a canopy bed presided over by an enormous pink bear.

'Okay, Jack, you're wondering where the money came from for it,' Felicia said. 'You been straight with me. I ain't going to lie to you. I'm doing a little tricking on the side. You're not going to turn me in and mess up Dawn's medical, I know.'

I could have said, *I wish you hadn't told me*, or, *Be careful, Felicia, prostitution is more dangerous than commercial fishing*, or, *Have you thought about what will happen to Dawn if something happens to you?* I said nothing.

'Thanks, Jack.' Felicia said. 'So?'

'So, you're taking too many chances. You took a chance telling me; what if you'd guessed wrong?'

'Then I'd say, "I know you think I'm pretty, Jack." I'd do you pro bono.'

Each night I'd swim out further. One becalmed night when I thought I'd swum as far as I could go and still had something in reserve for swimming back, I saw in the moonlight a body floating further out. It's an optical illusion, I told myself, only a log, but the longer I studied it, the more it looked like a body, and when fish began to jump around it – I'd never seen fish jump at night until then – I was sure they were feeding on it. I forced myself to swim towards it, but it moved further out, as if it was swimming too. I'd been already breathing hard when I first saw it, and now as I swam I could hear my breath echoing out over the water. I'd stroke closer, sure I was gaining, and then it would widen the gap between us again, and the thought came into my mind that it was the priest, and I gave up. I'd never catch him. I never swam out further than that.

Each night I'd swim far out and then, treading water, turn and gaze at the distant, luminous gold coast and the slums behind it. I'd think how, if a sudden power outage knocked the lights and plunged the city into darkness, I'd be confused as to the direction of shore, and that fear would get me swimming back.

On the night of the seiche, the campus was deserted, but then it was deserted most nights. I climbed to the flat roof of the shed and looked out over the oily oscillation of water. I estimated I was well above ten feet but wondered if I was doing something really stupid. I waited, watching and listening for the slightest change. The atmospheric pressure felt like the weight of moonlight. Lake Michigan gently sloshed the pebble beach below – the same beach I'd imagined the priest once launched from each morning. I looked for the gleam of a log or a body, or the leap of a fish, but the lake was undisturbed water. I didn't know much about seiches. I believed they could swell without warning, as if the basin of the lake suddenly tilted, or that the water lapping the beach might be sucked out as if a drain plug had been pulled, before rushing back in biblical proportions.

From where I perched I could see Madonna Della Strada, a church whose doorstep was the lake. Before I learned it meant Our Lady of the Way, I thought its name translated as Our Lady of the Streets, which sounded to me like a Virgin to whom whores might be able to pray. The still summer night made the memory of necking in a side doorway of the church all the more vivid. It was the winter of my junior year and the Phoenician girl and I huddled out of the slashing wind off the lake. She'd wrapped her green chenille scarf around us. Her dark hair kept blowing into our mouths until I gathered it in an ungloved hand and held it to steady us as we kissed. We thought we were alone, hidden in that doorway, but when I released her hair and we pulled apart, we were greeted by an enormous, wind-blown cheer. The alcove of our doorway faced the dormitory at Mundelein, a Catholic women's college, and the Mundelbundles, as students there were called, lined their dorm windows cheering and applauding.

I waited for the seiche until three a.m., every sense cocked, eyes straining in the darkness for the sight of the great wave rolling in. Even after I finally gave up and climbed down, I kept looking behind to make sure it wasn't gaining on me as I walked away. ■

GRANTA

Khalid

Alex Kotlowitz

Khalid with his brother Mohamed

Early one morning in July 2003 I was woken by a phone call from a young man who I'd known since he was twelve. He was out of breath. He told me that the night before, he and his brother had been driving in their neighbourhood – a rough part of the city's predominately African-American West Side – when a burgundy-coloured car pulled alongside them. The passenger in the car reached over to man the steering wheel while the driver pulled out a semi-automatic weapon and, with both hands, started shooting. Fortunately my friend outraced them, speeding under the El tracks on Lake Street, and though his car was wracked with bullet holes and the passenger window shattered, neither he nor his brother, who had curled up under the dashboard, were hit. Did you call the police? I asked. There was a pause. 'Uh, no,' he replied. Tell me where you are, I said, and I'll come get you. They had spent the night in their car in a neighbourhood on the South Side.

I took them to the local police station where they filed a report with the uniformed officer behind the desk. She admonished them for not coming to the police earlier. 'They could've put out an all alert and tried to stop the car,' she told them. 'Now it's too late.' She also told them the police could no longer collect evidence from the car, not even the bullet lodged in the dashboard. My friends said they could identify the assailant and thought the shooting was related to a murder allegedly committed by their younger brother who was in jail awaiting trial. She suggested that if they wanted some immediate action, they should go to the violent crimes unit on the West Side, where the incident had occurred, and then she leaned over the counter, smiled and offered a parting word of caution. 'Now, I don't want any of that tit for tat,' she told my friends. They nodded. As did I.

I drove them over to the West Side violent crimes unit, which sits on the second floor of the 11th District police station. We were directed to a detective, who was middle-aged, white and dressed in shirt and tie.

He also had a small silver stud in one ear. When we arrived he was on the phone, leaning back in his chair, his feet propped on his desk. We stood and waited. Still on the phone he covered the mouthpiece and turned to me. 'Who are you?' he asked. I tried to explain. A friend, I said. They'd just been shot at. 'No, who the fuck are you? A cop? A lawyer?' he demanded. I tried again, thinking that maybe describing me as a friend didn't really capture my relationship with these two young men. 'Well, see, I'm kind of like a father…' Before I could finish, he snorted, 'Yeah, I can see the resemblance.' He then heard me out, as I told him what had happened the previous night.

'Nothing we can do about it. We'll get the report in a few days, and look into it,' he told me.

'But these guys think they know who it was,' I said. They could even name the assailants.

'I just said, we'll get the report in a few days.'

'But they're worried these guys will try again.'

'What d'ya want us to do, provide protection to everyone who walks through these doors?' When we left, he was still on the phone, leaning back in his chair, his feet planted on his desk. He had never changed position.

This is Chicago. Or at least the parts where trust has evaporated because of the absolute, unmitigated destructive power of violence. These young men had no faith the police would come to their aid and the police, in turn, didn't take these young men seriously. Not to excuse his behaviour, but that detective had undoubtedly seen enough witnesses unwilling to testify. (I know of two young men who are paralysed, in wheelchairs, but refuse to finger the person who shot them.) And my friends had undoubtedly bumped into enough police officers who, like this detective, expressed indifference verging on annoyance. But this is what results in a city – or parts of a city – where shootings and stabbings (mostly shootings) have become so commonplace that death has taken on a jargon all its own. To 'peel back' someone's head is to kill them, a reference to an autopsy where the coroner peels back the skin on the skull of the deceased. A 'black cat' refers to a woman who has children fathered by at least two men who have been murdered. Death has become ritualized. Young men get tattoos in tribute to fallen friends, often simply reading RIP or MIA – and then the name of the victim. I know an artist who for years painted murals in the apartments of public housing residents; he was often asked to paint tombstones of lost friends on the cinderblock walls. But there are more visible memorials. It's not unusual to drive through the city's poorer neighbourhoods and see makeshift shrines to the deceased – usually flowers, balloons and stuffed animals if the victim is a child or empty liquor and beer bottles (the brands preferred by the dead) if the victim is an adult, their contents having been downed by family and friends at an informal memorial service on the street. In the summer, these markers are ubiquitous; their appearance as assured as perennials.

Last year I came across a memorial for a young man who had been shot eight times. He had collapsed and died in front of a small clothing store called Street Gear. The killing had occurred a few days earlier so by the time I arrived the balloons were deflated and the candles spent. Friends had left a dozen or so empty bottles of Hennessey cognac, Moët champagne and grapefruit juice. On two pieces of posterboard taped to the storefront, friends had left their thoughts:

MAN RAPP YOU IN A BETTER PLACE NOW AND KNOW MORE PAIN SO I JUST HAVE TO SAY MISS LOVE YOU RASCAL

WE LOST ONE. HEAVEN GAIN ONE RIP J-RAE

DEAR BRANDON I'M SO FUCKED UP RIGHT NOW. I CAN'T START 2 EXPLAIN. I WILL ALWAYS LOVE YOU. YOU WERE MY ALL BACK IN THE DAY. YOU DIDN'T DESERVE THIS. I LOVE YOU. YO PUMPKIN

When I happened by, there was a rally – one of many that periodically pops up around the city – to decry the violence. It was mostly middle-aged and older men, and as they walked around the block, they chanted, 'We own the land. We own the land.' It was, to be sure, an odd turn of phrase, but nonetheless pointed. Ownership – of community, of one's family, of one's fate – evaporates in an amalgam of neighbourhoods where last year there were an estimated 2,012 people shot, or, on average, five to six a day. Of those, 412 were fatal. The fighting in some instances is so open that it takes a purposeful effort to avoid it. Many years ago, I arrived at the public housing complex Rockwell Gardens just a few hours after a first-floor apartment had been firebombed by a gang from across the street. Turns out they got the wrong home. As I stood outside the building and the police gathered evidence, a young gang member came up to me with hat in hand. 'Contributions?' he asked. He was collecting money to buy weapons for a retaliatory strike.

Here's the thing about Chicago: It has long had a reputation for violence. The international symbol for the city are two index fingers formed to mimic a gun, a reference to the iconic Al Capone who, during prohibition, controlled both the distribution and sale of alcohol, as well as the leanings and votes of politicians. It was a turbulent time for the city, but it was all – or at least mostly – in the name of control. Control of alcohol distribution. Control of politics. Control of turf. It's this reputation for violence that everyone associates with Chicago, this muscular place, which on the one hand can feel exhilarating and lively, and on the other can appear exotic and dangerous.

American cities like Chicago saw an upsurge in street violence in the late 1960s, in the aftermath of the riots that devastated our urban centres, first those that occurred during the summer of 1967 and then again the following year in the wake of the assassination of Martin Luther King, Jr. President Lyndon B. Johnson appointed a commission to examine the origins of the disorders and Fred Harris, a US Senator from Oklahoma and one of the commission's members, coined the term 'quiet riots' to describe persistent high unemployment, poverty and crime in our central cities. In Chicago, homicide rates jumped precipitously in those years and Cook County Hospital became one of the first medical centres in the nation to create a trauma unit, in large part because of the growing number of gunshot and stab wounds they were treating.

Some of it could be attributed to the rise of first black – then Hispanic – street gangs. Initially, in the late 1960s, the black gangs had won some standing among the establishment, and the city's most notorious group, the El Rukns, were seen by some as a catalyst for positive growth in their neighbourhoods. The El Rukns received over $300,000 in federal grants for ostensible job training programmes, and their head, Jeff Fort, at the behest of a US Senator, was invited to attend Richard Nixon's inauguration. Before long, though, the neighbourhood gangs turned to big business: the marketing and selling of narcotics. They had such control over the city that Chicago was one of the last places to be overrun by crack cocaine; the gangs had kept it out fearing that it would open up the drug trade to small entrepreneurs and thus break their grip over the market. (Fort, who was originally convicted of conspiring to misapply federal funds, is now serving time in prison for both drug trafficking and terrorism charges; he was alleged to have had made a deal with Muammar al-Qaddafi in which the El Rukns were to receive $2.5 million to bomb buildings and airplanes in the US for the Libyan leader.)

In recent years, the black gangs have begun to splinter, and now rather than top-down organizations they tend to consist of what is referred to on the street as 'cliques', small groups of young men who band together on a block or in a neighbourhood and answer to no one but each other. The Hispanic gangs, though, are still intact, and while they're involved in the drug trade, they tend to be more connected by their desire to protect turf. But the violence, to be sure, isn't all gang related.

The here and now feels both threatening – *and* beguiling. Over the last twenty years, roughly 15,000 people have been murdered in the city, most of them shot, most of them African-American and Latino, most of them young men, most of them in impoverished neighbourhoods on the city's West and South sides. That's nearly three times the number of soldiers who have been killed in combat in Iraq and Afghanistan. And it's mostly over petty stuff. Some of it, of course, is the result of disputes over drug turf or drug deals gone awry, but just as often it's the result of an argument over a girl or a craps game, or a misconstrued glance or a stolen pair of sneakers. Or, as is too often the case, because someone is seeking revenge. Murders have their own DNA. Two recent shootings could be traced back to an incident five years ago involving a damaged car. I attended those two funerals and the young men there wore bulletproof vests under their shirts; they feared yet more retaliation.

Such street craziness is not unique to Chicago – nor does Chicago have the highest homicide rate in the US (that dubious distinction usually goes to New Orleans, both pre- and post-Katrina). In fact, the number of homicides in Chicago, which peaked in the early 1990s, has been steadily declining, and yet in certain parts of the city the violence remains omnipresent. For reasons no one can explain, Chicago has been the epicentre for murders by and of youth, some of them notorious. They've served as markers for the city.

On October 13, 1994 two boys, aged ten and eleven, dangled Eric Morse, who was five, out of a fourteenth-floor window at a public housing complex. Eric had refused to steal candy for them, and so they dropped him. Eric's eight-year-old brother raced down the fourteen flights hoping he might be able to catch him before he hit the ground. That same year, eleven-year-old Yummy Sandifer made the cover of *Time* magazine when his bloodied body was found under a viaduct. Sandifer, who was nicknamed Yummy because of his love for junk food, had shot and paralysed a rival gang member and mistakenly killed a young girl while aiming for someone else. His own gang members were afraid he might snitch, so they executed him. In 1998, two boys, aged seven and eight, were arrested for the sexual assault and murder of eleven-year-old Ryan Harris. Again, it made national news. It turns out that the real assailant was a man in his twenties, but virtually everyone in the city had become so accustomed to children killing children that they assumed the children were guilty. As I write this piece, the local news is reporting the death of a nine-year-old girl who was shot in the neck while helping her father wash his dogs by a group of young men driving by in a van. Three others were hit as well. They survived. Chastity Turner was the fortieth Chicago public school student killed this year; it's a tally which, sadly, the local press keeps track of, a kind of measuring stick for whether the city is having a good year or a bad year.

Not long ago, I visited with a long-time friend Don Sharp, the baptist pastor of Faith Tabernacle, a mid-size church in a middle-class, African-American neighbourhood. Class doesn't immunize the congregation from the street clashes. He told me that two summers ago he was preaching a Sunday service when a deacon from the church came to get him from the podium: Don's thirty-one-year-old grandson had been shot. Even now, Don is still not entirely clear what happened, maybe in part because his grandson isn't either. But as he understands it, his grandson and two friends were driving to the video store that morning when they passed a group of young men hanging out on the street corner. Something about them didn't feel right to Don's grandson, but for reasons he can't (or won't) explain, the friend drove the car back around. One of the young men then pulled out a semi-automatic weapon and started shooting and Don's grandson was shot in the head (the bullet's permanently lodged in his skull). The other passenger was killed. At the funeral, Don told a story from the Old Testament about a group of villagers who mistakenly used poisonous herbs while preparing a meal for the prophet Elijah. 'Our pot's been contaminated,' Don preached to the deceased friends and family.

Don, who is seventy-two, is broad-shouldered with a commanding, baritone voice. He has a preternatural ease about him, an infective calm, and so over the years I've leaned on him for advice and guidance. I jokingly call him my Baptist rabbi: he's a wise man. But when it comes to the violence, he's at a loss. 'Why is it that violence has such a glamour to it?,' he asked, not at all rhetorically. 'How is it that young men don't fear death? It's almost a blasé attitude to death; to violent death. It almost gives one esteem,' he said. 'They're angry, but they don't know why they're angry.' But anger doesn't necessarily explain the shootings and the killings. For over twenty years, I've wrestled with this, looking for theories, for explanations that make sense, but I'm still as perplexed as I was at the first funeral I attended in 1987, which was for a fifteen-year-old boy shot on the lawn outside his highrise. The numbers don't begin to capture the havoc wreaked on the soul of individuals and on neighbourhoods, nor do they tangle with the discomforting fact that the vast majority of the shootings are of African-Americans and Hispanics by African-Americans and Hispanics. What to make of all this? I don't know that I fully know myself, but what I've come to realize is that if you're black or Hispanic in Chicago, it's virtually impossible not to have been touched by the smell and sight of violent death. It's almost become routine, or at least expected.

Clearly, the entrenched poverty of these communities contributes: lousy schools, weary police, decrepit housing, absent fathers, the lack of jobs. It's a combustible combination. To be fair, though, the violence only perpetuates that poverty, and it's foolish to think about alleviating the poverty without simultaneously trying to figure out how to reduce the violence. Amidst all the shootings, businesses shutter, the good, hard-working residents flee (if they can) and school becomes a refuge rather than a place of learning. The availability of guns are a factor, but again, they're no more (or less) available to those in the inner city than they are to those in the suburbs.

What is clear is that there doesn't seem to be a sense of urgency, especially among the rest of us. 'We're in the midst of an epidemic,' Don said. 'If people were dying of some kind of disease, there'd be all kinds of alerts, but it's become a way of life for us, and that's dangerous.' I'm reminded of a *Chicago Sun-Times* front page from three years ago. The banner headline read: MURDER AT A GOOD ADDRESS. The story reported on a dermatologist who was discovered bound and brutally stabbed at his office on the luxurious Michigan

Avenue. I admired the headline for its brazenness and honesty. It was one of 467 murders that year in the city, though the others didn't warrant such attention, mostly because who would want to read a feature with the headline: MURDER AT A BAD ADDRESS? In Chicago, the wealthy and the well-heeled die headline deaths, and the poor and the rambling die in silence.

Two years ago, I met Afaf Ahmed, a tall, stately, open-faced Sudanese woman who came here as a refugee in 2004. Afaf, who speaks fluent English along with five other languages, including Arabic, French and even a little Bosnian, had been an interpreter in Sudan, working for a number of NGOs and then for a Norweigan shipping company. She grew up in the central part of the country, which, unlike the south, was reasonably strife free, but Afaf, who chafes at authority, took offence at the difficulties that relief agencies encountered in the country and after she helped a Red Cross official who was under threat of arrest by the government flee southern Sudan, she was detained and interrogated. She then fled the country for Cairo with her son, Khalid, and remained there for five years, counselling refugees from the Middle East who, like her, were fleeing the rigidity, and sometimes the brutality, of their respective governments. Finally, in 2004, she decided to leave. With Khalid, who was then thirteen, and Alaeldin Ahmed, her second husband, she came to the US and settled in Chicago. She was seven months pregnant. Before they left, Afaf told Khalid that this move was for him – that this was his opportunity at a better life. 'I expect you to be way better than me,' she told him. 'This is your chance.'

Afaf first settled in the Albany Park neighbourhood, a portal for new immigrants, but became concerned about the open-air drug dealing, so she moved to Logan Square, a traditionally Latino neighbourhood with handsome and sturdy brick homes. Over the past ten years or so, young professionals with children have moved in, though it remains an unusual mixture of classes, ethnic groups and generations and as a result is one of the city's more lively and interesting communities. Afaf rented an apartment on the first floor of a two-storey flat. Upstairs lived Mark Evans, her landlord, a man in his forties who had grown up on a farm in central Illinois. Afaf quickly befriended Evans and the two of them periodically shared meals together, with Afaf cooking traditional Sudanese dishes or Evans barbecuing in the backyard.

It soon became clear to Afaf that her son was having trouble fitting in. His English was spotty at best, and so he felt like an outsider. He was convinced that others at school were laughing at him; he felt bullied and on one occasion he came home with a broken middle finger after another student tried to wrest a dollar bill from his closed fist. Afaf and Alaeldin worked hard to teach Khalid English and would try not to speak much Arabic at home. Khalid, not surprisingly, found comfort in the presence of other new immigrants, and so Afaf enrolled him in an after-school circus programme which catered to new arrivals. There, while learning to ride a unicycle and to juggle, he took English classes. On the street, he began hanging around with young Latinos, most of them immigrants from Mexico, though he also became friends with two brothers who had emigrated from Cuba. On the street, Khalid became known as 'Egypt' because as he learned English he talked endlessly about the country – about swimming in the Mediterranean, about riding camels in the Pyramids – to anyone who would listen. Most of his friends didn't know his real name.

As it turned out, the two brothers from Cuba belonged to the Maniac Latin Disciples, one of a score of street gangs in the city, and one afternoon as Khalid was driving with two other members of the MLDs (as they're referred to on the street), they got pulled over by the police. One of the older gang members handed his pistol to Khalid, assuring him that since he was underage he'd be treated leniently. Afaf, though, pleaded with the juvenile court judge to lock him up and Khalid spent thirty days behind bars. She felt he needed to be off the streets, away from the ruffians he was hanging out with. Then Afaf moved out of Logan Square to an apartment building farther north, hoping to extradite Khalid's ties with the gang. 'If I was running a gang,' Afaf told me, 'I wouldn't want Khalid. He was very childish. He just wanted to fit in.'

On the evening of July 7, 2006, Khalid left his mother's house. It was a Friday and he told Afaf that he planned to spend the weekend at an evangelical Christian camp in Indiana. Given the large number of refugees and immigrants in Chicago, missionaries ply their craft and every Saturday morning the presiding minister of the camp in Indiana would send a bus into Chicago to pick up youngsters for a weekend of activities. Afaf had already lost a friend to street violence and so she was attentive to her son, making sure he was not spending time on the streets, especially not with the brothers from Cuba, one of whom – Jorge Pena – had taken Khalid under his wing. Jorge was a baby faced, ponytailed young man whose street name was, like Khalid's, the name of his last home, 'Cuba'. 'He had eyes like a snake,' Afaf told me. 'They were without expression.' She did what she could to discourage Khalid from spending time with him. She worried about the streets, especially because a month earlier Mark Evans had been murdered, apparently forced out of his apartment late at night in a robbery attempt, shot three times and left to die in the middle of the street by his home.

That Sunday, Afaf got a call from a friend of Khalid's saying that her son had been arrested. She began phoning police stations on the North Side. By the time Monday came around, she was directed to the morgue, where she learned that sometime over the weekend her son had been shot, six times – two of the bullets penetrating his chest, a third lodged in his abdomen.

I first met Afaf six months after Khalid's murder. We began to see one another regularly, often for lunch at a local Ethiopian restaurant where the cooking made Afaf feel close to home. She was constantly agitated, angry at anyone she thought wasn't working hard or fast enough to solve her son's killing. She had so alienated the young detective in the case that an older detective had to step in to act as an intermediary. Afaf made repeated visits to the site of the murder, a desolate spot behind a garage in an alley. On her first visit, she found fifty candles laid out, fresh flowers and writings of farewell scrawled on the garage door. There she ran into a petite thirteen-year-old girl, Genassia, who had attached a quarter-sized, battery-operated green light to the garage door. She told Afaf that Khalid had told her about the Muslim religion's affinity for the colour green (it signifies nature and is incorporated into many flags of Muslim nations). Aside from the murderer, Genassia, it turned out, had been the last to see Khalid alive. They'd been walking together late that Friday night and she had tried to get him to join her at Burger King, but he said he needed to be somewhere. He then went down this alley and Genassia, as she walked away, heard six shots. Afaf gave Genassia's name to the police.

Afaf seemed invigorated by her own private detective work, but that soon dissipated as the case stalled, and in the weeks and months to come she pulled into herself, her face tightening like a fist. There would be afternoons I'd stop by and she'd still be in her nightgown, curled up on the couch in her compact living room, smoking, her hair uncombed. She looked as if she were wilting. Unwashed dishes lay cluttered around the kitchen sink. In need of money, she sold various items from the house, including her television and some furniture. The house got emptier and emptier. She said, 'If I can't protect my son, I'm worth nothing.' At one point, she checked herself into a psychiatric ward at a local hospital. She seemed uncharacteristically impatient with her other son Mohamed, who was not quite two when Khalid died. She became so depressed, so inward, so sour that – and I'm not proud to admit this – I began to go around less.

Let me state the obvious: Murder of a loved one or friend can sap the life out of an otherwise spirited person. It depletes the soul. How does one try to make sense of the nonsensical? Last year, shortly after two students at the Community Christian Alternative Academy in North Lawndale were killed on the streets within six weeks of each other, the school's principal, Myra Sampson, told me she was at a loss as to what to do. 'I can't tell you the number of kids who have stopped me in the hallway and told me "I'm going to be next",' she said. 'They're in such a heightened state of arousal, they can't learn.' One boy had to be hospitalized; he was having auditory hallucinations that one of the deceased students was talking to him. 'What's going to be the impact of having a group of young adults who shut off?'

Too often these neighbourhoods are compared to war zones, but that feels too glib, too facile. There are significant differences. Unlike those at war, people living in neighbourhoods like Chicago's Englewood or Garfield Park or Logan Square, demonstrate no belief that someday there may be a resolution. There is no promise of victory or threat of defeat; there is no sense of a people coalescing around a cause. To the contrary, people disappear into themselves. They retreat. They stay indoors. They don't talk with neighbours. They keep friends to an absolute minimum (often children speak of having 'associates' not friends). This is precisely what happened to Afaf. 'I was a very funny, very pleasant person, but this has consumed me,' she said, apologizing for not being better company. 'I'm alone now. Nobody wants to be with me. It's like lenses. I see everything through this tragedy.'

Finally, the police arrested Jorge Pena, but even this brought Afaf surprisingly little solace. Moreover, the story behind the killing made Afaf defensive, if not angry and confused. The police had learned that Cuba, Khalid and two others had gone to Mark Evans's house to rob him and tried to march him to an ATM machine. When Evans ran, Cuba allegedly shot him multiple times. Khalid was clearly shaken by the incident (according to one of the participants, Khalid wet his pants right after the shooting) and in the following days he hinted to friends about the murder. He couldn't help himself. It was as if he needed to relieve himself of it. Cuba repeatedly warned Khalid to remain quiet about the incident, once allegedly admonishing him, 'You talk too much. Shut the fuck up.' But Khalid couldn't. Around midnight on July 7, Cuba lured Khalid into the alley and shot him six times, his body eventually resting by the blood-spattered garage door. As he lay dying, Cuba allegedly held him and whispered, 'I love you, Khalid. But I had to do it.'

After the arrest Afaf withdrew. She no longer had her amateur detective work to occupy her and she lost her job working with immigrant children. She then decided to open a small Sudanese restaurant and she and Alaeldin leased a narrow storefront across the street from a local high school and spent much of the summer of 2008 fixing it up, painting the walls and installing a used sink and refrigerator. But as it turned out they didn't have the money for a licence nor, for that matter, for the personnel and equipment, and so had to abandon the idea before the restuarant ever opened. Afaf stopped answering the phone and when she did she'd decline my (increasingly infrequent) invitations for lunch. I offered to bring food by but she said she had an appetite only for sand.

For weeks, Afaf had had a bitter, almost metallic, taste in her mouth. She couldn't rid herself of it and it only intensified when she ate, so she stopped eating. She told me that the only thing that helped was candy she could suck on, but even that only diminished the bitterness and didn't erase it. One day when she had taken Mohamed to Lake Michigan, she reached into her pockets and realized she'd forgotten to bring any candy. The metallic taste was unusually strong so she scooped up a small handful of sand and slowly sucked on it. It took away the bitterness. The sand gave her taste. It is, I suppose, the equivalent of finding solace in an empty room. It was the only joy – albeit a muted one – she could find. She purchased bags of play sand from Home Depot and told her husband it was for their son to play in, but when he discovered that she had been eating it, he began cooking elaborate Sudanese meals, mostly lamb, which Afaf ordinarily savoured, but nothing kept that bitterness away like the sand. She had to stop a few months later when her doctor informed her of an alarming iron deficiency. 'This tragedy is like my shadow,' she told me, 'I'm trying to save what is left of me.'

As the attorneys selected a jury at the first day of Jorge Pena's trial this past summer, Afaf and I sat in a windowless room in the prosecutor's office. Afaf looked surprisingly refreshed, resplendent in a black turtleneck and a black-and-white scarf wrapped elegantly about her neck. Afaf is nearly six feet, and yet I don't think I had ever fully noticed her height. She stood straight backed, proud, her braided hair pulled back into a ponytail, not unlike the photographs she had shown me of her in Cairo in a colourful *tob* and headdress, when she seemed almost defiant as she towered over her friends. We were soon joined by Genassia, the girl who was the last to see Khalid. She's now sixteen, still waiflike and nervous – talking fast, cracking knuckles – but with an admirable straightness about her, an innocent bluntness.

'Did Egypt have a little brother?' Genassia asked. 'He used to talk about him all the time.'

Afaf began to cry. 'Why'd you come forward?' she asked. Genassia told her that the night of the murder she had trouble sleeping. Eventually she fell asleep on the couch where she dreamed that Khalid asked for her help. Genassia also told us that Pena had warned her against cooperating with the police, but she chose to anyway. (When she later took the stand, she couldn't look at Pena, not even to identify him, and was clearly nervous, one leg bouncing with such force it shook her whole body.) She told Afaf that she had a baby last year. Afaf covered her face in dismay. 'So young,' she muttered. 'Who's the father?'

'He's in jail,' Genassia replied.

'Who is he, one of Khalid's friends?'

'No, I met him in school.'

'Are you breastfeeding?'

'No, I was smoking cigarettes so they didn't want me to.'

Afaf offered Genassia to stay with her for a while, at least to hide from Pena and his family. 'I will call you,' Afaf told Genassia. 'And help take care of your baby.' Afaf paused. 'Why did he kill Khalid?'

'They used to pick on him all the time,' Genassia said. 'If he had money, they'd take it. I told him to stop hanging out with them but he said, "No, no, they like me".' (At the trial, Genassia testified that Khalid ordered her not to follow him into the alley; Afaf suspects he knew what awaited him.) Afaf repeated her offer to have Genassia and her baby stay with her for a while, especially because it would get her out of the neighbourhood, away from Pena's fellow gang members.

It is, I suppose, the paradox of murder, of the ultimate act one human being can commit against another. It breaks apart families, communities, the human spirit. But in unexpected ways it can also connect us. I know of a rural white police officer in Michigan who once discovered a young black man, a shooting victim, dumped along a local highway. Since the victim was from Grand Rapids, the officer had to travel an hour south to investigate the killing and in the process he befriended the victim's sister. They helped each other and once he solved the case, the two became quite close, this rural white cop and this urban African-American woman. They became like father and daughter. He attended her wedding and she comes to speak to a criminal justice class he teaches at the local community college. She calls him 'dad'. Afaf seemed rejuvenated by the trial and while she says it was because she so desperately wanted some kind of justice, I suspect it also made her feel less alone.

The next day of the trial, she met the parents of Mark Evans. Until that day, Afaf had seemed unable to accept her son's role in Mark Evans's murder, and for Evans's parents it had been a difficult two years. In their grief, they leaned on a group called Parents of Murdered Children, a peculiarly American assemblage. Both are retired farmers and told me they weren't sure how they'd feel about meeting Afaf, but very quickly it became apparent they needed each other. Afaf embraced Pattie Evans outside the courtroom, not wanting to let go; she relayed her stories about their son, about his generosity and good nature (about how he didn't ask for a security deposit from Afaf and how forgiving he was when she couldn't pay the rent on time). Throughout parts of the trial, Afaf and Pattie sat next to each other, hand in hand. Pattie, at one point, told me she wasn't sure how she would receive Afaf, but her presence, she told me, 'was a reassurance. We were just two grieving mothers'.

During the trial, when the prosecution was about to present the jury with photographs of the crime scene, a woman from the prosecutor's office tapped Afaf on the shoulder and suggested that she might want to step out of the courtroom. Afaf shook her head. ('The thing about Africans, we move on,' she later said.) The photographs

GRANTA
THE MAGAZINE OF NEW WRITING

Make a gift of good writing with a Granta subscription
– fiction, reportage, memoir, biography and photography five times a year

Buy a twelve-month subscription for a friend and receive, with our compliments, a *Granta* special-edition **MOLESKINE**® notebook

Subscribe online at **www.granta.com** or on **Freephone 0500 004 033** or fill in the **back of this card** and send to us

'With each new issue, Granta *enhances its reputation for presenting, in unequalled range and depth, the best contemporary writers in journalism and fiction.'*
SUNDAY TIMES

USE THIS CARD IF YOU ARE SUBSCRIBING FROM THE UK, EUROPE AND THE REST OF THE WORLD (WITH THE EXCEPTION OF THE USA, CANADA, CENTRAL AND SOUTH AMERICA.)

Gift subscription offer: take out an annual subscription as a gift and you will also receive a complimentary *Granta* special-edition **MOLESKINE**® notebook

GIFT SUBSCRIPTION 1

Address:

TITLE: INITIAL: SURNAME:

ADDRESS:

POSTCODE:

TELEPHONE: EMAIL:

GIFT SUBSCRIPTION 2

Address:

TITLE: INITIAL: SURNAME:

ADDRESS:

POSTCODE:

TELEPHONE: EMAIL:

YOUR ADDRESS FOR BILLING

TITLE: INITIAL: SURNAME:

ADDRESS:

POSTCODE:

TELEPHONE: EMAIL:

NUMBER OF SUBSCRIPTIONS	DELIVERY REGION	PRICE	
☐	UK	£34.95	All prices include delivery
☐	Europe	£39.95	YOUR TWELVE-MONTH SUBSCRIPTION
☐	Rest of World	£45.95	WILL INCLUDE FOUR ISSUES

I would like my subscription to start from:
☐ the current issue   ☐ the next issue

PAYMENT DETAILS

☐ I enclose a cheque payable to '*Granta*' for £ _____ for ____ subscriptions to *Granta*

☐ Please debit my ☐ MASTERCARD ☐ VISA ☐ AMEX for £_____ for ____ subscriptions

NUMBER ☐☐☐☐ ☐☐☐☐ ☐☐☐☐ ☐☐☐☐   SECURITY CODE ☐☐☐

EXPIRY DATE ☐☐ / ☐☐   SIGNED _____   DATE _____

☐ Please tick this box if you would like to receive special offers from *Granta*
☐ Please tick this box if you would like to receive offers from organizations selected by *Granta*

Please return this form to: **Granta Subscriptions, PO Box 2068, Bushey, Herts, WD23 3ZF, UK, call Freephone 0500 004 033** or go to **www.granta.com**

Please quote the following promotion code when ordering online: **GBIUK108** depicted Khalid lying on his back against the garage door, which was splattered with his blood. In one of the photos, you could make out Khalid's right hand, his index finger raised. Afaf whispered to me, 'He died like a man.' She later told me that it's a symbol of a Muslim's pronouncement of faith. This was undoubtedly his final act.

Over the fourth of July holiday, as Afaf waited for Monday's closing arguments, sixty-three people were shot in the city, eleven of them fatally. Afaf watched the news that weekend as the body count mounted. 'I don't get it,' she told me. No one does. James Highsmith, a former drug dealer in his fifties who now works for the violence prevention programme CeaseFire, once told me, 'It's not a norm in America that we have such rampant violence. It done got to the point where it affects every aspect of the community.' When Highsmith got out of prison, he was hired by a developer to rent out apartments in the Englewood neighbourhood on the South Side. The first question potential renters asked was: Who's running the block? 'They wanted to know if they could get their kids to and from school safely, or if a grown son could visit them,' Highsmith explained. He told me of a small gang in his neighbourhood that calls itself 'Brain Dead'. He shook his head in wonderment. 'What the hell you gonna call yourself brain dead for?'

It took the jury one hour to find Jorge Pena guilty of killing Afaf's son, Khalid. He faces a minimum sentence of forty-five years and he'll soon be tried for the murder of Mark Evans. As Afaf walked out of the court building, she spotted Pena's mother in the distance, a heavy woman in a black pantsuit, her shoulders sunken. Folded over her right arm was the oversized black suit her son had worn during the trial. 'I did my suffering. Now it is her turn,' Afaf muttered. There was no joy in her voice; she was just stating a fact.

Not long ago, I visited with Afaf in her apartment. It was mid-morning and she was still in her nightgown, but the apartment was unusually clean, the furniture rearranged. She sat on a chair, one leg curled beneath her, her voice full and vibrant. 'The hard part is that my country has the longest civil war,' she told me. 'They take everyone at nineteen in the army. I thought it would be easier to have him come to America. I don't know. It's God's will.' She was having trouble tracing her thoughts. 'I am his parent. I couldn't find a good place for him.' She told me that when Mohamed, who's now five, reaches adolescence, she plans to send him to Sudan to live with her mother. 'I will try to make him safe,' she said. ■

Hampstead Theatre

50
YEARS
1959 - 2009

Autumn 2009
0th Anniversary Season

September - 17 October

22 October - 7 November

28 October - 7 November

he Fastest
lock in the
Universe
Philip Ridley

What
Fatima
Did...
by Atiha Sen Gupta

Daring
Pairings 3

90s revival: Philip Ridley's edgy and vocative drama caused a sensation en it premiered at Hampstead Theatre 1992, winning the Evening Standard ard for Most Promising Newcomer to Stage and the Meyer Whitworth Prize. now regarded as a contemporary classic.

New Hampstead Theatre commission: *What Fatima Did...* is a main stage debut for a young writer who has been learning her craft with Hampstead Theatre since her early teens.

Hampstead Theatre's third New Writing Festival: A series of unexpected collaborations, featuring work by The Factory, Nabokov Theatre, heat&light – Hampstead Theatre's young company, Central School of Speech and Drama, and Hampstead Theatre's five writers on attachment.

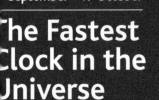

ckets: **£15 - £25**

ox Office: **020 7722 9301**

ook Online: **www.hampsteadtheatre.com**

Swiss Cottage, Jubilee Line (exit 2)

He was sitting on the deck of a rented beach house about a thousand miles east of Chicago. This is not where I'd expected to see Nelson Algren.

Sand, ocean, sunburn – and something Nelson hadn't expected. This part of the island lacked electricity.

He was supposed to be working on a book, non-fiction, called *Notes from a Sea Diary*. And he could not use his electric typewriter. That's where I came in, a guy in his mid-twenties who was also supposed to be working on a book, fiction, my first novel – but getting nowhere.

After Nelson and I met and he explained his predicament, I was happy to let him borrow my old battered manual typewriter.

Nelson was friendly and generous, reading a couple of my short stories, offering helpful advice. He was the voice of experience – that great Chicago voice – warm, funny, sometimes operatic in his recital of various complaints, protests, grievances.

Isolated scenes: Nelson in his workshirt and baggy pants sitting on the beach watching young women in gleaming bikinis come bouncing out of the surf.

Nelson throwing a coffee cake at a temporary house-sharer – a man who thought Nelson ought to take his turn tidying up the kitchen.

Nelson and I and two women playing a comical game of poker – chips worth up to ten thousand dollars each.

Nelson pretending to confuse Saul Bellow's novel *Herzog* with an old ball player, Buck Herzog, who finished his career with the Cubs.

We kept in touch, exchanged some letters. I still have a Polaroid photograph of Nelson taken among friends in New York – rumpled shirt, wolfish smile, hair appearing windblown. And I kept a souvenir of that evening – one of his losing tickets at the racetrack. Nine horse in the sixth race at Bay Meadows.

ART SHAY

Nelson Algren, 1949

When I met him, I'd just finished reading *Never Come Morning*. I still have all the ancient paperbacks, including *A Walk on the Wild Side* – third Crest printing, May 1960, fifty cents.

And bearing the famous Hemingway quote: 'This is a man writing. Mr Algren can hit with both hands and move around and he will kill you if you are not careful.'

But he wasn't a killer, was he? He was a writer of enormous compassion whose work carried the voices and longings of people in the jails, the shanties, the backstreets –

'Where only yesterday,' he wrote, 'the evening crow crossed only lonely tepee fires, now the slender arc-lamps burn.' ∎

POETRY
POETRY
ETRY POETRY POE
ETRY POETRY
POETRY POET
POETRYP
POETRYPO
POETRY

The Lightless Room

Nelson Algren

Nelson Algren punching a heavy bag in the Division Street Y, Chicago, 1950

PITTSBURGH, PA (AP)... Coroner's physician Ed Biddeson disclosed today that the death of Frank ('Blackie') Cavanaugh, Chicago welterweight pugilist, was caused by cerebral hemorrhage sustained when he was knocked out in the third round of a scheduled eight-round preliminary with Benny Speciale of this city, at Sportsmen's Arena Saturday night. Ringside spectators assert that Cavanaugh's head struck the canvas as he fell and that he may have been dead before having been fully counted out. Dr Biddeson's postmortem serves to substantiate this opinion. Coroner Markheim has ordered a thorough investigation into the death. –*News Dispatch*

Cavanaugh's Girlfriend

We was always suppose to get married, right from the start, but I don't think we would of ever, even if this hadn't happened. Now that he's gone I can say it better: Blackie never meant a thing he said, he lied to me more often than not. I woulda married him any time he woulda just give the word so's I could go home again and hold up my head to Pa like a Christian and say I was now lawfully wed.

But it would have had to have been at St Columbanus to please Pa, with Father Ryan officiatin'. And Father Ryan wouldn't even confess Blackie no more, far less marry him to a really church-going girl like me. Father Ryan always thought so highly of me. So no matter how you figure it, it couldn't hardly ever of been, 'cause Blackie just wasn't the kind to change his ways for a woman, he'd had so many of them. Even after me and him started going together so steady that folks would hint around to find out if we was married secret, he'd still brag up other women, about the places he took them he wouldn't be seen in with me. And what he done with them just as easy as with me, every time.

73

Once, when we was first going together, Blackie knocked out a nigger, and Judge Costello came down in the locker room and give him ten dollars for training expenses and called him the White Hope of White City. The next afternoon at three o'clock sharp I met him in front of the Woodlawn. He kissed me that time and said we would now be lawfully wed, and on the way to the El we stopped in at John O'Connor's.

I couldn't any more stop him from drinking than I could have from fighting when he was mad. The drink was in him like the fighting, and not me nor him nor his father and brothers nor Father Ryan hisself could put any sort of a stop to either one. I begged O'Connor he should give Blackie no more, that we was that day to be lawfully wed. But all O'Connor done was quit selling to me, saying I was more drunk than Blackie. That may well have been, I *have* been known to overdo it. The middle of the week and this *was* the middle of the week; but I yet knew better what it was I wanted, drunk or sober, than Blackie ever did. It was him shouldn't have been having the gins that time and not me. And when it got so late I knew full well we would never make the City Hall that day and it might be six months or a year or never before ever we had another ten-spot between us again, I slapped him hard, in the dark of the booth, and walked out praying Mary he wouldn't let me go.

At the corner I let him catch up, holding a half-empty beer glass and his shirt-tails out. 'I'm a fool for mistreatin' a good woman,' he said, and that black curly hair was in his eyes till I could have kissed him right there on the public street. 'We'll be wed by Judge Costello hisself this very night.' Then he threw the beer in my eyes and shoved me flat against a store-glass like forcing a man on to the ropes. I heard the glass begin cracking above me, but he was too weak from the drink to shove me through. I shoved him off and ran, with him kicking me from behind – that's a shameful thing for a woman to have to remember, any woman. Two blocks I ran, down 63rd, till there was no breath left in me, and people just making room instead of stopping him, men passing and one or two laughing even, and myself not well able to see any more where I was running, for the beer burning my eyes. And being that heartbroke.

And that's how he would do: pretend he was crazy about me till he got me believing it all over again, and then right off act like an infidel, like he hated me something terrible. And which was how he really felt, I never did learn, and I doubt Frank knew hisself.

But those ones who laughed on the street that time – Lord how ever I held up my head that Sunday Mass I can't say to this hour. But maybe you do see now, when his friends show me the sport page so I can see for myself it is so, that I've the same feeling I had when I prayed Mary every night for something to happen that Pa said never could be. And then it happen just the same, and Pa was that proud of me in front of people as he's never once been since. I really hope you don't mind my saying Frank was no good, but – just between you and me and Father Ryan of course – he didn't care, one way or another, whether he lived or he died, and I do forgive him in my heart. Unless he's just bad hurt and gets better or so paralysed drunk again they can't tell he's not dead.

His Father

When an Irishman is bad, he's very bad, he's simply no good a-tall. The boys are all fine boys, I've been a sober hard-working man all my days. Frank was our first, the only one born in the Old World. And the only one to turn out bad.

Simply no good a-tall.

Saul Singer, His Manager

Well, Blackie won't be around Coulon's this winter, lazying against the ropes when he ought to be in there mixing it and getting the booze out of his system. Loafing on the rubbing table in them trunks with the shamrock my own wife sewed on for him. Chewing the fat and always razzing the boys who are going somewhere some day, telling everybody how they ain't going nowheres, ever. Betting even the promising boys they'll be walking on their heels after their next fight, always roughing it up or holding on or fighting in a shell when he should ought to be in there mixing it clean, never taking the cigarette out of his puss in workouts unless I took it out for him.

Honest, I couldn't tell you straight if Blackie was a contender or a bum. I couldn't never find out myself, and it's about killed me trying to. He'd *never* show me what he really had, he was forever holding something out on me. Right up to last Saturday night.

It does seem though that it almost had to be Blackie if it was anyone. The way he was always squawking he was going to quit on me just as soon as he could get on cash relief – that was how he really felt.

He was the only one of the boys around Coulon's who seemed to know he wasn't going nowheres.

Well, he was right, I can see now, but I wasn't so certain then. And it's bad to think of him not being around in that faded green sweater comin out at the elbows and the faded letter they'd give him out at Fenger High a dozen years ago. Not pickin up pins at the White City bowlin alleys for his supper and a ten-dollar four-rounder on Monday night or knocking off clay pigeons for a snort of bar whiskey behind the stands, challenging the boys who run the concessions, and settin on the newsstand at 63rd and South Park like that first time I seen him, wavin a red toy cane in one hand and a Popeye kewpie in the other, barrelhouse drunk and cussing out everyone walking past him. He'd just lost to Bruno Meleska, a good boy I was handling at the time, and he yelled over at me I was just one more flannel-mouth Polack and did I want a piece of what he had give Meleska. You would have thought he had beat Bruno to hear him. I came over to see what he looked like up close and told him I'd like some of it too, just to see what he'd do. He just sat there waving that Popeye and the red cane around and yelling he'd go out of his class and lick every flannel-mouth Polack on Chicago Av'noo.

I picked him up a few days later just for his cockiness. He never did come through any more in the fights I got him though he come through that night. But it does make me feel low thinkin how I won't never see him yank off a tablecloth in O'Connor's, beers and all on to the floor again, and then call O'Connor a underfed shoneen. He'd get hisself and everybody with him thrown out of some place, and then back in and argue till they tossed him out again. 'I liked that,' he'd say as soon as he caught his wind on the sidewalk. 'Give me some more of that, O'Connor you filth' – and out he'd come flying again, and keep it up till O'Connor either closed the place or called the squad. I won't pass no tavern no more and hear him shoutin around inside for the biggest shot on 63rd Street, even if he was orderin it somewheres in Blue Island or Gary. Or meet him weavin down 57th at nine o'clock of a Sunday morning with a half-gallon empty under either arm, brushing folks out of his way and panhandling every Irish face he passed. The good Irish on their way to Mass would keep right on going when he'd offer to give them the empties for half the price of the refund on them.

Maybe we brought him along too fast. Maybe he was overmatched. His feet wouldn't follow his punches through, ever; though he was fast enough when he was right. If he'd been right a little more often, if he'd of lived right even three days of the week before a fight, say, this never would have happened. It only happened because deep inside him he wanted it to.

I had that feeling that he'd been holding out the whole time. Looking down at his casket in the open grave with five shots of good Irish whiskey inside of me, I tossed the empty bottle in against the edge of the casket and bust it. And all at once it just seemed to me this was just a new way Blackie had thought up of holding back on me. If I'd had one more and the casket would have still been open, I would have bust the bottle on his stubborn skull. It's four days now since the wake and I can't seem to care about the things I got to do, one way or another, any more than *he* ever did.

If I'd never crossed the street that night after he lost to Bruno Meleska to talk to the tramp, I'd be settin on top of the world this minute, instead of where I am.

His Mother

Of all the money that lad made at gambling and fighting, even stealing for all I might have known and setting such an example to his younger brothers as more than once made me wish him out of the house to stay, he never so much as once brought a dollar home or bought his mother so much as a flimsy house dress. All he ever brought me home was that night cat Marge of his, to sleep with him in the roomer's bed after the roomer had went off to work. And leave me to make their sheets up afters. Then back they'd go to their boozing and helling and whoring back of White City soon. As ever the streets were darkening and the little lights coming on.

So 'tis just as well I say, for he was the sort of lad who'd strike his own mother, once the will took him. And I say Father Ryan was right in washing his hands of the lad, his own father and brothers was right in throwing him out when his breath smelt of the drink. And the lad would best have died in his cradle in Cork. And I'm a church woman in good standing that's saying this.

I thank the Virgin not one of his brothers are fighters and gamblers, they're good boys every one and it was Mary's blessing, nothing less, that made him the one to go. I thank the Saviour he'll not be bringing home that little simpering thing to sleep with him in the roomer's bed, be leaving the sheets for me to make up afters and then to have her crossing herself like a nun and saying a Novena at my own table soon as ever it's getting dark in the streets again.

Cavanaugh

I was fit that night. Hadn't had me a drop all day nor a woman all the week. Feeling good too I was and knowing I could win, and weighed myself in feeling high as any lark.

It weren't till the night and the great lights comin on in the streets, and the little sign-lights in between beginnin their flickerin off and on, and everythin else gettin dark again, like the only way I remember Cork, as though nothing might ever be light again. Then I sat alone in the hotel room recalling what a fool I been all my days, and what foolish things I'm still after doin. The foolish women always in my way, the foolish drink and all. And all the while the great night comin on the other side of the little window. And the foolish way I've wasted my strength on those streets.

What small difference could it make after all then, I asked myself, did myself or this I-talian lad win tonight? I asked it out loud, being there so alone by myself, and it seemed in that moment there was no other human voice in that whole great hotel. Nor anythin quite human on the street below. Nor in that whole great city. And how my own mother no longer cared in her heart, as she used to when I was a child in Cork and her only one, did I die on the street this very night.

And the whole great city I'd never been in before and nobody in it any longer knowin or carin. And my own manager, for all I could tell, bettin my own money against me, and me with no certain way of finding him out for sure. I looked then once at myself in the cracked dresser mirror. And even to myself then, I saw I looked like a ragged stranger. The unclane kind you send his ways before he finishes his whimperin just for the very foul look of him. And none of them, not even Sol Singer, knowin the sort of thing I wanted the whole time. And myself with no real way of showing them at all.

It was a sort of place I wanted, all my own mind you, a kind of a room I must have been inside of, one time or another far back, a very small sort of room it must have been and I a very small sort of child. For I first recall wishing to be back within it with mother, when we were yet in Cork. A small room, surely, quiet in there and warm, with no small sign-lights going on and off in the street below. And no way of getting dark in there as though nothing at all could be light again.

Surely it was only for the wanting of such a place that I loved the drink instead. It would take four good preliminaries in New York, Sol would say, and me in the best shape of my career, to pay the rent of a month of such a place as often as I told him I wanted, the best way I could tell him. And how it was all he could do to keep getting me on once or twice a month at White City. Had he just not brought me

along that fast, had it just not been for the drink and that holy-talkin
Marge, perhaps then I might well have gotten those New York fights
and even won them too. Then I would have set up in contracting with
the old man, I should of clane forgot the drink. I should of set with my
feet on the desk like Judge Costello hisself and never be after gettin my
mouth bust open of a Monday night off some Chicago Av'noo Polack
for twelve dollars and expenses, just because a crowd likes to see an
Irishman take it. I would've got myself married to some quiet sort from
around St Columbanus. But no one like that holy Marge – how is a
man supposed to respect a woman he has his own way with all the
time, any night of the week, every night he has nothing to do and time
on his hands, in the park or the fun house at Riverview or out at
Danceland when they dim the lights? I had my way with Marge the
first night ever I seen her, up at the Merry Gardens it was, and many's
the night since I've wished I'd not gone dancin that night. The very
righteous way she'd carry on about getting married and all, when all I
wanted was peace and quiet and some little way of livin, of gettin along
just from day to day without getting my puss bust in of a Monday. But
she cared for nothing, nothing at all; save the gossiping tongue of that
Father Ryan.

Pa was the first started saying I wouldn't ever be nothin but a
poolroom pug because of the drink, that everybody should try to be
champ of whatever line he was in, and he never would stop to figure
out how maybe I loved the drink only after I grew to know.

Speciale wasn't tough, he wasn't even a little tough. He was strong,
he was strong in both hands. But no way so strong as myself. It was the
smart lads who beat me, the strong ones with nothing but strong in
their hands were the very ones I fought best. I could be mean with the
foulest of them, and cared more for fighting the ill-tempered low-
hitting lads than ever I did for the easy-natured, claner ones. I liked this
Speciale. Just for the low surly look of him.

He hit me with an overhand right when I came out – caught me
square on the side of the jaw with everything in the house behind it,
and I shook it off before he got hisself set again from the force of his

own great blow. I snapped his head back with a short left, not to hurt him but just to show him he couldn't be hurting myself. He must have struck me twelve/fifteen times with that overhand right, me stopping a few in the air with Elbows McFadden's old trick, and then just letting them come on. That gave me the chance to hit him and to show him I cared not at all for the strength he had in his hands. That made him a little wild the rest of the round.

That's how them I-talians are, and the Blackamoors as well: they get a little mixed in their minds, or scared a little, and they no longer hit so sharp. They start throwing all that they have, that's why they burn out so fast. 'Tis the Jew fighters that kape their heads: it's when they're losing that they fight better and better. But to do it he has to first lose the first four rounds, or get hisself knocked down once or twice. Then he gets up so very calm, and begins, once in a while, to swing. But he never swings once till he's counted it first: he never pulls that trigger, as they say, till he sees it's likely to ring the jackpot. And so it is, with a fighter like that, he has his fight hopelessly lost and as yet he's hardly swung his hands – then of a sudden he does, and the fight is all over right then.

I never felt so calm in all my life as after that first round, when the crowd thought I was hurt. I wasn't, and Sol knew I wasn't, and Speciale knew I wasn't too. I wasn't near so tired as him, settin across from him with my head thrun back listenin at him givin me the line about roughin him against the ropes and gettin the old thumb in his eye and the heel of the glove across his teeth comin out of the clinch. I opened my eyes at the warning buzzer and stood up too soon, just to show how fresh I was, and Sol took off the stool and I looked straight up to get the bends out of my neck – and way up there in the rafters, up there in the great dark with but one small light shinin on it and small flags flying about it, a sign said PARK AS LONG AS YOU LIKE IN A LOT OF YOUR OWN.

And all the little flags waved a little, like there was a breeze up there you couldn't even feel down where me and Speciale was. Then the lights was shinin hot on my back and Speciale was thrown that overhand right, mixin low lefts at my short-ribs, and I knocked him down with one I slung from the fourth row flush into his gut. When he got up I knocked him down with two straight lefts into his teeth. He spat out his mouthpiece at six, his front teeth was come too loose to gulp it well, and he come up at nine. The boo-boo birds in the back of the park, the iron-throated lads, begun yellin I should finish him while I was able.

I could not. He was too fast to find, and still too strong. He went into his shell and stayed there, and I threw what I had, and it wasn't enough. Beside, I wanted to get back to the corner to take another look at the sign with the little light on it and the small cool breeze going past. It had to do with the thing I always wanted, I needed to see it once more.

Sol squatted before me then, workin on my legs and so not seein where my eyes were: PARK AS LONG AS YOU LIKE IN A LOT OF YOUR OWN. I had never thought of it that way before, and surely it was the very thing I'd been wantin all my days and yet not knowin, peace and quiet and a place all my own where I could just lay on my back all the day doin nothin just so long as I liked, and not a scoldin holy voice anywhere near. More than havin a system on the dice or the horses and being married to a wife not named Marge.

'What's eatin on you?' Sol asks me, lookin up worried-like but not slowin his rubbin, 'What are you holdin out on me for when the fellow is out on his feet? I don't know what it is you're dreamin of, Blackie, but it's unfair to myself.' And he starts in a-tellin the many fine things he is soon to do for me, him and myself is going to take in a few nightclubs this very night if I just finish this boy the next round. But even going out on a binge sounded sort of fake to me then, surely I had no heart left in me at all, not even for the drink.

'You act like you're scared,' Sol tells me, 'the wobblier he gets the scareder you look. Are you sick, Blackie? Are you drunk?' And he had the impudence then to smell my breath.

Then he looked pretty scared hisself.

But I just looked straight up at them rafters at that cool small breeze stirrin all them little flags and said just with my lips, like I used to in

Cork when I was a tot and so's Sol couldn't hear, 'Yes, I'm so scared I'm sick, but I like it that way.' Then I crossed myself for the first time since Father Ryan forbade me the church, and went out under the lights laughin to myself. And Speciale hit me with a hand like a housebrick clane between the eyes.

I could hear them yellin, I could feel them standin up, in the rows out there in the dark. They was all far away and goin farther. And I knew I could shake it off, like any other time. Only I didn't, for that high wind that seemed closer. I liked it, that feelin, it was like the boo-boo birds was going far away for the last time, like this time they was never coming back at all, and I was happy to feel them going – and then I seen myself just as plain, like I was one of the boys way up in the bleachers myself, lookin through opera glasses – I was down there under the great lights in pants with a shamrock on one corner, leanin all my weight on Speciale to make him shove me off and my pants hangin too low and my head wobbling blow-like side to side and my hands too low ever to get them up in time again.

Then all the sounds came back like a great wave. I felt clear just one moment, with everything right up close as never before. The great lights swelled up all over the whole house, till the place was filled with one big white hot light shinin straight down through my eyes, so even them being closed didn't keep out the whiteness and the burnin. Then some good fellow pulled the switch, I heard him pull it, far back in my head. And all the lights everywhere in the world began going out one by one till there wasn't but one little flickering one, for all the world like a vigil light, right over the ring, and no sound, not a whisper even, nobody around at all, and nothing to do save to keep watchin that one small flickering thing. But I let the big cool wind come down and blow it out like a puff. Then it was just me and the big cool dark and no wind near at all, as still, as small and safe and warm as the place where I laid as a small sick child. ■

BEST EUROPEAN FICTION 2010

EDITED BY ALEKSANDAR HEMON

PREFACE BY ZADIE SMITH

IN STORES NOVEMBER 2009

This project is supported by cultural agencies throughout Europe and the US, and with primary support from Arts Council England.

WWW.DALKEYARCHIVE.COM

Saint Jane

Elaine Showalter

Jane Addams with children in Chicago, date unknown

I n his *Chicago Poems* (1916), Carl Sandburg memorably celebrated the Midwestern capital as the 'Hog Butcher for the World... Stormy, husky, brawling/City of the Big Shoulders'. Chicago was a roughneck town, a place for a young man who was 'alive and coarse', a 'tall bold slugger set vivid against the little soft cities'. Yet one of the movers and shakers of this hyper-masculine city was a short, refined, middle-aged lady, the opposite of everything Sandburg saw as virile and progressive. According to her biographer Allen Davis, Jane Addams, founder and director of the inner-city Chicago settlement Hull House, was 'venerated and worshipped' in the period just before the First World War, as 'no woman in any period of American history has been'. An indefatigable social activist, who never saw an urban problem she didn't want to fix, Addams was hailed as 'the only saint America has produced', and a female saint to boot.

Even by Sandburg's standards, however, Addams was tough and energetic. She belonged to 173 civic organizations, and allied herself with numerous reform groups to support progressive legislation on child labour, juvenile justice, housing regulations, sanitation, prostitution, unemployment insurance, fair working hours and trade unions. Constantly sought after as a speaker and writer, she was also asked to deliver babies and officiate at weddings and funerals. Addams kept herself going with short power naps and a streamlined personal style; she could get dressed and do her hair in five minutes in the dark without a mirror. She did not like to be idle, crocheted during meetings and lectures and calmed her nerves by moving furniture. As one resident of Hull House observed, 'Miss Addams is low in her mind today. She is rehanging all the pictures.' Yet Addams was amused by those who saw her as a noble and saintly being; as she wryly noted, she could feel visitors to Hull House 'positively...peering into my face to detect spirituality.'

That spirituality certainly did not come in a denominational package. Although she prudently joined the Presbyterian Church a month before she moved into Hull House, Addams was no missionary, and did not use the settlement to evangelize or proselytize. In a predominately Catholic neighbourhood, with many Jewish, Greek and Arab residents, she wisely avoided any controversial religious education or identification with a church or clergyman; as one Jewish girl remembered, 'No religion was introduced into any of the clubs or classes, with the exception of the annual Christmas party which became a sort of folklore tradition.' Addams's priority was that everyone should feel welcome, and that differences should be acknowledged and respected. In contrast to St Teresa and her European sisters, Addams was a very American kind of saint; practical, pragmatic, dynamic and secular. An heiress from rural Illinois, she brought her own cultural values and standards of efficiency to the project of social uplift. Above all, Addams was a shrewd businesswoman and a brilliant negotiator who instinctively understood the basic principle of avoiding ultimatums. She balanced morality with diplomacy, refusing to take sides on divisive political issues such as strikes.

As a woman, Addams was not only conspicuous among the beef and newspaper barons, the fiery radicals and rugged working-men who became urban heroes at the turn of the century, but also had some advantages over them. Their domain was the meat-packing plants, the stockyards and the roaring streets; hers was the well-scrubbed settlement house. But as a refined and petite woman, who always said how much she admired Louisa May Alcott while she also idolized Lincoln and Tolstoy, Addams could get away with some radical programmes and ideals. Hull House offered its clientele such genteel pursuits as a madrigal society, and a book club where Italian immigrants read George Eliot's *Romola*, but Addams also launched a Working People's Social Science Club, which hosted anarchists, trade unionists, socialists and lecturers, including W. E. B. Du Bois. Arriving in Chicago three years before the University of Chicago opened its doors, she forged strong alliances with progressive social scientists on the faculty, especially John Dewey, who named his daughter after her.

Moreover, because she was unmarried, and had no husband or children to neglect, Addams was an acceptable spokeswoman for feminism. Her authority depended on her public role as a traditionally self-sacrificing maternal caretaker. As the historian Jill Conway notes, 'She embodied in her person a solution to the problem of the role of women which was acceptable for both men and women, for her active public career carried with it no threat to the accepted fabric of society.' Like Addams, American 'New Women' at the turn of the century were often products of the new women's colleges, drawn from small towns to urban centres and work in settlement houses, and in rebellion against marriage and conventional domesticity. For many of these women, the acute shortage of compatible New Men led to heartbreak. But finding a male companion was never a priority for Jane Addams. From adolescence on, she never expressed any romantic interest in a man, and satisfied her emotional needs first in a productive partnership with an exuberant college classmate, Ellen Gates Starr, and then in a forty-year 'Boston marriage' with wealthy Mary Rozet Smith, who also provided financial support for many projects at Hull House and donated the pipe organ for its theatre. Addams was both free of family obligations and had a wife of her own to handle domestic comforts.

'Miss Addams has walked a long road,' wrote a journalist in *Harper's Bazaar* in 1904, to a 'plateau of high altitude, where a wonderful peace lies brooding.' How did she travel from the insignificant small town of Cedarville, Illinois to the slums of Chicago and national celebrity? Like many American feminist intellectuals, Addams idolized her father, an Illinois state senator and successful businessman. She was first educated in her father's library, reading Ruskin, Carlyle, De Quincey, Browning, Whitman and George Eliot, and internalizing high-Victorian stories of aspiration and moral struggle. As a sickly and introspective child, she identified with her favourite fairy-tale character, Andersen's 'Ugly Duckling', and thought of herself as 'pigeon-toed' and 'crooked'. Judging from photographs, in fact, Addams was actually a pretty girl with curly hair and a decided cleft chin. But after an adolescent period of vanity, when she had pierced ears and wore long dangly earrings, she turned against jewellery and other frivolities of fashion and pulled her hair back in a bun. Already she was preparing herself for a professional life, and indeed, as she admitted in her autobiography *Twenty Years at Hull-House* (1910), she had become 'a girl...of serious not to say priggish tendency'.

Addams had hoped to attend Smith College, newly opened in 1871 for the higher education of women, but her father insisted that she enrol instead near home at Rockford Female Seminary. At first she was disappointed by this 'humdrum' local school, but she made the most of its opportunities, studying maths, Greek and history, and even experimenting with opium to understand her beloved De Quincey. (Disappointingly, she writes, 'No mental reorientation took place, and the suspense and excitement did not even permit us to get sleepy.') As valedictorian of the class of 1881, she delivered an oration titled 'Cassandra'. Florence Nightingale too had chosen Cassandra as the tragic symbol of the brilliant woman doomed always to be a prophetess of truth and yet always to be 'disbelieved and rejected'. Yet Addams had a very different perception of Cassandra's dilemma than the self-pitying one of Nightingale and other nineteenth-century feminists. In her view, Cassandra was cursed because she had failed to make herself intelligible in the language of men. A modern Cassandra, Addams instructed her classmates, must discipline herself to test her intuition against reason, study science, and 'attain authority through trained intelligence' rather than claims to feminine intuition.

Addams left Rockford full of plans for her own further training as a doctor. Even after her father's sudden death from appendicitis in August 1881, she left home in the fall to study medicine at the Women's Medical College in Philadelphia. It was a disaster. Neurasthenic breakdown was a standard feature of the experience of educated young women; doctors in the United States and England even argued that higher education took a heavy toll on feminine nervous and reproductive strength. But Addams had realized that she did not actually like the discipline of scientific training, and in February she stopped being a medical student and became a patient of Dr Silas Weir Mitchell at the Hospital of Orthopaedic and Nervous Diseases.

The American inventor of the 'rest cure' for nervous women, who would include Charlotte Perkins Gilman and Edith Wharton, Weir Mitchell treated his thin and anxious patients with seclusion, massage, complete inactivity, bed rest and a rich diet. The rest cure didn't do Addams any harm, but didn't do her any good either; she became impatient with the various restrictions, and concluded that 'nervous people...do not crave rest but activity of a certain kind'. Addams was in search of this meaningful activity for herself. 'I was absolutely at sea so far as any moral purpose was concerned,' but she knew that she wanted to be engaged rather than academic, to 'live in a really living world', rather than a 'shadowy intellectual or aesthetic reflection of it.'

Medical practice would not be her moral purpose, and in two lengthy trips to Europe in the 1880s, she searched for a vocational replacement. The answer seemed to be in the East End of London. In 1883, she had been haunted by watching the Saturday night auction of decaying vegetables to starving people on the Mile End Road. Addams never forgot the image of 'myriads of hands, empty, pathetic, nerveless and workworn, showing white in the uncertain light of the street, and clutching forward for food which was already unfit to eat'. In her autobiography she wrote: 'I have never since been able to see a number of hands held upward...without a certain revival of this memory, a clutching at heart reminiscent of the despair and resentment which seized me then.' In 1888, she returned to London and heard about Toynbee Hall, a house where university graduates lived among the poor, 'yet in the same style they would live in their own circle. It is so free from "professional doing good," so unaffectedly sincere and so productive of good results in its classes and libraries that it seems perfectly ideal.'

Addams emerged from her time in London determined to create a Toynbee Hall in Chicago, which would be 'an experimental effort to aid in the solution of the social and industrial problems which are engendered by the modern conditions of life in a great city'. Although other Americans were starting settlements in the older slums of New York and Boston, Addams chose Chicago because of its huge industrial growth at the end of the nineteenth century and the predominance of first-generation immigrants among the poor. 'It is much easier,' she believed, 'to deal with the first generation of crowded city life than with the second or third.' The major problems Addams identified were social isolation and lack of community. Immigrants in the big cities were 'clannish' – what we would now call ghettoized – fearful, unable to speak English, and thus cut off from encounters with their neighbours and with American society as a whole. Women were particularly vulnerable; one Italian woman she later met in Chicago did not even know that there were roses in America; although she lived near a park and florist shop, she had never ventured out to them.

By 1889, Addams and Ellen Starr had moved to Chicago, decided to pool their resources, approach various urban charities and start a settlement in the 19th Ward, where several immigrant colonies intersected: Italians, Germans, Polish and Russian Jews; Bohemians, Irish and French Canadians. They found an old mansion that had survived the fire of 1871 but was now engulfed by slums and had been turned into a saloon and a funeral home. As Addams described it, Hull House was:

> an ample old residence, well built and somewhat ornately decorated after the manner of its time… Its wide hall and open fires always insure it a gracious aspect. It once stood in the suburbs but the city has grown up around it…the streets are inexpressibly dirty, the number of schools inadequate, factory legislation unenforced, the street lighting bad, the paving miserable and altogether lacking in the alleys and smaller streets, and the stables defy all laws of sanitation.

In short, a perfect location.

The women moved in with all their dowry, including fine pictures, a Mason oak sideboard, the family silver to put in it and expensive draperies. The *Chicago Times* reported that 'the halls were done in delicate terra-cotta tints and the rooms in ivory and gold. The floors were polished and laid with rugs from the orient. There was the music room with its classic simplicity, the dainty piano and soft etchings and water colors on the walls. The library blossomed forth with rows of books in scented leather bindings and in dusky niches flashed the snowy marble of rare statuary.' Addams quickly returned the draperies to her married sister, but her intention had always been to provide the slum-dwellers with elegant rather than merely serviceable furnishings.

By 1907, Hull House had expanded to thirteen buildings over a full block, including a coffee house, gymnasium, kindergarten and a residence for working women called the Jane Club. The most important cultural centre was the theatre. Addams believed that performing and watching plays was an ideal way to counteract isolation. For the lonely and alienated worker, theatre provided 'a sense of companionship with the experience of others'. She encouraged various immigrant colonies to perform the 'immortal dramas' of their own nation; the Greeks staged Sophocles's *Ajax* and *Electra*; Germans did adaptations of Wagner; children not only performed fairy tales and patriotic American pageants for Thanksgiving, but also Shakespeare, Molière and Schiller. Any Jewish, or Italian, or Lithuanian patriarch watching dramas about 'Americanized sons and old country parents' was relieved to find 'that others had had the same experience as himself', and freed both 'from a sense of isolation' and belief 'that his children were the worst of all'.

Alongside the activities of the settlement, Hull House pioneered cooperative housing for working and professional women, with a central kitchen. By 1911, there were fifty-one residents, including twenty men. In the United States, where over 400 settlements had been founded by this time, mixed-gender residences for volunteers, working-women and paid staff were common (in Britain they were rare). Moreover, even when there were male residents, women were in charge. Henrietta Barnett, who came to visit from Toynbee Hall, observed that in most of the American settlements she saw, 'the grey mare was the better horse of the pair'. Fabian leader Beatrice Webb was even franker about the power differential of American settlements: 'the residents consist...of strong-minded energetic women, bustling about their various enterprises and professions, interspersed with earnest-faced self-subordinating and mild-mannered men, who slide from room to room apologetically.'

Among the early male residents of Hull House were Edward Burchard, who enjoyed knitting caps for cancer patients; the journalist Francis Hackett who called Hull House a haven for the 'sexually unemployed'; and Henry Standing Bear, the son of a Sioux chief who worked there as a handyman for a year on his way back from school in Pennsylvania to his reservation in South Dakota. As Ellen Starr bragged to her family: 'if there were one single Indian in the city...we would get him.' Beatrice Webb found the communal dining room 'higgledy-piggledy', but other visitors admired its convenience and the liveliness of conversation.

Other American feminists of the Progressive period of the early twentieth century shared Addams's vision of urban democracy and female empowerment, but none had her stamina and courage. Charlotte Perkins Gilman lived an identical lifespan (1860–1935) but found her vocation as a feminist writer and theorist. She came to live in Hull House for three months in 1896, and was frightened by the environment of Chicago's North Side, a neighbourhood called Little Hell, in which Addams wanted her to start another settlement. 'The loathly river flowed sluggishly nearby, thick and ill-smelling,' Perkins wrote. 'Everywhere a heavy dinginess, low, dark brick factories and gloomy wooden dwellings often below the level of the street; foul plank sidewalks, rotten and full of holes; black mud underfoot, damp soot drifting steadily down over everything.' Pleading ill health, Gilman fled to California. 'My interest was in all humanity, not merely the under side of it, in sociology, not social pathology.'

Addams's sainthood did not last long. In a speech at Carnegie Hall in July 1915, she not only came forward as an anti-war spokeswoman for the Women's Peace Party but claimed to have heard that young British and French soldiers on the front had to be doped or drunk with rum or absinthe before they could conduct a bayonet charge. The outraged public response to the insinuation that soldiers were not brave and patriotic but stupefied and blind was swift. One newspaper called Addams 'a foolish, garrulous woman'. Another attacked her as 'a silly, vain impertinent old maid'. The qualities of idealism and pacifism that had won her adoration as an urban saint brought her down when she applied them to masculine mythologies in wartime. On the other hand, she did not stand in the way of military recruiting at Hull House; six male residents enlisted and were sent overseas, while another ran the Hull House draft board.

Addams's reputation never recovered. The British pacifist Maude Royden was shocked to witness the complete eclipse of her fame after the war. 'Her popularity had swiftly and completely vanished.' During the 1920s she remained active as a campaigner for the Women's International League for Peace and Freedom, and there was some measure of rehabilitation after her seventieth birthday in 1930, when she was honoured as a distinguished American. But when she received the Nobel Peace Prize in 1931 along with the educator, diplomat and politician Nicholas Murray Butler, she was too ill to go to Oslo to receive it.

Yet Addams's vision for community in Chicago had its own momentum. In the 1960s, the theatre she had started at Hull House was revived as a place where fierce new realist plays were staged. One of its alumni was David Mamet, who remembered the pride of the community company 'to be engaged in the business of a collaborative art.' The road from Saint Jane to *Sexual Perversity in Chicago* was long indeed, but at the end, Jane Addams, like her heroine Cassandra, made herself heard in the language of men. ∎

NEW FICTION FROM GRAYWOLF PRESS

THE HEYDAY OF THE INSENSITIVE BASTARDS by ROBERT BOSWELL

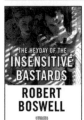

"An unnerving, fascinating collection."
—*O, THE OPRAH MAGAZINE*, 25 Books You Can't Put Down

"Heartbreakers from a writer who knows how to do it right."
—*KIRKUS*

Robert Boswell's extraordinary range is on full display in this crackling new collection. Set mainly in small, gritty American cities, each of these stories is a world unto itself.

I AM NOT SIDNEY POITIER by PERCIVAL EVERETT

"Everett effortlessly entertains…and refuses to be shy about speaking his mind."
—*TIME OUT NEW YORK*

[*I Am Not Sidney Poitier*] is full of feeling, and it says a great deal about our nominally postracial America. It's also very, very funny."
—*VERY SHORT LIST*

Percival Everett's hilarious new novel follows the tumultous and extraordinary life of a young man named Not Sidney, as he scrambles to balance his skin color with his fabulous wealth.

THE ACCORDIONIST'S SON by BERNARDO ATXAGA

"The most accomplished novel to date by an internationally celebrated writer."
—*BOOKFORUM*

"A gorgeous and ambitious story about the Basque land and language."
—*PUBLISHERS WEEKLY*, starred review

David's pastoral childhood in Obaba is ruptured when he finds a letter implicating his father in fascist activities during the Spanish Civil War, including the execution of local republican sympathizers. Obaba's history slowly cracks open to reveal to David the political tensions still raw beneath the surface, and the long shadow cast by the war. *A Lannan Translation Series Selection.*

NOW AVAILABLE ONLINE AND AT YOUR LOCAL BOOKSTORE

WWW.GRAYWOLFPRESS.ORG

Gift subscription offer: take out an annual subscription as a gift and you will also receive a complimentary *Granta* special-edition **MOLESKINE®** notebook

GIFT SUBSCRIPTION 1

Address:

FIRST NAME:	LAST NAME:
ADDRESS:	
CITY:	STATE:
COUNTRY:	ZIP CODE:
TELEPHONE:	EMAIL:

GIFT SUBSCRIPTION 2

Address:

FIRST NAME:	LAST NAME:
ADDRESS:	
CITY:	STATE:
COUNTRY:	ZIP CODE:
TELEPHONE:	EMAIL:

YOUR ADDRESS FOR BILLING

FIRST NAME:	LAST NAME:	
ADDRESS:		CITY:
STATE:	COUNTRY:	ZIP CODE:
TELEPHONE:	EMAIL:	

NUMBER OF SUBSCRIPTIONS	DELIVERY REGION	PRICE	SAVINGS	
☐	USA	$45.99	32%	All prices include delivery
☐	Canada	$57.99	32%	YOUR TWELVE-MONTH
☐	Rest of World	$65.99	32%	SUBSCRIPTION WILL INCLUDE FOUR ISSUES

I would like these subscriptions to start from:
☐ the current issue ☐ the next issue

PAYMENT DETAILS

☐ I enclose a check payable to '*Granta*' for $_____ for ____ subscriptions to *Granta*

☐ Please charge my ☐ MASTERCARD ☐ VISA ☐ AMEX for $_____ for ____ subscriptions

NUMBER ☐☐☐☐ ☐☐☐☐ ☐☐☐☐ ☐☐☐☐ SECURITY CODE ☐☐☐

EXPIRATION ☐☐ / ☐☐ SIGNED _____ DATE _____

☐ Please check this box if you would like to receive special offers from *Granta*
☐ Please check this box if you would like to receive offers from organizations selected by *Granta*

Please return this form to: **Granta Subscriptions, PO Box 359, Congers, NY 10920-0359, Call toll-free 1-866-438-6150** or go to **www.granta.com**
Please quote the following promotion code when ordering online: **BUS108PMG**

Chicago's Great Expositor

Wole Soyinka

It is not a complete man now dominating the affairs of the world from a historic mansion appropriately named the White House, although a case can be made that he comes close enough. Taking the American Founding Fathers' arithmetic – which counted every slave as three-fifths of a free man – to its logical conclusion, Barack Obama's human valuation should rate approximately seven-eighths of an American white; the white line of his ancestry elevating his status from the mere three-fifths. In practice, however, the logic of racism renders that line of social bleaching irrelevant. Obama thus remains three-fifths of a man. Morbidly fascinated by the unusual spectrum of the current occupancy of the White House, I co-opted my figure-bound son and ventured deeper into the fractional realm of human valuations. We came up with the following result: given a full-blooded African-American wife, plus their two (approximate) octoroon children, the First Family of the United States of America, so rapturously embraced throughout the world, from the Soviet Union to Papua New Guinea, is a mere .63125 equivalent of the constitutional family unit for a White House incumbency. Yet – annus mirabilis! – not only did the Americans install these fractional intruders, but almost everyone, of every racial stock I have met, and across partisan lines, inclines to the view that, in relation to Obama's immediate predecessor of eight years, it would be an act of charity towards that last incumbent to merely reverse the figures.

It is indeed a remarkable journey on which the Americans, as one people, have embarked, despite repeated and costly faltering, since Martin Luther King's Sermon on the Mount – *I Have a Dream*. The attainment of that dream has become vested in the person of the forty-fourth President of the United States, Barack Obama, a man of supreme self-confidence and infectious human rapport who decided that all procrastination or diffidence had come to an end as he launched his bid to ascend the thorned mountain slopes of Martin Luther King's vision.

I had the opportunity of travelling across much of the land mass of his nation from the party primaries to the final battle and found this the most distinctive aspect of his presidential campaign, and a window into Obama's very character: a total lack of diffidence which allows him to detect the moment of a critical mass. It led to a campaign strategy that completely neutralized all considerations, positive or negative, of an ancestry shared with the barely tolerated, and socio-politically marginalized minority group of his nation. Never once did the race card surface in the course of his campaign, except, of course, when others evoked it – ironically his own racial colleagues who tried to suggest that he was not 'black' enough to be the flag bearer for what they perceived as the moment of possible racial restitution. Then, his response was quick, effective and dismissive.

Nonetheless, the totality of that – literally – chequered background had dogged his maturation, contributing a crucial dimension to the personal formation and world outlook of America's forty-fourth president. What the American people – and the world – have surely discerned by now is the multi-textured promise of a national leader whose background has enabled him to identify, on a human level, with the history, mores, cultures, values and *aspirations* of others, beginning, logically, with his own origins.

Of course many African-Americans, especially today, take pride in tracing their roots. Fortunately for Obama, those roots were very accessible, literally above ground – more sturdy branches than roots – so his quest did not involve DNA, or a journey into the unknown à la Alex Haley. That advantage, in addition to the close, formative contacts with other societies and cultures during the impressionable phase of childhood, makes Obama stand out in stark contrast to his predecessors in the White House. It makes a difference when a journey of self-discovery is undertaken, not as an abstract exercise of lineage curiosity, or to add ancestral texture to the image of an already established political legitimacy – as with Robert Kennedy – but in circumstances that provoke a need to grasp the essence of one's individuality, as a product shaped by, but also as inquisitor of, one's very social environment. Needless to say, the parameters of such enquiry need not be racial; in Obama's case, race was inevitable. It was his lived actuality.

These are indeed strange times for American society. Obama's candid, unfiltered intimacy with his origins – a vibrant, intensely present past, so vividly captured in his *Dreams from My Father* – weaves an indefinable aura around the White House about which many Americans remain uncertain, despite the unquestioned enthusiasm that swept him to power. It is not simply that he consciously placed some distance between his candidacy – now incumbency – and the ancient aristocracy of the black struggle, there is also the fact that he is an outsider twice removed. First, one takes note of the heritage of exclusionism that he shares with all others of his racial complexion. The more intriguing dimension, however, is the fact that he is not even a product of the indigenous history of that exclusion, being born and raised outside the slave lineage. Despite shared humiliations – a Kenyan grandfather, revered as a village elder but a lifelong 'boy' to his British employers – Obama has no claims on the full scatology of the black American memory. In addition, his habit of introspection, of micro-dissection of observed individual and group conduct, attitudes, responses and motives, appears to have placed him on a personal trajectory where, unlike many of his racial compatriots, he admits no simplistic, black-and-white answers, preferring to delineate the fault lines between pros and cons, however stridently projected or simply habitually embraced. *That's the way it is; that's the way it goes.* Not for Obama, right from college days, leading to his abandonment of a legal career for a deep immersion in community activism.

It went beyond lessons from his father's tribulations at the hands of *his own kind*, where Africans were already in control of their own affairs. Obama simply asked questions that others preferred to brush aside. His ruminations on race issues are an endless revelation. Sometimes they read as if he has internalized his legal training – a flurry of *Obama* vs. *Obama* encounters, cross-examinations, one Obama appearing for the plaintiffs and yet another for the defendants.

Bringing this habit of mind to issues has left commentators in no doubt that, in Obama, the White House is restored, after a near decade-long hiatus, to a 'thinking' president.

If they still doubt it, Africans do not, certainly after his address on the Ghanaian platform in July this year. Few American presidents have tackled the specifics of a continental dilemma with such eloquent directness, even as he placed the issues within a universal context of responsibility and evasion. The following is vintage Obama, and it is clearly an applied extension of his formative lessons on race, as narrated in *Dreams from My Father:*

> Now, it's easy to point fingers and to pin the blame of these problems on others. Yes, a colonial map that made little sense helped to breed conflict. The West has often approached Africa as a patron or a source of resources rather than a partner. But the West is not responsible for the destruction of the Zimbabwean economy over the last decade, or wars in which children are enlisted as combatants. In my father's life, it was partly tribalism and patronage and nepotism in an independent Kenya that for a long stretch derailed his career, and we know that this kind of corruption is still a daily fact of life for far too many.

Substitute 'a colonial map' with the geography of slavery and the consistent fidelity to the deductions of those years of immersion in America's own sociology is transparent.

I consider the American nation extremely fortunate. The god of timing was definitely on its side. For a nation that has preached diversity more in the breach than in the observance, the election was indeed the moment of positive reversals, but not simply as a one-off, isolated gesture. So much potential resides in a personality that has been shaped by childhood recognition of a diverse world. The ability to act upon such data intelligently is a different matter, and what the American electorate began to deduce, at first with some scepticism but early enough along the campaign trail, was that this 'unknown quantity' was both knowledgeable and knowing. His opponents realized this much too late. In addition to his mental acuity, he had done his homework, and in some depth; a disciplined routine that was abundantly manifested even before he began his post-election outreach to the various warring blocs – including the religious – that have coalesced to fill the vacuum left by the demise of the Cold War.

A fortunate timing for the nation, no doubt, but despite his evident self-confidence, if Obama had a choice, this would not rate as the most auspicious time to be elected into office. Or perhaps he relishes that fact. He comes through sometimes as one of those cases of benign masochism which revels in daunting challenges. Still, a nation once universally deemed powerful but clearly declining – first morally, then materially – bogged down in external wars of dubious motivation and questionable judgement, reviled on several fronts, even among traditional allies, is not the ideal initiation ground for an untested candidate, most of all an outsider with centuries of prejudice against the very composition of his humanity. There are sectors within the United States, even today, where the mere thought of the rise to the highest office of such a candidate is not merely unthinkable but treasonable.

And yet it happened, the culmination of putative efforts in the direction of a national redemption, the repudiation of a centuries-old mental conditioning. It promises an end to a career of costly contradictions – the closure of the abyss between catechism and practice: 'the land of the free', 'all men are created equal', the American Dream; all contributory mantras to the faith that makes immigrants brave oceans and cross deserts, suffocate in containers, dodge rabid bloodhounds and their vigilante handlers on border patrol – the last oblivious to the irony of their own claims to indigenous citizenship within a mongrel nation. Still, these are the contradictions which, as experienced by the outside world, have earned the nation a suspect regard, despite her obvious wealth, power and advertised openness. Now, with the unprecedented mongrelization of power at its very pinnacle, the once disapproving world permits itself to sniff an incoming season of change, remains suspended on a bridge of great expectations. Alas for the border patrols, their legwork is certain to be kept even busier than ever.

F or the African continent, such expectations may be said to fall into several categories. First, there is the sense of proprietorship, a natural reaction, given the background of the incumbent. With that sentiment of 'owning' a part of this individual goes – or at least went – the mood of quantifiable expectations: that the African continent would become a priority with the new American government, and not merely in rhetoric, but in deed. The more politically pragmatic have warned that the man called Barack Hussein Obama was elected as, and will remain, president of a distant country called the United States, not of the African continent or any nation within it. Not to be denied, however, is the political fillip that could be seized upon and exploited by nearly everyone on that continent – itself a continent of blighted expectations – galvanizing movements for democratic and participatory civic life. Its best expression is perhaps encountered in a song that immediately hit the airways in Kenya, Obama's paternal country, after his election. Its lyrics went thus: *It is easier for a Luo to become president of the United States than of his own Kenyan nation.* African leaders such as Robert Mugabe, Jammeh of Gambia, Omar al-Bashir of Sudan and others of that ilk know that this is not a lament but a challenge. The dictators and despoilers of the African continent are no longer at ease.

Most noticeable is the change in the accustomed tone of earlier presidential visits. Obama was not unaware of the special advantage of his African origin while on African soil, and the only question was to what effect he would use that right of belonging. The signs were already clear. Obama's policy statements on America's new regard for, and attitude towards, African and other zones of misgovernance were the mere expository icing on the cake. As with Iran, the consciousness of a potential 'Obama effect' was manifest from the moment of recognition of his closeness to power, and undoubtedly began to create contradictory, unpredictable responses within different zones of illegitimate or irresponsible incumbencies. Some, like Zimbabwe, will perhaps continue to pursue face-saving formulae to rein in their excesses; others, such as Iran, have speeded up the battening of hatches.

For the African continent, his very choice of Ghana – more than merely implicitly loaded with the rejection of self-preening 'giants' such as Nigeria as an 'obvious' first port of call – was already eloquent, but Obama is not the kind to leave loopholes, even for a glossed or denied inference: 'We have a responsibility to support those who act responsibly, and to isolate those who do not, and that is exactly what America will do.'

Backed by unmistakable references, and even the occasional direct naming, Obama's Ghana address was the infliction of some unpalatable home truths on home grounds. Not content with giving faces to individual efforts – non-governmental – that sustain the banner for positive change by naming them in his Ghana address, Obama sealed his open snub to corrupt and undemocratic governance by ensuring that some prominent opposition voices from neighbouring Nigeria were openly invited to his Ghanaian banquet. Such gestures guarantee, at the minimum, symptoms of disorientation, even temporary seizure among the cheerleaders and upholders of a corrupt state. They act as a curb on the flaunting of impunity. Again, this was a first. Traditionally on such visits, any concession to opposition voices studiously avoided gestures that might 'give offence' to the incumbent power, however nauseous its existence – a tokenist mention here and there, or a commiserating handshake and a few seconds of platitudes, nothing more. Barack Obama has broken that mould; the effects should not be underestimated.

Outside the African continent, there is no question but that a number of repressive forces are in a quandary. The easy recourse to the negative emotionalism of the past – i.e. identifying 'World Enemy No. 1', then heaping the internal problems of nation, region or religion on that one source – will clearly undergo some attrition. The restless forces that challenge corrupt, unrepresentative power within such troubled regions no longer feel isolated, and will prove far less inhibited by routine demonization of the 'common enemy' just outside the door. The features of a once starkly projected foe, in diabolical outlines, become blurred when unexpectedly progressive pronouncements, backed by motions of reaching out, issue from the home of the Great Satan. 'Let's-wait-and-see' periods will vary from place to place, from situation to situation, but the facile definition of a global adversary will clearly undergo some loss in credibility. Quite accurate, in my view, is an analysis of the Iranian situation that I have encountered: that the ham-fisted manipulation of the recent presidential elections by the theocratic dictators was a predictable response to the potential threat of what is termed 'the Obama effect'. The Iranian rulers are confronted by a phenomenon whose effects, in global politics, are as yet difficult to gauge but impossible to ignore. The vast slave encampment known as North Korea has already taken fright and reacted in the only way its leaders know – bluster and threat – creating a momentum that spells grave danger beyond that region.

Even within the United Nations I suspect we shall see workings on the subjective level among Third World, and indeed 'non-aligned', nations, born of sentiment, undoubtedly. Voting patterns will undergo noticeable changes, the votes of African nations – 'traditionally' allied with the rest of the Third World – can no longer be taken for granted. Overtly expressed or not, there will be the factor of sentimental identification – all other considerations being equal of course – with the balance tilted in favour of the American president over issues that can hardly be regarded as minor or inconsequential. I believe we shall observe more listening than ranting. Bloc automatism will be whittled down and may even become a thing of the mindless past. It goes beyond sentiment, however; there is the awareness that, after a prolonged hiatus, a sense of vision has returned to the American presidency, and that efforts to redress the errors of the past merit dispassionate attention. Indeed, that shift was apparent long before Obama's landmark Cairo speech in June.

That speech brings us back to what one is moved to identify as a conditioned empathy with a lived reality, especially in the sphere of traditions – conditioned, indeed reasoned, because such empathy stems from experience, not from any abstracted idealism. This is clearly a crucial asset that the head of a world power must possess. At the same time, however, it constitutes its own peril, capable of breeding an all too ready accommodation with contestable aspects of such traditions, and the opportunism of their proponents. Nowhere is such a danger more likely than in the case of a leader who is determined to end the dismal record of a nation that attempted so arrogantly to be not only the world's policeman but its political moralist. The gesture towards conciliation, within the rubric of the traditions of other lands, other societies, and their applications, was of course unexceptionable, and Obama was right in his Cario address to erect a bridge across differences.

However, the limitations of that speech, in which he cast the hijab as a personal choice protected by law, are glaring. The world has numerous interlocking constituencies well outside those of nation boundaries, and when a constituency in question accounts for no less than fifty per cent of the world's population – its women – there is great need for circumspection.

The right of women to veil or not veil is not in question; indeed, is not *the* question. The question is whether or not any practice is transparently founded on choice or imposition. The veil, even beyond its function as a physical act of separatism, is a metaphor for much else that is actual, some of which involves consequences predicated on freedom and slavery, life and death, and thus impinges on the province of human volition and dignity. We are living in a world, sections of which, unfortunately, take pride in perpetuating traditions of sectarian control, marginalization and dehumanization made possible only through the denial of choice to their citizens; where members of that 'lower constituency' are harassed, publicly lashed, imprisoned, stoned to death – sometimes for showing an inch or two of flesh beyond the eye slits graciously permitted for the practical purposes of navigation. It would have been preferable had Obama either avoided the veil as a sign of his affirmation of the right to cultural differences or else proceeded to make a determination also on issues of personal choice and group compulsion.

If Americans dubbed Ronald Reagan the Great Communicator,

Obama is fast proving to be the Great Expositor. Thus profound issues such as the existential condition of women in society – any society – deserve more than a point of view dictated by only one 'tradition', most especially when there are also available contradicting traditions within that same Tradition. The Talibanic view of women is a far call from the Moroccan or Algerian, the Indonesian from the Iranian etc., and the human arithmetic of Obama's ascension must be held to apply universally, or not at all – one-half of the world's population cannot be equal to only three-fifths of the rest, and far less in many instances.

And then there are the minuscule fractions within each constitutency. The Somali jihadists have introduced public amputations of hands and feet as punishment for petty theft, a habit that stigmatizes, by association, even victims of abnormal circumstances – war, accidents, disease etc. In any case, this form of punishment calls into question the very act of permanently disfiguring a human being for one infraction or another. No, these are certainly not issues in which an American president should become personally embroiled, but the evocation of an aggressive symbol of subjugation, such as the veil – and its variations – cannot help but expand the parameters of its cultural significations and consequences for a section of humanity. In Somalia, for instance, in areas already controlled by extreme zealots, stoning to death for adultery is a mere stone's throw away from the present. No, interventionism is not the issue. What matters is the consciousness that wherever a field of discourse provokes such considerations, the articulation of a credo that gives no joy to the enemies of human dignity becomes a moral obligation.

Once evoked, the ramifications of such a symbol as the veil fall within the realm of legitimate discourse. The undeniable differences within even so-called traditions call attention to a large variety of options in interpretation and practice, even within supposedly hermetic theologies. That gesture of moral relief to the endangered species within societies of inequality was an avoidable omission in a context that was, after all, of Obama's own instigation. Sadly, it was left to President Sarkozy of France to seize, within that same month of

June, the high ground of egalitarian morality, as he bluntly voiced his detestation of the 'degradation' of women through sartorial confinement.

There will be, unquestionably, more moments like this and, paradoxically, perhaps more so for the Obama leadership temperament than for the less idealistic, sensitive or discerning. However, in the years to come, as the world moves to judge whether the Great Expositor from Chicago has fully mastered the navigational skills required for the passage between Scylla and Charybdis, it is the existence of a consistent, clear-cut political philosophy, progressively enunciated, with its promise of finely calibrated action, that will continue to ring in the ears of a troubled world, from the Congo to Beslan, resonating with a deep urgency that is most pertinent for the African continent:

> That is why we must stand up to inhumanity in our midst. It is never justified, never justifiable to target innocents in the name of ideology. It is the death sentence of a society to force children to kill in wars. It is the ultimate mark of criminality and cowardice to condemn women to relentless and systemic rape. We must bear witness to the value of every child in Darfur and the dignity of every woman in the Congo. No faith or culture should condone the outrages against them... When there's a genocide in Darfur or terrorists in Somalia, these are not simply African problems – they are global security challenges, and they demand a global response. ■

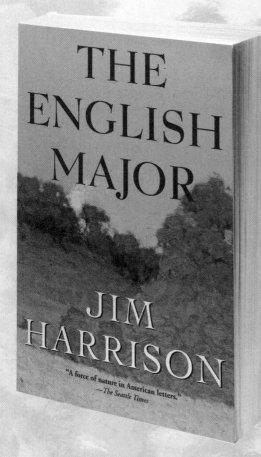

"A ribald, questing, utterly charming and Zen-serious novel . . .

THE BOOK OF THE YEAR."

—Alan Cheuse, *Chicago Tribune*

"*The English Major* is to midlife crisis what *The Catcher in the Rye* is to adolescence."
—*Los Angeles Times*

"[Harrison's] sentences . . . FUSE ON THE PAGE WITH A POWER AND BLUNT BEAUTY. . . . *The English Major* . . . is tragedy recast as comedy. . . . Harrison creates delicious comic tension."
—Jennifer Egan, *The New York Times Book Review*

"[A] WISTFULLY COMIC NOVEL . . . Harrison has created a character of such appeal and self-deprecating wisdom that even the more fantastical episodes —a nubile young woman cavorting in the nude for his pleasure —acquire a charmingly philosophical air."
—*The New Yorker*

Mr Harris

Tony D'Souza

Once when I was sixteen I went down to North Avenue Beach to hook up with two West Side Hispanic girls I'd met at a rave. It was summer, I had a car, money from cutting lawns in my neighbourhood and three bottles of Boone's Farm Strawberry Hill. The plan was to get the girls drunk, hook up with one or both of them. But after we'd finished the bottles and smoked some weed, the skinny girl lay back in the sand and said she was going to be sick. Then the darker, prettier girl started worrying that they should get home, and that was the end of it. The lake wind had been blasting us all evening anyway; the whole thing had been an enormous waste of time.

The girls had come in on the El and they asked me for a ride home. I was a North Side prep; the West Side was a place I didn't go. Except for a few safe enclaves, the West Side was black. Then the pretty girl batted her mascaraed eyes at me with her hair pulled back tight and sexy and that was it. I told them to hop in the car.

The car was brand new, a six-cylinder Corsica that my parents had bought for me. The pretty girl ran her hand on the dash and liked it. We were listening to Led Zeppelin, which they didn't usually listen to, but it was my car and so they did. The skinny girl who had ruined everything was in the back, getting sicker by the minute. Then we were up on the Ike and the midnight traffic was wall to wall, cherries lighting up ahead of me, everything stop and go. The girl in back kept saying, 'I'm going be sick, I'm going to be sick in your car.' And I kept turning around to tell her to hang on. I did this half a dozen times, and half a dozen times I almost hit the car in front of me. Then I finally did.

The girls were instantly sober; so was I. The car that I hit was lit up in my headlights; in it I could see a whole family of people reaching for their necks. That the car was a junker with patches of missing paint all over the trunk meant something bad. That the bumper was hanging off was worse.

The driver and I got out at the same time. He was black, older, not a big man; I noticed right away how small he was. He was holding his neck and wincing in pain. We stood together in the middle lane of traffic with the cars lined up behind us blaring their horns. 'Damn you hit me,' the man said, holding his neck. I looked at my car. There was no damage. But he was looking at his car. He said, 'Damn you knocked off my bumper.' I could see that the bumper had been held in place with electrical wire, was still held in place by wire on the one side. I said to him, 'You just have to rewire it.' He looked at it and said, 'Man you knocked my bumper off my car.'

This is why you don't go to the West Side, I told myself. This is why everyone you've ever known has told you again and again you don't go to the South Side, the West Side ever ever ever. Poor poor poor. Black black black. You'll get robbed and murdered. You'll never get home again.

The man said to me, 'Man we got to call the cops and have the cops come and look at this.' I shook my head. I said, 'My dad can't find out.' He said, 'Well, we got to figure something out then.'

He took longer than he needed to find a pen and paper in his car. The whole time he did the black faces in the windows turned to look at me as they rubbed their necks. He wrote down my address from my driver's licence and then my phone number, which I told him. Then he said, 'Man you'll hear from me soon,' and got back in his car. Back in my car I was shaking. Anything else that happened in that ride I don't remember other than the girl who had ruined everything hadn't gotten sick.

The phone rang the next afternoon. My father was playing golf, thank God, but my mother was home and she took the call. She came into my room where I had secluded myself in dread; she had her worried look on her face. She said, 'There's a man on the phone for you.'

I picked up the phone in our back atrium. The view was of our yard, the flowers blooming in the beds. The man on the phone was the man I hit, his voice was deep and black. I understood right away that my mother knew that a black man was calling me; black people never called our house. He said to me, 'I took the car in and had them look at it.' I thought to myself, 'On a Sunday?' Then he said, 'It's going to cost a thousand dollars to fix the car.'

'A thousand dollars?' I said. 'I don't have a thousand dollars.'

Without even pausing he said, 'How much do you have?'

'Two hundred dollars,' I told him.

'Well maybe you can ask your father for some money.'

'If I ask my father for money he'll talk to his lawyer.'

'Oh yeah well you're the guy who hit my car.'

'I know I hit your car but I don't have a thousand dollars.'

'Then how much do you have?'

'I have two hundred dollars.'

'Then maybe I should call back until I get your father.'

'My father is away.'

'Then maybe I can keep calling back every single day until I get your father.'

The room became small around me, the colours of the beds of flowers too strange to understand. I said, 'Maybe I can find more money.'

'Yeah well how much can you find?'

'How much to fix your car?'

'I can probably fix it for four hundred dollars.'

'I can probably get four hundred dollars.'

'Okay, Anthony, I got to talk to my wife. I'll call you back.'

My mother was listening at the door of course. She looked stricken when I came out of the room. She said to me, 'Is it about drugs?' 'It isn't about drugs,' I told her. Then I told her what had happened. After she had a moment to think about it, my mother said, 'You shouldn't have been on the West Side.'

The man's name was Mr Harris. He called back every day. If he thought he'd get my father on the phone, he didn't because my father was always at work. He tried once to get my mother into it, but my mother told him it wasn't her problem to deal with, that if it had been her she would have waited for the police. Then she passed the phone to me.

Mr Harris explained to me that his wife didn't want $400, she wanted $1,000 because she had whiplash. He said that if I didn't get them $1,000 by the end of the next week, they were going to call their lawyer. Because, Mr Harris told me, us people up in Park Ridge weren't the only people in the world who had lawyers. Because they had lawyers on the West Side too. And not only did his wife have whiplash, but his cousin and his cousin's kids had whiplash, too. So for $1,000 I was getting off easy.

I don't know why, but after the initial day of it, I wasn't scared by him. I knew it would be a thing of money, that a sum would be agreed and paid and that it would come to an end. I don't know how I knew it, but I knew as well that if I decided to not pay him anything, I could get away with that, too. I knew Mr Harris couldn't come to our house in Park Ridge in that beat-up car of his without getting one of our neighbourhood cops on his tail. I knew he couldn't come up where we lived without getting arrested. Because a black man in a tattered suit had come to our door soliciting once when I was young. My mother had told him 'no' and looked out the drapes at him as he left. She said to me, 'He's not going to make it three more doors before they call the police on him.' Ten minutes later we heard the sirens and when we went out to look, they were handcuffing him up against the trunk of an oak tree while all the mothers and their kids stood in the doorways to see.

After a dozen more calls, Mr Harris and I settled on $400. I would get him a money order and mail it to him so that I wouldn't have to go down there, and so that I could have a receipt, like my mother said. My mother gave me half the money; I took the rest out of my account. When the teller asked me who to make it out to, I told her 'Mr Harris'. Then I put the envelope in the mailbox outside the bank and was done with it. School was starting again in two more weeks. Early golf team practices would begin that weekend; I still had summer league tennis matches to play at our club. I'd learned a valuable lesson about messing around in the city and that was it. I wouldn't mess around like that again.

Except that wasn't the end of it. From his side of the city, Mr Harris called me the next Saturday in the afternoon and he was angry. He said he was at the cheque-cashing place and they wouldn't cash the money order because it was made out to Mr Harris. He said, 'Who makes out a cheque to somebody like that? Mr Harris. Mr Harris. Don't you know that people have two names?'

Mr Harris put the cheque-cashing lady on the phone. She was also black. She said to me, 'Are you Anthony?' 'I'm Anthony,' I said. She said, 'Anthony, is this the Mr Harris you meant to give this money order to?' 'Yes it's him,' I said. She didn't say anything for a long moment and then she said, 'I can't cash this cheque for him this way. You have to come down here and write his first name on the money order and initial it.' Then she put Mr Harris back on the line. He said, 'You have to come down here Anthony.'

'I'm not coming down there,' I told him.

'How am I supposed to get my money? How am I supposed to get my money?'

'I don't know.'

'Why would you put Mr Harris?'

'You didn't tell me any other name.'

'Why wouldn't you ask?'

'I don't know.'

'You have to come down here and do this.'

'I'm not coming down there.'

'You're the one who hit me.'

'I'm not coming down there.'

'Man you have got to come down here. Man please. I'll give you a hundred bucks back.'

He told me where he was at. I took the Kennedy, then the Ike. The city loomed up at me on the way down and then it passed. I got off at Racine. It was a nightmare world down there. Burnt-out buildings, burnt-out cars, dogs running loose, gangsters on the corners. I pulled into the gas station where Mr Harris was waiting, and there was the car I had hit, the crappiness of it, the peeling paint. The bumper was again attached by wires. There was another black man with Mr Harris in the car and he was drinking from a brown-paper bag.

Mr Harris got into my passenger seat. His face was older than I remembered, his eyes yellow, his hair speckled with lint; his hands were ashy and worn, he smelled of alcohol and cigarettes. He put the same money order that I had sent to him on the dash; now it was smudged with fingerprints. He said to me, 'Write Michael Harris on this.'

'Who writes Mr Harris on a cheque?' Mr Harris said to me as I wrote. Then he said to me in a relieved voice, 'It's okay now. It's over. Just follow us to the place so I can give you the hundred bucks.' Then he got out of my car, into his, started it, pulled away. I didn't follow him. ∎

THE ✦ TIMES
CHELTENHAMFESTIVALS

LITERATURE09

60
1949 - 2009

in association with

Waterstone's

Monica Ali
Chimamanda Ngozi Adichie
Simon Armitage
Diana Athill
Kate Atkinson
Sebastian Barry
Iain Banks
John Carey
Jonathan Coe
Antonia Fraser
Maggie Gee
Susan Hill
Armando Iannucci
John Irving
A L Kennedy
Colum McCann
Jon McGregor
Audrey Niffenegger
Edna O'Brien
Stephen Poliakoff
Owen Sheers
Nicholas Stern
Colm Tóibín
Sarah Waters
Fay Weldon

Booking opens 10 August
9 – 18 October
Box Office 0844 576 7979
cheltenhamfestivals.com

Charity No. 251765

Jardine's Restaurant sat on a hill in Oak Forest, a southern suburb. On a clear night you could see Chicago. Part of our Jardine's dining ritual was to pause at the door, have a look at the skyline.

There it was: small but bright, like a white fire in the Forest Preserve.

Comiskey Park was in there somewhere. Wrigley Field was there. Blackhawks jerseys, the most beautiful in sports, hung dignified in Chicago Stadium lockers. The major heroes of Chicago sport were there: Luis Aparicio, Bobby Hull, Dick Butkus. Also the minor: the Maki Brothers (Chico and Wayne), Jerry Sloan, Wilbur Wood, chubbiest pitcher in all of baseball, his knuckleball having rendered his physique irrelevant.

Mayor Daley was there, jowly, in his pyjamas, nicer at home than at work.

My intellectual heroes were there: Studs Terkel; the columnist Mike Royko; his creation, Slats Grobnik, who I assumed was a real guy. My uncle John and his brothers were there, arguing politics like radicals out of Dostoyevsky, only eating White Castles. The Old Town folk music scene was there: Steve Goodman, John Prine. Someday, when I could drive, I'd head downtown. Prine and Goodman would approach, go: You play guitar?

A little, I'd say.

Come with us, they'd say. We need some fresh ideas. And you seem pretty cool.

The Museum of Science and Industry was there: the Pickled Babies swam in their jars of green formaldehyde, even Full-Term, his head mushed down by the lid of his jar for all eternity; the talking mannequins of the Bell Telephone Exhibit waited creepily and silently for morning, when they could once again begin mechanically extolling the Virtues of Telephonic Communication.

Marquette Park was there, where crazy protesting Lithuanians had climbed into trees with flares the night Dr King came to town. As Dad drove us through, I'd seen a guy reeling in a tree, face red-lit by his flare, fat branch between his legs, like an animatron in a ride called Race-Hatred Forest.

Grant Park was there, sanctified by the recent Convention protests. The lilac-covered wire fence in Gram's backyard was there. Fifty-fifth Street was there, the ghost of General MacArthur driving along it in his ghost-car, on the way in from Midway. The Greek grocery was there, its gumball machine laced with plastic balls redeemable for candy bars. Uncle Bill and Aunt Anna's pipe-ceilinged basement apartment was there, on Mozart Street, where he'd studied the teachings of the Rosicrucians so devotedly that one night he accidentally astral-projected himself to the Palmer House, where he worked as a janitor. (Next day some of his co-workers swore they'd seen him, though in fact he'd never left his bed.)

The lake was there, heaving in the dark. The alewives were there, waiting to wash ashore.

Roses were there, clustered around fading Virgin Marys in crèches slightly askew. The Black Panthers were there, signalling secret meetings with African drums. The Nabisco plant was there, filling the night with the smell of vanilla. Lake Shore Drive was there, worrying me with its famous S-curve: When old enough to drive, would I be one of the dicks who drove into the lake?

Wide avenues of spreading oaks were there. Moss-covered park lagoons were there. Narrow gangways were there, smelling of wet brick. The Magikist Lips were there, always kissing. A decommissioned DC-9 sat atop a restaurant on Cicero, so working South-Siders with no hope of vacationing anywhere but the Dells could have the experience of eating on a plane.

Porn showed in the grand old theatres; pigeons nested on the new Picasso statue; old babushkas sat alone, watching *The Munsters* on Channel 32; guys clomped down North Rush Street in early disco shoes. Harold Drumm was there, a boy who'd lost his arm in a trash compactor and haunted my dreams because, it had said in the *Chicago American*, he'd run home, arm in hand, calling for his mother.

Petersen Coal, where Dad worked, was there. The flophouse lobby where he'd been held at gunpoint by a crazed conspiracy theorist was there. Division Street was there, down which an angry heartbroken mob of black high-school kids had marched the day of the King assassination, breaking out store windows with rocks and bricks, closing in on Dad's car when the Chicago cops intervened, firing their guns in the air. The famous racist Trent brothers were there – slumlords and customers of Petersen Coal – who'd mounted a machine gun in their office across from the Taylor Homes, anticipating the Uprising. They'd thrust delinquent black tenants into basement boilers head first, and, when they felt it necessary, they'd shove the guy all the way in and walk off, leaving him to burn.

Chinatown was there, Greektown was there, the Ukranian, Polish, Irish, and Mexican enclaves were there. Dad knew them all, down to the intersection where one ended and the other began.

We'd moved out too early. In truth I didn't know the city well at all. But some day I would. I'd move down there, live on Lake Shore Drive. That would be my base of operations. Yes: some day that burning white fire would know me too. I'd move around it with confidence, taking cabs, tipping bartenders who knew me by name, hanging out with Royko, who'd see me as his protégé, the real thing, a true Chicago kid.

Why live there, people would ask me. Why not Paris? Why not New York?

Why, it is my city, I would reply. It contains everything one could ever desire.

But now it was time to eat.

The entire city could be blocked out with the thumb. That was part of the pre-Jardine's ritual: you held up your hand and blocked out Chicago with your thumb.

But because you were a kid, and Chicago was all you knew, it was in your heart, and stayed there forever, the yardstick against which the rest of the universe was judged. ■

Snark *David Denby*

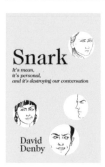

Snark – (noun)
Snark: a tone of teasing, snide, undermining abuse that's spreading through the media. In this sharp and witty polemic, David Denby takes on the snarkers. He identifies the nine principles of snark, tracing its history from personal insult in the drinking clubs of ancient Athens, through components as diverse as *Private Eye* and Tom Wolfe to its arrival in the age of the Internet.

Picador

Apology for the Woman Writing *Jenny Diski*

So overwhelmed was Marie de Gournay by the work of French essayist and philosopher Michel de Montaigne, that when she met him, she stabbed herself with a hairpin until the blood ran in order to show her devotion. 'An exceedingly literary novel... Diski's cool, modulated prose exhibits the moderation so prized by Montaigne, a warning to those of us who love books that there can be a danger in loving them too much.' Michael Arditti, *Independent*
jennydiski.co.uk

Virago £7.99

The Empty Throne *Tony Scotland*

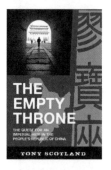

Travelogue, detective story, imperial saga, genealogical search; inspired by Bertolucci's *The Last Emperor*, Tony Scotland's quest for an imperial heir to the Dragon Throne in the People's Republic of China is a fascinating and fabulous read in every way. Now updated and with a new epilogue. 'A minor classic. Written in a rousing style, hilarious and sad by turns... absolutely gripping.' *The Spectator*
www.chalkstreambooks.com

Chalkstream Books £8.99

The Paris Review

Since *The Paris Review* was founded in 1953, it has given us invaluable conversations with the greatest writers of our age. This fourth collection of brilliant interviews is indispensable reading for all those interested in what makes our greatest writers tick. Introduced by Salman Rushdie, this volume includes interviews with Haruki Murakami, Marilynne Robinson, Philip Roth, Maya Angelou, Orhan Pamuk and many others.

Canongate £14.99, November 2009

GRANTA

Once Upon a Time the Zhou Brothers

Bei Dao

TRANSLATED BY JEFFREY YANG

When I first came to America in the autumn of 1988, I met the Zhou brothers in Chicago. At that point they'd only lived in the city for a couple of years, yet they were already practising their amplified version of traditional hospitality. The two of them kept me company for three days as we descended into Chinese restaurants and rose into bars in the sky. Chicago was heaven to me. They were generous, gracious, never allowing a word of protest, always whisking the cheque away.

On my next visit, in the summer of 1991, I fell from heaven into hell. I had come back to take part in a symposium at Chicago University and would be in the city for more than a month. There was regional discrimination among the participants right from the start: those from Taiwan and Hong Kong were put up in high-class hotels; others, like me, who were from mainland China, were checked into student dorms. I slept on a sofa in a communal lounge and didn't dare turn over once, even in my nightmares. But outside was where the real nightmares began: the roads were in ruins, the street lights were dim, everywhere people acted suspiciously, including me.

Then the Zhou brothers, liberators, appeared, and once again we were living the American dream. They had recently bought a club from some Polish people to convert into artists' studios and here they held a grand party for us – genuine red-lantern, green-wine, debauched revelry – with a host of waiters and a live American band. It was as if the wind had swept the clouds away, leaving us foreigners wide-eyed in wonder.

When the conference ended, I moved out of the dorm and in with the brothers. Besides playing games on the computer with Shan Zuo's son, Mo Hu ('Ink Tiger'), I wandered around nearby Chinatown. Shan Zuo's wife, Xiu Ling, handled all the household affairs, and the brothers, despite their slightly eccentric outward appearance, were naturally open and kind, letting the glow of their goodwill fall freely on those around them. Since then I've had one more home in the world, and have come to Chicago nearly every year, always staying with them. We don't keep in touch otherwise, but once we see each other, it's as if we only parted yesterday. Often I bring other friends with me: a dozen or so more mouths to feed, yet we drink plenty, eat more, crash for the night – nobody is treated like an outsider. As it is written: 'Within the four seas all are brothers.' In the world of contemporary art the generosity and benevolence of these two have become legendary. Every time they go to New York, it's said they throw a huge party for all the poverty-stricken Chinese artists in the city, each one rushing to tell another, so they can all be a part of what is more like a magnificent festival.

Even in Chicago, where they've lived now for nearly twenty-five years, Shan Zuo and Da Huang are still an unusual sight. Neither one is particularly tall, but they're both stocky and nearly bald on top, with long dark tresses that float down their backs like beards. Their eyes gleam like torches and usually they are dressed in black. To me they look like Wulin heroes straight out of the mountains and forests of ancient China.

On closer inspection, Shan Zuo possesses an inner calm and Da Huang a detached arrogance. Over the years, passing through Chicago, I've come to know something of their lives. Shan Zuo's original name is Shao Li, Da Huang's is Shao Ning. They are Zhuang ethnic minorities and were born in the city of Nanning, in the Guangxi Zhuang Autonomous Region of south-east China where it borders Vietnam. Their maternal grandmother, Zhou Jin Hua, started Wuming County's first girls' school. She was the principal and taught music and fine arts there. Her staunchly feudalistic husband, however, didn't agree with his wife's liberal outlook and this caused trouble between them. One day, Zhou Jin Hua left home taking their only daughter, Yi Xing, with her. When she grew up, Yi Xing became a teacher like her mother. This grandmother, Zhou Jin Hua, was the backbone of the family. She taught her two grandsons calligraphy from when they were very small, using the eighteenth-century *Mustard Seed Garden Manual of Painting* as a guide.

But a shadow hung over the family in the figure of Yi Xing's husband, Meng Yuan. He was a poetry scholar who drank heavily and had a wide circle of friends. Not long after Da Huang was born, Meng Yuan walked into a Party propaganda session and announced, 'These neophytes shouldn't be leading specialists...' and proceeded to rant drunkenly against the state. After the session, he went to buy Da Huang a little sweater and came home to find a pair of handcuffs waiting for him. He was sentenced and sent to a criminal reform camp. After that Yi Xing allowed her children to change their surnames to their grandmother's: Zhou. From then on, her teaching salary of only forty yuan a month had to take care of two adults and five children. Meng Yuan disappeared from the family forever.

In the time I've known them, the brothers have rarely brought up their father. Of the two, I've spent more time with Shan Zuo – but he's uncomfortable speaking about matters of the heart, while his capacity for alcohol surpasses that of anyone I know. It's obvious that he's inherited both his romantic nature and his love of drink from his father.

Each time I visit Chicago, it's as if the Zhou brothers deliberately conjure up new astonishments for me: they've bought a house for the land in order to design a private garden, set up a foundation, established a cultural centre, given financial aid to young artists and, most extraordinary of all, bought 160 hectares of forest land by Lake Michigan to create their own sculpture park. In these dreamless times, this is surely a kind of dream-making power.

One night not too long ago a group of friends converged in the bar in their home. Among them was a Metropolitan Opera bass-baritone, a group of black Broadway singers, some American businessmen who have dealings in China and bosses of the local Chinese newspaper. Once the music stopped people started to wander off and I walked with Shan Zuo to the studio to drink some more. We talked about the Cultural Revolution and Jia Yi's Han Dynasty essay, 'The Faults of Qin', and then the conversation turned to his father. During the War of Resistance, he said, there was a day when the Japanese bombed the school and his father brought home more than a hundred teachers and students to give them food, drink and shelter. 'Whenever my grandmother talked about this she'd always complain about it,' Shan Zuo said, 'but that's just the kind of person she was.'

I thought of the fate of the two generations: one drunken slip from Meng Yuan from which, it seemed, ten thousand generations could never recover. From then on, the two brothers had feared they might never escape the shadow of their father's fate.

In the late Sixties, Shan Zuo left home. He walked a hundred miles to a mountain village where he settled and found work. Saying little to those around him, he started painting portraits of Chairman Mao to earn money so that he could travel and see the world. In the early Seventies, when some colleges were recruiting worker-peasant-soldier students, Shan Zuo applied twice and was twice rejected because of his family background. In 1973 he returned home. His grandmother had died and the small house was dilapidated, but he was reunited with his brother, and in their elation they were inspired to make their first oil painting together. In the painting, two people row a small leaf of a boat that cuts forward through the waves, as if trying to break out of the frame – the dream vision of two children taking on the world outside.

For the next few years, Shan Zuo and Da Huang took temporary work as designers for the Guangxi Cai Diao Opera Troupe and for the province's Song and Dance Troupe. Then, in 1978, Shan Zuo was finally accepted into the stage design department of the Shanghai Theatre Academy. Da Huang stayed behind in Nanning. He wrote despondently to his older brother, 'Since you left for Shanghai, I've felt utterly alone, constantly lost. I often go to the places where we used to walk together. I'm full of selfish worries for the future, what to do – it's as if fate's strangling me... We brothers must carve out a new path together, we must struggle for art's ultimate aspirations.'

Da Huang told Shan Zuo he had decided to become a 'visiting student' at the Shanghai Theatre Academy, and he didn't wait for his older brother's letter in reply before leaving.

Da Huang arrived at the Shanghai Theatre Academy on March 3,

1979. As Shan Zuo only had one tight bunk space, the brothers decided to take turns sleeping. Shan Zuo went to classes during the day while Da Huang slept; then in the evening Shan Zuo rehashed the key points of each lecture for him. Da Huang painted for the rest of the night while Shan Zuo slept, returning to his older brother's bunk in the morning. But their double act was soon exposed. Their teachers, however, were so moved by the brothers' determination that they decided to let Da Huang sit in on classes. Not long after this, because a television was stolen from a classroom, stronger security measures were put in place and only officially registered students were allowed into the dorms. So Da Huang spent his nights outside, sleeping by the side of the road, or in a playground, curled up on the platform at the top of the slide. Later he rented a bunk in a public bathhouse that locked its doors at ten and opened at six a.m.

Those two years, between 1978 and 1980, marked a significant turning point in the history of Chinese art as it began to fall under the influence of Western movements. Like most of the other students studying art at the time, the Zhou brothers were excited by everything they saw and heard. It was as if that first oil painting, which they'd titled *Waves*, had been a sign; as if the boat was propelled by the energy of the changing times and was actually leading them outside the frame.

After their studies ended in Shanghai they made a pilgrimage along the Silk Road, standing awestruck before the cave paintings at Dunhuang and the stone carvings at Longmen. When they returned to Nanning, they found the oppressive atmosphere of the provincial capital unbearable. They converted a deserted warehouse owned by the Ministry of Culture into a secret art studio and abandoned themselves to their work day and night.

In February 1980 the Zhou brothers found a new source of inspiration close to home. The rock murals of Flower Mountain, painted by Zhuang people over two thousand years ago, stretch along the cliff face for more than 150 miles. The largest is forty-four metres high by 170 metres wide, and there are more than fifteen hundred primitive images in all. The significance of these murals, which date back to the Warring States period between 476 and 221 BC, is deeply ingrained in the Zhuang people's consciousness.

To study them, the brothers sailed down the river on a bamboo raft and roped together bamboo ladders to scale the cliffs. They slept on the raft or on the shore, caught fish, gathered wild herbs and drank sorghum wine. Gradually they filled scores of notebooks with sketches. On their return, from these sketches, the two brothers made over four thousand rock-mural paintings. Visitors to their studio were surprised to discover only images of nude men and women, and when reports of their work began to spread, the brothers found themselves blacklisted and in trouble once again.

But time brought a swift reprieve. In October 1982, carrying a letter of introduction, the brothers made a special trip to Beijing to meet the Dean of the Central Academy of Fine Arts, Zhang Ding. He was a great admirer of their rock-mural paintings and organized an exhibition in the Academy's galleries. Zhang Ding was the one who completely altered the brothers' fate. In February 1983 they returned to Beijing and enrolled at the Central Academy to continue their studies. In February 1985 they curated an exhibition of Flower Mountain murals at the National Art Museum of China. On the day of the opening ceremony, Zhang Ding was in Shijiazhuang on business. He spent the whole day worrying about some unforeseen disaster until he watched the CCTV report about the exhibition that night and his heart returned to its normal rhythm.

I can remember the day in 1985 that the exhibition closed; the memory is buried somewhere among the blur of my wife's labour and our baby's first cries. I had been riding my bike past the National Art Museum on the way to the Union Medical Hospital for the past few days and I'd seen 'Exhibition of the Murals of Flower Mountain' on the promotional banner. Because these two otherwise unrelated events became linked by the birth, I remembered the two brothers with the strange names.

When the Zhous came to America in 1986, after being invited to show their work in Chicago, they had thirty dollars and fifty paintings between them. Their English was non-existent. After a month they were brave enough to be interviewed on American television, but Da Huang told me that they hadn't even been able to understand the questions. It didn't take them long to infiltrate many of the best art galleries. At the Chicago International Art Fair in 1988 they showed dozens of works, nearly all of which sold, including one that broke the $300,000 barrier. 'That feeling of waking up overnight to world acclaim,' Shan Zuo told me, 'only people who've really known suffering can comprehend it.'

In January 2000 the Zhou brothers were invited to the World Economic Forum in Davos, Switzerland, where for the opening ceremony they improvised a live painting in front of an audience of world leaders and economists. On a canvas three metres high and nine metres wide, the brothers painted their simple, gestural motifs as if intoxicated, moving swiftly and deliberately. The whole process took forty-five minutes as the hall filled with applause and cheers. President Clinton was one of the many heads of state who later invited them to dinner.

Most modern success stories are the same except for a few details: the usual mixture of packaging and self-promotion. I've seen several of my friends sink and decay into wealth and fame, but not the Zhou brothers. Wearing their flat, sharp leather shoes, they've ridden the wave of success with astonishing skill. Actually, what surprises me the most is how two destitute boys managed to make their way out of China's interior into the rest of the world. Chance has certainly played its part, but one thing that's certain is their inner compulsion – and the stronger the compulsion, the further one goes. It must have something do with what their grandmother taught them by her example, with their mother's perseverance and their father's romantic nature, as well as his lingering shadow. I think it also has something to do with their ethnic-minority blood. Compared to the Han civilization which has already passed into decline, ethnic-minority cultures still possess a fighting spirit and a will to make memorable life-works. So that inner compulsion is perhaps a summoning of the blood that in their case goes back to those ancient rock paintings.

There is no doubt that the Zhou brothers' work has also been influenced by Abstract Expressionism, the post-Second World War movement that was so central to the New York art scene. Their spontaneous paintings have the same energy and improvisational quality that marked out the New York school in the Fifties. And in the same way that Western artists often found inspiration in 'exotic lands' and 'primitive cultures', the Zhou brothers have brought the Chinese tradition of impressionistic brush painting and the ancient signs of Chinese murals into the context of modernist Western art. Perhaps this kind of exchange is just another means of self-preservation in an increasingly homogeneous global culture. But it makes it easier to understand the Zhou brothers' art: the vast amount of white space, the ingenious touches of the brush, the free use of primitive signs that make up their paintings. When looking at them, one thinks of the works of the great Chinese painter Bada Shanren and the calligraphy and ancient pictographs of China.

And yet perhaps the greatest mystery is the way the brothers paint collaboratively. I asked them once if any conflict occurred during their creative process. Da Huang replied, 'Conflict is a kind of tension – in the whole of the painting it is transformed into an equivalent harmony.'

As I've spent more time with Da Huang, I've discovered that his savage energy perfectly balances Shan Zuo's passionate nature. Without his older brother's voice to temper it, Da Huang's energy risks a certain ruinous quality; without his younger brother's voice, Shan Zuo lacks a necessary fierceness.

At four in the morning, Shan Zuo and I were rapidly hitting the bottom of a bottle of Cognac. The primitive figures in the painting on the wall had begun to dance and leap about. I stumbled back to my room wondering why I couldn't walk straight. Shan Zuo held me up, leading me on as, staggering and tumbling, we made our way through the darkness. ■

Big Money

Dinaw Mengestu

When I returned to my father's small and slightly dilapidated office on the near South Side of Chicago in 2003 for the first time in several years, the most commonly spoken words by both him and the two drivers still left employed in his messenger service were 'big money'. Everyone in the office said it, my father included: 'big money', with extra emphasis on the 'b' so that the word, despite its natural brevity, always came out sounding as if it consisted of two syllables. Money was always the object of the sentence, even if it was only implied, but to hear the men in my father's office speak of it, it was only its size that mattered. If there was such a thing as 'little money', and in my father's messenger service there was plenty, it was hardly, if ever, spoken of, even though it comprised the vast majority of everyone's day, from the envelope that needed to be delivered from the South Loop to the north-west suburbs in no particular rush, to the lone box waiting to be ferried three blocks away. These minor deliveries were what kept the company running, and what paid the weekly, tax-free salaries of the constantly rotating list of drivers who could be found sprawled out in various positions on the few chairs that had been scavenged for the office. And yet like anything else on a small scale, they were generally hated by the drivers, who saw them only as a distraction from the potential big payday waiting in the shape of a fifty-box rush-hour delivery that was bound to come.

In a city as sprawling and as proud of its architectural grandeur as Chicago, such an emphasis on size seemed only fitting. Everything surrounding my father's office was big, and the men working with him rested in that shadow. The office was on the second floor of a two-storey building, just around the corner from a fast-food Greek takeout restaurant and a strip mall better suited to the suburbs, and yet less than a quarter of a mile away stood the Sears Tower and a dozen other skyscrapers whose shadows were literally cast over the office and road every afternoon. Size was paramount in a city like that, and if the immigrant men working with my father had to share only one word in common, it would have certainly been 'big'. What else could they say about the city they now found themselves in and about their dreams, and all the things that threatened to derail them, except that they were big?

The messenger service had been around for close to a decade by the time I returned to briefly manage it. My father at sixty had been diagnosed during a CAT scan with a large, cancerous tumour in his left lung. He never smoked. His drinking was confined to a weekly beer and, on even more rare moments, a glass of Scotch or cognac. His work kept him in solid shape; his arms and legs were even now still lithe and stronger than mine. He chided me constantly to eat more fruit and to pray – his twin pillars to having a long and healthy life – and yet bad luck, genetics, or unknown environmental factors won out, and he was scheduled to have at least one lobe of his lung removed.

I knew the general outlines of how the business worked, and who my father's major clients were, having briefly participated in the time-honoured tradition common to all small-business owners of taking their sons to work with them. In junior and in high school I spent at least the first month of each summer working with my father. I would help him or one of his drivers with the occasional delivery, or if my father was busy with the phones, which according to his rules always had to be answered by the third ring at the latest. I would wake up at seven a.m. or earlier each morning and dress in my father's clothes. I'd take a cleanly starched white shirt from his closet and socks from his bottom drawer, and while he always wore a full suit, I was allowed to get away with slacks or khakis, so long as they were ironed.

Our house in the suburbs was three blocks from the expressway and only one mile away from the city's border, so within minutes of leaving home we were heading straight towards the Sears Tower, which stood at the end of Interstate 290 the way I imagine castles must have once stood with an air of magnificent grandeur above the petty villages beneath them. Along the way we would listen to the morning news and once we had reached downtown, stop for doughnuts and coffee near the Chicago Mercantile Exchange. The half-hour journey was one of the few rituals that we ever shared and, even at the time, seemed to be especially poignant precisely because of that. While my father and I were hardly strangers there was a gap between us that was not only generational but also cultural: having been raised almost entirely in the Midwest, thousands of miles away from Ethiopia, I spoke of dreams and privileges that he could have never even considered.

During the first years of what I now think of as my accidental apprenticeship, my father often took me to meet his clients. While I stood next to him, dressed in miniature, he would proudly introduce me as his son, who, at the age of thirteen, was certain to become a doctor and was a straight-A student, even if at the time I no longer was. As I grew older and more familiar with the routines, I watched him slip thin white envelopes with a hundred dollars or less in them to the young men and women who were responsible for deciding which messenger service deserved their company's business, one of the facts of life that ranged from menstruation to his inevitable death that he no longer tried to shield me from. He called the women 'dear' and the men 'buddy' while flattering all of them equally.

Afterwards I would watch him descend from the twentieth- or thirtieth-floor mail room with a package in his hand, wrapped in a small rage as he spoke of the crooks and thieves that made business almost impossible and yet he knew he could never do without. At the end of each week, if all went well and his clients had paid their invoices on time, I was given a cheque disproportionately larger than what I deserved and perhaps even disproportionately larger than what he could afford. At the very most I had helped carry a few boxes, or perhaps I had sat in the driver's seat of a car while it was illegally parked and had kept him or one of his drivers from getting yet another ticket, which leads me now to believe that more than anything my father was paying me to witness his life, and in more specific terms his life in that city so that I would know what to expect when I was older, so that I harboured no illusions or false sentiments of just exactly how all of this worked.

I had always planned on never returning to Chicago. It was one of those private vows made without ever having to be formally declared, but that nonetheless exist in their own right, like the desire to some day get married or have children. From the moment I left for college I considered my break with the city irrevocable. Despite its size and diversity, I thought of the city as provincial; as a place of tight, confined borders from which people rarely ventured, and where a distinct brand of Midwestern racism and ignorance lived and thrived. These were the general terms on which I had experienced the city as a child and to which I still, however unfairly, held it. By the time I was old enough to leave, several close friends had slipped into a temporary life of drugs and gangs, while plenty of others remained permanently rooted, either through teenage pregnancies or short-lived high-school careers, to the small-town suburbs in which we had grown up. I had been called a nigger dozens of times in high school, and with bigger, and meaner, friends taking the lead I had later gone out of my way to frighten young white couples walking along the lake shore. And while of course I knew at the time that none of this was unique to Chicago, I was convinced that the city itself was somehow guilty of creating at least some of the anger and contempt I often felt, if only because there had to be something more specific than human nature to blame.

Chicago was not a small Midwestern town, although on the many nights I spent fantasizing about my future life somewhere along the east coast or in Europe, I treated it again, however unfairly, as if it were. I still loved the city for its aesthetics and even though at that time I had travelled to only a handful of other places in America, I was right in assuming that few could match the splendour of driving north along Lake Shore Drive and watching the skyscrapers and Lake Michigan gradually unfold in almost competing strains of beauty – the city all towering glass and stone with the massive lake, almost always flat and placid, lapping up against it.

When my father's diagnosis came in I was living in Brooklyn and working part-time for a well-known writer and her son. I had just finished my MFA at Columbia University and was working on the fourth revision of a novel set, appropriately enough, in a small Midwestern town destroyed in a flood. I spent my evenings going to readings and parties or at various bars with friends, drunkenly imagining our own bright literary futures as we heaped lavish praise on the writers we adored and indulged in mocking all of the others. My girlfriend at the time, an aspiring human rights lawyer who had reared herself out of poverty and into law school, stood sceptically to the side.

'There's nothing real to what you're doing,' she told me more than once, describing my life at times as self-indulgent, at other times as pretentious and overly romantic, which of course it was, in part because that was precisely what I had sought – a life of intellectual languor, where days and nights were spent in the company of big ideas that were stifled only by the constant presence of a hangover.

Despite how enamoured I thought I might have been with my life, the only private debate I had with myself about returning to Chicago was for how long. My father and I never discussed what role I would play when I was there. We said nothing at all about the business or who would take care of it while he recovered. During the one phone conversation that we had before I returned, he simply said he was going to be fine and I need not worry. He handed the phone back to my mother and it was to her that I said I was going to find a one-way ticket to Chicago in the following days, and that I would take leave from work or even quit my job so I could stay as long as needed. She briefly insisted that this wasn't necessary. She said that I could come home for the surgery and then return to New York shortly afterwards, but her protests were only half-hearted and didn't last long. I would like to say that this happened because I had been faithfully reared to believe in small sacrifices and the preservation of family above all else, and while there may have been some of that in my abrupt departure for home, there was also a greater unacknowledged understanding that my life was still not formed, that I was in danger of wasting it and that, more likely than not, after never having held down a real, stable job, I probably needed some money.

K arl was one of the last full-time drivers working in my father's office when I arrived. A large, middle-aged recent immigrant from Poland with fine blond hair and a thick accent, Karl was responsible for coining the phrase 'big money' and as a result claimed a certain pride in ownership over the words. He employed them almost hourly, sometimes on multiple occasions over the course of a single sentence. He told me often, especially during my first few days in the office, before my father was admitted into the hospital, that, 'This is not big money. *This* is big money.' He had only been in America for a handful of years, just long enough to take a critical, if not contemptuous, view of most things concerning the business and to be convinced that regardless of the circumstances, he could surely do better.

In the days before my father's surgery, when he was still checking into the office daily, the two would often have rambling arguments over the lack of work coming in or which routes were best for getting to a particular suburb during rush hour. Each was righteous in his own particular way. Karl, in a near rage which could just as easily be disassembled or assembled, would complain about the lack of big money coming into his pockets. My father would try and assure him that big money was coming, if not now, then soon. On at least one occasion I remember that their argument was interrupted by a phone call from one of their clients requesting an immediate pickup of a number of heavy boxes that needed to be transported twenty miles away to an office outpost in the suburbs. I remember my father hung up the phone, stood up and with a big smile repeated the order directly to Karl: 'Twenty boxes. Pickup from Lower Wacker to Winnetka. Rush.'

There was no need to say anything else. The significance of twenty boxes going from downtown Chicago to the far northern suburbs as a rush-order delivery was so self-evident that they could just as easily have continued to stand there grinning at one another, but it seemed as if the moment wouldn't have been complete unless they fully acknowledged it. Perhaps Karl said it first, although in this case it would have more likely been my father, who had an instinctive sense of how to appease his drivers. 'Big money,' he said, to which Karl responded back, even more enthusiastically, 'Big money.' Whatever argument they were having was temporarily suspended, if not forgotten. Karl rushed out the door and my father sat back down to better enjoy his reprieve.

From the beginning I imagined Karl and me becoming if not friends, then at least solid drinking partners. Once my father was in the hospital I pictured myself saying to Karl at the end of the day, 'Let's go have a beer. I'm buying.' When Karl was busy handling a major, big-money run, I took care of the small deliveries around the city, which in the beginning took me twice as long as they should have. Occasionally if Karl was still in the office when I left to make a run he would tell me the fastest way to get to the intersection of Dearborn and Jackson, where to park the van so as to avoid a traffic ticket while making a delivery, or how to find a particular loading dock on Lower Wacker. Our shared vocabulary consisted initially almost entirely of logistics.

Eventually we made several large deliveries together, experiences that bonded us close enough for Karl to share with me occasional fragments of his life in Poland before he came to America. He was unabashed in his nostalgia for home and like my father spoke often about the things he loved and missed and was certain to never find here, things that ranged from family, to love to decency, integrity and honesty. There was none of that in Chicago and in America, as far as he could tell. What there was here, though, was work, work that could lead to big money, which Karl was committed to.

After only a few days at the office with Karl I began to think of my life in Chicago as the temporary manager of a small business as more real than anything I had done before. The hours spent delivering packages, answering the phone or talking with Karl seemed to have an inherently greater substance than the life I'd been living in New York, which in comparison now seemed like all smoke and mirrors; child's play that had been extended into a second decade of life and would perhaps some day be extended a third. Chicago was a realer city – more down to earth and normal, a place where men worked hard and drank beer, a ritual of which I was now part. I was shuttling daily between the hospital, my father's office and whatever small deliveries fell to me to complete. I had never anticipated it, but I began to pass the hours spent in traffic wondering how I could help improve the business. I tried to think of business contacts I could drum up from college; new technology I could investigate and advertisements I could write in search of new drivers. It would take months, if not years, to do all that and as far as I could see at the time, that was just fine. I was finding my way around the city again. I was having dinner with old friends in neighbourhoods I had rarely visited before. It was fall and the city, weather and evening light were glorious, and as if that weren't enough, the Chicago Cubs, historically the worst team in baseball since the second half of the twentieth century, were in first place and seemed like serious contenders for the World Series.

Either by luck or by serious efforts of the imagination, sometimes seemingly disparate events converge, through which we try and find a pattern. That fall I took the Cubs' unexpected winning season and drained it for all possible meaning. It had been ninety-five years since the Cubs had won the World Series and almost sixty since they had made it to the finals, and yet in the fall of 2003 they were one of the best teams in the country. The significance behind this was obvious to me. The Cubs were on the rise and as their good fortune extended, so would my family's. It was a simple one-to-three ratio: the Cubs would win the World Series, my father would emerge cancer-free, business would thrive and I would later be able to say that I was there to have witnessed it all.

The fact that I had never really cared about baseball hardly mattered. As a child I went to three or four Cubs games a year. I cheered them passionately while they were in plain view and mostly forgot about them shortly afterwards. Starting that September, I became a devoted fan. I read, watched or listened to every game, sometimes rushing between deliveries to my new favourite bar in the Ukrainian Village to watch a couple of innings before heading back to work. I had become fully invested in the myth and lore of baseball's most heartbreaking team, with its sad-luck string of losers and occasional heroes. I found myself able to slip easily into conversations about baseball and the Cubs' chances of winning the division and making it into the World Series with strangers at a bar. I said things like, *The new pitching staff is remarkable, perhaps the best in baseball. Kerry Woods is the best young pitcher in the league. Sammy Sosa is inconsistent in the play-offs: a great but greedy player who likes to only hit home runs. Dusty Baker is the best manager in baseball, and the Cubs should be thanking the gods daily for giving him to them.*

I often had these conversations in the same bar I now frequented, where in keeping with the spirit of the time I drank cheap bottles of Pabst Blue Ribbon, the official beer of the Chicago Cubs, known for its flat, watery consistency and popularity, instead of the rail Scotch that had sustained me in New York. It was part of a rapid transformation that I imagined I was making from New York literary life to that of the now mythical blue-collared American worker. I found pleasure in rushing to finish a beer and cigarette while watching a game in order to fill a last-minute delivery for one of the law firms we regularly worked for. This was real life and real work, and, with the exception of my drive-by bar stops, how my father and his drivers spent most of their days.

On the afternoon my father was scheduled to come out of surgery I was sitting in traffic, less than a mile away from Wrigley Field. I was supposed to be at the hospital with my mother and sister when the doctor came out, but a call had come in at the last second and with Karl already away on another delivery, it was mine to handle. I had turned on to the wrong highway (I should have taken the local streets instead) and now found myself in lurching gridlock traffic that made it impossible to arrive on time. I say this only by way of measuring the sometimes stark divides between our competing desires. Part of why I had returned to Chicago was to be there in that moment when the doctor stepped out and announced to my family that either all was well or that there was still more bad news to come. I had steeled myself for the latter and even though all was expected to turn out well, my father and I had even briefly tried to discuss how, should anything go wrong, it would be up to me now to see my mother and sister through.

There may not have been much truth in what we said – my mother is more resilient and capable than both of us combined – but we indulged in our old-world fantasies of men as protectors and providers nonetheless. When it was clear I would never make it back in time, and when my mother called to say the surgeon was waiting to see her and that she would go in and talk to him alone, I felt that separation acutely in ways my father must have felt a dozen times before when his obligation to a business that he had forged more out of necessity than desire kept him away. It was never so much that he was called from our lives at critical points, although of course this certainly must have happened, but that more often than not he was unable to do or say anything other than respond affirmatively when his cellphone, always perched nearby, rang. His drivers often rejected his calls, especially those that came late at night just after they had finally settled home and had finished dinner and were sleeping away some of their exhaustion in front of the television. If no other driver picked up, he would rise and occasionally he would ask me to come along for company. He made sacrifices to his body and, just as critically, to his time in ways that, despite my efforts to understand him, had always eluded me, until now.

I remember briefly pressing down furiously on the horn after I spoke to my mother, even though that would change nothing, and then turning up the music loud so as to not be able to hear the other drivers doing the same. I let my mind wander into worst-case scenarios in which the strict, towering surgeon with the slight German accent told my mother in the same dispassionate voice in which he said everything; that despite their best efforts, my father had failed to make it through, or that he had made it through, but really to no good purpose since the cancer had indeed spread and was now clearly in his lymph nodes running rampant through other parts of his body.

Such fantasies either serve to prove our own helplessness against the body's steady march towards death, or they reward us with our own images of how we would stand courageous in the face of that fact. Not being there meant imagining the worst and quickly I began to pile on the indignities. I was twenty-three, an aspiring writer with multiple degrees, and until a few weeks before had been employed by a well-known writer, and yet I was now spending my days in mail rooms across the city, picking up boxes and being told that I was running late. My father was lying in the hospital and my mother and sister were in a waiting room, and whatever pleasure I may have previously found in the honesty of my labour evaporated. I hated where I was and what I had to do and, by extension, what my father had always done to play his role in keeping us afloat, in part for the work itself, but more importantly because in order for it continue, it had to come before everything else.

When I spoke to my mother less than an hour later she told me rather calmly that all had gone well. They had removed a significant portion of my father's left lung. The surgery had been a success and there was ample reason to believe that they had caught all of the cancer. It was exactly what we had been told to expect. I can trace the break with my fantasies about real work and real life to that day. After that I tried to spend less time in the office and more in the hospital, even if that meant a few calls had to initially go unanswered or a couple of packages had to be delivered late. As my father recovered I read to him Gogol's *Diary of a Madman*, employing some of the same theatrical techniques he had once used when he invented stories for my sister and me when we were children. There was something about the escape into literature that we both found comforting and edifying, and if there had been no business to worry about I would have spent every afternoon doing only that. Now when I was called away to make a delivery I hated it. I could find nothing redeeming in the work, except that it was important to my father. While picking up a stack of boxes late one night from a law firm, I found myself wanting to explain to the young lawyers that this was not really me they were seeing, a thought which, despite its honesty, I still find contemptible.

W ith my father recovering, Karl began to transfer his complaints about the lack of big money on to me. Unlike my father, however, I had no natural way of responding. I couldn't promise him that big money was coming and I didn't particularly care if it did. One afternoon he confided in me out of nowhere that there had, in fact, never been such a thing as the Holocaust. It was an invention of the Jews who were also running America. We argued briefly, but of course there was no way of winning and I was certain that if I had probed deeper I would have found a host of other things that he hated or looked down on, including – even if my father and I had been been excluded – blacks. It was easy to make sure I never had a sustained conversation with him again.

I still held on to the Cubs, however, even though the pattern I thought I had detected had proved itself to be as foolish as I had always suspected. From the same bar in the Ukrainian Village I drank and cheered as if much more were personally at stake as they won their division. All they had to do now was beat the Florida Marlins in a seven-game series to make it into the World Series. By mid-October they were up three games to one and everyone in the city was elated. The Cubs were just one game away from taking the conference championship, the second best thing to winning the World Series itself. When they lost game five some of that elation vanished and there was an encroaching sense that perhaps we were all being set up for yet another disappointment. On the television and on the radio announcers talked frequently about the Curse of the Goat, a story dating back to 1945 when Billy Sianis and his goat were allegedly kicked out of Wrigley Field during game four of the World Series. Sianis, after being evicted, reportedly said that the Cubs *ain't gonna win any more*; fifty-eight years later millions of people across Chicago seemed to be busy speculating as to whether or not that was still going to be true.

The last two games of the series, which only a week earlier had seemed unnecessary, were scheduled to be played in Chicago. An old childhood friend who now worked as a reporter for the *Chicago Tribune,* and with whom I had spent much of the past month watching the games, called me on the day of game six to say he had won two tickets through his office lottery. I considered it more than just an act of good luck or fortune that we were going, and even though I may not have been willing to admit it to myself at the time, I'm sure I saw it as a form of compensation for what had been a long and difficult month. The Cubs were going to win and the equation I had concocted earlier would finally work itself out to my satisfaction.

The first eight innings of game six were the best moments in baseball that I will most likely ever see live. The Cubs' pitching kept the Marlins from scoring a single run while the rest of the team added one glorious point after another. Every hit or deep fly ball was a minor victory, with everyone in the stands erupting accordingly. We were hoarse from screaming and singing and, of course, drunk on beer. When the eighth inning began we were up 3–0 and anyone there would have said that only a cruel act of God could have stopped us.

What happens next is now already part of the city's lore. In the eighth inning, with two outs, Luis Castillo, batting for the Marlins, hits a high fly ball to left field. The Cubs outfielder, Moisés Alou, jumps to grab it at the same time that a fan leans over the stands to reach for the ball, making it almost impossible to catch. The Cubs' management cries for a call of fan interference, but the umpires are unmoved. Rather than a third and final out, Castillo remains at the plate. He's walked on a wild pitch, sending him to first base and another runner to third. Two more batters come to the plate, each one driving home at least one run so that by the time the inning is over the game is tied and a stadium full of Cubs fans are pointing to left field at the fan who leaned over the railing and are chanting 'asshole' in unison. The Cubs, in a manner and style that seem wholly unique to them, go down quickly. They give up five more runs in the final inning, losing the game 8–3. The following day they are crushed again in game seven, bringing their almost glorious season to what in retrospect seems like a fitting, if not inevitable, end.

Three weeks after that game I returned to New York, at least one month earlier and, in my mind, several years older than I had expected. While the Cubs had blown it, my father's recovery had moved along steadily. The surgeon even later reported how lucky they were in catching the tumour when they did since it was just millimetres away from attacking the lymph nodes. He predicted a full and rapid recovery and by the end of October my father was already managing most of the business with his cellphone from his bed. Even though I was no longer responsible for answering the calls, I felt a pull inside my stomach and heart every time the phone rang.

I would like to say that my father returned to work effortlessly, but that seems unlikely. I'm sure that it took a great amount of effort and will to do so, certainly even more than before. I stayed around long enough to understand that he would manage just fine without me before I left to go back to New York. I returned to my normal life with a slightly naive promise to myself that I would return to Chicago frequently, in part to be reminded of the great efforts taken by my parents on their children's behalf. I sometimes joked with my friends that it was hard returning to the real world: real work, real life, real responsibilities, which was to say by extension that everything else was artifice, a sentiment which I still partly believe in even as I'm quick to reject it.

Before we moved to Chicago we spent our first seven years in America living three hours south in Peoria, Illinois. We attended a Southern Baptist church; my father worked in a Caterpillar factory, famous for making tractors, and my mother worked at the local university. A summer night out was to a drive-through ice-cream stand that also had benches near the side of the road. When I lived in Chicago, I often thought of that time in Peoria as somehow having been more authentic to what we think of when we picture life in America because of its seemingly wholesome nature; because I could tick off all the boxes that came with that picture of an earnest and hard-working American family. Chicago was too big, too aggressive and violent to fall into that category, until, of course, I moved away and returned and saw a fraction of it from my father's perspective. Now, even though no one in our family lives there any more, Chicago still seems to me like the very heart of the heartland, for reasons having nothing to do with geography and nothing to do with size. ∎

You'll have heard how the city once ended in fire, and around these parts, it threatens to end in ice every few years or so. But once, not too long ago, Chicago flirted with ending in water, an entirely preventable man-made inundation that few saw but everybody felt – a two-billion-dollar sucker-punch tsunami that weighed in among the dozen most costly floods in American history.

The groundwork for the Great Flood of 1992 was laid a century before, when the Illinois (later Chicago) Tunnel Company built a series of semi-official, semi-clandestine tunnels under almost every street downtown. The tunnels were only supposed to house telephone cables, but in a nice Pynchonian twist, the operators covertly decided to install a narrow-gauge railway for delivering freight, as well. The dirt hauled out of the tunnels filled in the lakefront and formed all the land now under Grant Park, the Field Museum, Soldier Field and McCormick Place. You'd think that amount of landfill ought to have tipped off more than a few officials that something besides phone cables was going in underground.

In fact – show me another city so coarse and strong and cunning! – all the phone cables came right out again, just half a dozen years later, leaving the several dozen miles of illegal underground railroad system to haul coal, ashes and freight to and from buildings all over the downtown. When the tunnel company finally went bust after another forty years, they abandoned the tunnels, which fell into limbo. Because the passages violated all kinds of private property lines, nobody really owned them and the city never assumed full responsibility.

Now cut to September 1991, when another semi-regulated private company was driving piles into the Chicago River (the river that this city, in one of history's all-time mind-boggling engineering feats, persuaded to run backwards). The dolphin pilings were supposed to keep barges and tourist boats from smacking into the foundations of the Kinzie Street drawbridge. But somebody forgot to remind the pile-drivers about the long-neglected passages honeycombing not far below, and a misgauged piling compromised the walls of a tunnel directly under the river.

Now comes the distinctive Chicagoan twist: cable television workers down in the tunnels a couple of months later actually saw the leak, videotaped it oozing mud and water, and sent the urgent evidence to City Hall. The staff of Mayor Daley – Hizzoner the Second – promptly set out…to take bids from other private companies, to see who could patch things up the most cheaply. Three months later, the tunnel walls at last collapsed, and overnight the river came pouring in.

The abandoned freight tunnels filled quickly, soon taking in about a quarter of a billion gallons. Water passed easily through old concrete barriers and soon began to fill the city's subway system tunnels as well. Businesses that had forgotten about their illegal freight-tunnel hook-ups a half a century earlier were shocked to find their foundations filling with up to forty feet of water. The power grid began to short out, the Board of Trade and Mercantile Exchange suspended trading when waters began to percolate up through their basements, and the entire downtown and financial district were eventually shut down and evacuated.

Weirdly, at street level, there was no trace of the subterranean deluge. Only this once in a lifetime thing, water flowing underground…

City officials scrambled to find the cause, nobody quite piecing the flood together with the video reports from months before. Work crews began shutting down the city's largest water mains, trying to stop the surging tide, but only compounding the disastrous loss of utilities and services. Meanwhile, WMAQ radio's night-time crime reporter, tipped off to the fact that the aquarium seemed to have relocated to the basement of the Merchandise Mart, went on air early that morning, saying:

> I have found something very interesting in the Chicago River on the east side of the Kinzie Bridge. I see swirling water that looks like a giant drain… I am hearing reports that fish are swimming in the

basement of the Mart just feet from the swirl! I do not see any
emergency crews near this spinning swirl, but I think they may want
to take a look. In fact I think someone should wake up the Mayor!

The city emergency teams showed up at the swirling bathtub drain
shortly thereafter.

But it took three days, sealing off and lowering the Chicago River;
dumping sixty-five truckloads of rock, cement and mattresses into the
now-gaping hole; and punching a release sluice from the flooded
clandestine tunnels into the Chicago Deep Tunnel system at massive
expense before the downtown drained out enough for life to resume.
Some skyscrapers stayed closed for weeks. The full, compounded costs
of the disaster are impossible to calculate, but the wrangling over
insurance and legal responsibility, needless to say, went on for years.

And the Pynchonian secret-freight tunnels? They stayed popular
well into the twenty-first century with the real-life Dungeons and
Dragons urban-explorer set, who used them to go spelunking and
building-hacking. Then a terrorist threat from a deranged member of
the Chicago Urban Exploration club led to the tunnels' final sealing a
few years ago. But the sixty miles of twisting passageways are still down
there, awaiting their accidental rediscovery by some unwitting private
company half a century from now. Until then My Kind of Town stands
ready again for any fresh elemental disaster, forever bareheaded,
shovelling, wrecking, planning, building, breaking, rebuilding… Okay:
maybe a little light on the planning. ∎

The Projects

Camilo José Vergara

View north from 4555 South State Street, Chicago, Robert Taylor Homes, 1995

C hicago was the first large American city I visited after I came to the United States from my home country, Chile. I arrived in the Windy City at five in the morning, one day in October 1965, having travelled there overnight from Baltimore on a Greyhound bus. My first impression was of the downtown as I wandered along the empty streets waiting for the banks to open. The streets seemed narrow and dark and the buildings soared to great heights leaving only a small sliver of sky visible. There were several billboards with huge pictures of camels on them but no words or writing. I thought I was hallucinating.

As a photographer I have followed Chicago's progress for nearly four decades, focusing, as I do in other cities, on the poorest and most segregated neighbourhoods. Over the years Chicago has reinvented itself in many ways. The city has spent lavishly on its downtown, adding the Sears Tower and the Hancock Tower which have transformed its already magnificent skyline; it has also demolished tens of thousands of vacant homes and hundreds of large factories, and put up a large number of new buildings to replace them. Trees and flowers have been planted throughout the city. But from my point of view the most dramatic development has been the demolition of most of the city's high-rise public housing projects, built in the 1950s and 1960s.

While I was a student in the late 1960s at Notre Dame University, Indiana, about a hundred miles to the east, I thought of Chicago as a place to visit for fun and excitement. Driving towards the city, the stink of Gary, Indiana always let you know you were getting close. Nearer to downtown the famous skyline came into view and right there along the Dan Ryan Expressway stood something even more remarkable: the twenty-eight towers of the Robert Taylor Homes, each one a sixteen-storey slab of reinforced concrete, stretching for two and a half miles along the highway. Seen from a speeding automobile, the repeating forms of the projects were for me a defining feature of Chicago. Twenty years later I would look at the Dan Ryan Expressway from the rooftops of the Robert Taylor Homes. In 2009 seagulls fly where the towers used to be.

After the demolition of the Pruitt Igoe housing projects in St Louis in 1972, the Chicago projects became the nadir of ghetto living. By the late 1970s the Robert Taylor Homes, as well as other large-scale public housing projects in Chicago such as the infamous Cabrini Green and Henry Horner Homes, were national symbols of poverty, segregation and crime. Life in these buildings grew increasingly dangerous and difficult as their residents grew poorer. Not only that, but by the middle of the decade the families that lived in them were overwhelmingly African-American, often headed by women living on public assistance. Those who could, moved out, leaving those behind ever more helpless and isolated.

As the years passed I began to notice the signs of dereliction and desertion: black smoke outlined windows of apartments that had caught fire, windows were boarded up, the older boards, dark and dull, contrasting with the shinier newer ones. Wire mesh covered the exterior hallways linking the apartments – what the architects had originally called 'sidewalks in the sky'. Extensive graffiti as well as the dangling wires for cable and satellite television transformed the once clean grid-like facades into a jumble of tangled lines. In the 1980s some blocks were 'consolidated', that is, their top floors were closed and sealed off from the lower floors. Children grew up in them without ever visiting the top half.

I began to make portraits of the most notorious projects and to re-photograph them every time I visited Chicago, which was twice a year if I could manage it. On occasion there were tense moments since drug dealers were often 'clocking' at the entrances. With the camera on the roof of a car, I faced the buildings squarely and photographed them with an architectural lens so their sides remained parallel. I didn't think of them as simply buildings, but as human faces whose signs of visible ageing I wanted to record.

I thought my pictures would provide answers to questions I had, such as which were the best and worst blocks in a complex, which floors had the most fires, did it make a difference if there was a police station on the ground floor? While I always wanted to capture the unexpected in the projects, I never imagined that I was going to document their demise and demolition.

From the late 1980s I would be escorted by public housing officials, maintenance workers or security guards so I could gain access to and photograph from the roof. I became familiar with dreary office lobbies where I waited for hours until someone appeared to accompany me to the top. From my guides I learned how to enter the buildings without being hit by heavy objects thrown from the upper floors. At times I had to stand awkwardly by as the security people reassured gang members that I didn't work for the police. Everywhere I went I eavesdropped and wrote down what I heard.

At the Henry Horner Homes management office a dishevelled man looking like a prophet, named Nathaniel, yelled, 'They want us to have diseases, they want us to die out.' Nathaniel was there with a small elderly woman to complain about a leak in their apartment. After they left, the receptionist explained that he was an alcoholic and a drug addict, adding, 'The women sit by the window and throw out Pampers, bloody napkins and pipes. You have four people on the ground but only three can work, the fourth has to look up all the time to warn others about things coming out of the windows. Nobody wants to come here and work in this hellhole. I think this is the worst development in Chicago.'

Written on walls and among people I met I discovered nicknames I never knew existed, such as Lil'-Roach, Lil' Nell, Creep #1, A Dog, D-Dog, Nike Dog, T-Bone, Lord Radar and Solid World. And first names such as Bakarus, Shaterse, Marshon, Jevale, Dijo, Lamario, Davetta and Toimail. I collected these names in the early 1990s as evidence that in their architecture and lifestyle the ghettos were a fundamentally different environment from the rest of America.

For many local residents projects were proof that slavery had not ended in 1865 with the Union victory in the Civil War. I frequently heard references to slavery and prisons, but I understood them to mean that projects were built to keep African-Americans segregated and inferior. In 2009, in a South Side store by the name of Wild Wild, I found commemorative T-shirts with images of mostly disappeared buildings in notorious developments in Chicago. Written above the images of public housing buildings was '1865'.

On my way up to the rooftops I inspected mostly broken mailboxes and barely functioning elevators where the smell of urine always came through despite the liberal application of cleaning fluid. I examined the hallways and went inside apartments with maintenance workers to look at the problems they were supposed to fix. I passed through dark elevator penthouses and heard water dripping there along with the clanking and screeching of the poorly maintained machinery. Good setting for a horror movie, I thought.

The elevators were often dark and slow. Little light came out of their cabin lamps since the plastic covers were smeared with smoke. Rides were made longer because of frequent breakdowns. If I chose to use the stairs instead, here I would surely encounter graffiti-covered walls, and find piles of mattresses and crack vials littering the way. The maintenance staff often cooked food in the small closets where they kept their tools. They were proud of their heavy stews and would invite their co-workers to eat with them. Once I was offered a pig's ear sandwich on white bread, with part of the ear covered in black sauce protruding from between the slices.

Foul smells lingered in these high rises and followed me during my visits throughout the buildings. Often garbage was piled up at the lobby as well as on every floor. Nothing was properly cleaned so that semi-solid layers of filth accumulated everywhere contributing to the overall stench. The smell of the Chicago projects lives on in my memory to this day.

It was always a relief to reach the roof. From there I could see Lake Michigan, the Chicago skyline, the other housing projects with areas of decay surrounding them, stretching off into the distance. Wild flowers and sometimes even bushes grew up there. Once on the roof of the ABLA Homes in the city's West Side, I followed a monarch butterfly as it flew from flower to flower.

During my visits to Chicago, I would regularly drive down the old commercial streets such as West Madison Street – badly scarred from the 1968 riot that followed Martin Luther King's assassination – as well as Ogden Avenue, Ashland Avenue and other thoroughfares where most businesses have been destroyed by fire or closed down.

On Ogden Avenue in the 1980s I came across an Oldsmobile dealership with a huge neon rocket sign out front. The dealership had closed long ago and of course the sign didn't light up any more. The building was being used for storage, its large display windows sealed with cinder blocks. Later the neon sign was dismantled to prevent passers-by from being accidentally hit by the falling rocket. On a recent visit, earlier this year, I found the building itself was gone, yet walking around I could still see the terrazzo floor of the showroom and imagine families driving out of it in their new automobiles. Just down the road, Ogden Avenue became Route 66, beckoning them all the way to California.

Running off Fifth Avenue I found something rare for Chicago: a winding street with a continental look. This is West Monroe Street, and many of the houses here had turrets, which were once a popular architectural feature in the city, especially for buildings on corners. These turrets were prone to rot, and often started to fall apart, forcing their owners to remake them but without the rich original detailing that gave them their charm. West Monroe Street appeared to have lost most of its trees, but this year I saw new saplings growing from small beds in the grass-covered sidewalks.

Travelling the rusting El, the train line that rattles and screeches its way over commercial streets along Chicago's South Side, I revisited the same empty lots I had first photographed twenty-one years ago. Here the city looked pretty much the same except this time, instead of the ground covered with snow, there were fields of green grass. The old A&P Supermarket at Ellis Avenue and Forty-third Street, which was abandoned by 1992, had been demolished and a new retro-style apartment building erected in its place. This intersection is about ten blocks north of President Obama's Chicago home.

Crime has not decreased here as much as it seems to have done in other cities such as New York. DON'T SHOOT! billboards can still be seen in areas such as Englewood in the South Side where gang activity and crime are still widespread. Avenues such as Ashland and Halsted are now as dangerous as State Street and Division Street, running along where the housing projects used to be. This year I saw that the Department of Homeland Security was sponsoring billboards which asked: WHERE IS YOUR FAMILY? Dereliction and decay have spread to encompass sections of older ghettos such as Englewood and Lawndale and even the suburbs beyond.

Tall smokestacks, reminders of Chicago's industrial past, are disappearing from the landscape as factories are demolished and the city gets cleaned up. For those who enjoy the beauty of decaying iron and steel, Chicago has its movable bridges and the El. Its iron structure frames the street below as it runs into the distance and its shadows form intricate patterns on the pavement.

Under the vacant lots left behind when the factories and workshops are demolished lie basements and tunnels. Metal footings for machinery protrude through the concrete floors. Today one needs to be an archaeologist to understand what went on in these places. But there is no doubt that the great industrial era of Chicagoland is gone. ■

Chicago 1981–2009: Photographs

Camilo José Vergara

Robert Taylor Homes, view north east from 4500 South Federal Street, 1988

Robert Taylor Homes, view north east from 4500 South Federal Street, 2000

View north east from 4500 South Federal Street, 2009

Cabrini Green, West Division Street at North Cleveland Avenue, 1988

Cabrini Green, West Division Street at North Cleveland Avenue, 1995

West Division Street at North Cleveland Avenue, 2004

Cabrini Green, West Division Street at North Cleveland Avenue, 2001

West Division Street at North Cleveland Avenue, 2009

1117 North Cleveland Avenue, 1988

1117 North Cleveland Avenue, 1995

1117 North Cleveland Avenue, 1998

West Taylor Street from South Washtenaw Avenue, 1988

View north east from West Taylor Street at South Washtenaw Avenue, 1993

View north east from West Taylor Street at South Washtenaw Avenue, 2006

View north east from West Taylor Street at South Washtenaw Avenue, 1994

View north east from West Taylor Street at South Washtenaw Avenue, 2009

Former Oldsmobile dealership at West Odgen Avenue and South Drake Avenue, 1987

Corner of West Odgen Avenue and South Drake Avenue, 2009

2051 West Lake Street, demolition of Henry Horner Homes, 1995

Fifth Avenue and Monroe Street, 1981

Fifth Avenue and Monroe Street, 1991

Fifth Avenue and Monroe Street, 1997

Fifth Avenue and Monroe Street, 2000

Fifth Avenue and Monroe Street, 2006

Fifth Avenue and Monroe Street, 2009

West Madison Street towards Hoyne Avenue, 1988

West Madison Street towards Hoyne Avenue, 2006

West Madison Street towards Hoyne Avenue, 1994

West Madison Street towards Hoyne Avenue, 2009

View north west from East 43rd Street at South Ellis Avenue, 1992

View north west from East 43rd Street at South Ellis Avenue, 2009

Prairie Avenue between East 36th and East 37th Street, 1988

View north east towards Prairie Avenue from East 53rd Street, 1993

Prairie Avenue between East 36th and East 37th Street, 2009

View north east towards Praire Avenue from East 53rd Street, 2009

North west corner of 78th Street and Ashland Avenue, 2004

North west corner of 78th Street and Ashland Avenue, 2009

USE THIS CARD IF YOU ARE SUBSCRIBING FROM THE UK, EUROPE AND THE REST OF THE WORLD (WITH THE EXCEPTION OF THE USA, CANADA, CENTRAL AND SOUTH AMERICA.)

Yes, I would like to take out an annual subscription to *Granta*.

YOUR ADDRESS FOR DELIVERY

Your address:

TITLE: INITIAL: SURNAME:

ADDRESS:

POSTCODE:

TELEPHONE: EMAIL:

Billing address if different:

TITLE: INITIAL: SURNAME:

ADDRESS:

POSTCODE:

TELEPHONE: EMAIL:

NUMBER OF SUBSCRIPTIONS	DELIVERY REGION	PRICE	DIRECT DEBIT PRICE (UK ONLY)
	UK	£34.95	£29.95
	Europe	£39.95	
	Rest of World	£45.95	All prices include delivery

I would like my subscription to start from:

☐ the current issue   ☐ the next issue

YOUR TWELVE-MONTH SUBSCRIPTION WILL INCLUDE FOUR ISSUES

PAYMENT DETAILS

☐ I enclose a cheque payable to '*Granta*' for £ _____ for _____ subscriptions to *Granta*

☐ Please debit my ☐ MASTERCARD ☐ VISA ☐ AMEX for £ _____ for _____ subscriptions

NUMBER ☐☐☐☐ ☐☐☐☐ ☐☐☐☐ ☐☐☐☐   SECURITY CODE ☐☐☐

EXPIRY DATE ☐☐ / ☐☐   SIGNED _____   DATE _____

Instructions to your bank or building society to pay by Direct Debit

DIRECT Debit

TO THE MANAGER:

(BANK OR BUILDING SOCIETY NAME)

ADDRESS:

POSTCODE:

ACCOUNT IN NAME(S) OF:

SIGNED: DATE:

Instructions to your bank or building society Please pay Granta Publications Direct Debits from the account detailed in this instruction subject to the safeguards assured by the Direct Debit Guarantee. I understand that this instruction may remain with Granta and, if so, details will be passed electronically to my bank/ building society.

Banks and building societies may not accept Direct Debit instructions from some types of account

BANK/BUILDING SOCIETY ACCOUNT NUMBER
☐☐☐☐☐☐☐☐

SORT CODE
☐☐ ☐☐ ☐☐

ORIGINATOR'S IDENTIFICATION
9 1 3 1 3 3

☐ Please tick this box if you would like to receive special offers from *Granta*
☐ Please tick this box if you would like to receive offers from organizations selected by *Granta*

Please return this form to: **Granta Subscriptions, PO Box 2068, Bushey, Herts, WD23 3ZF, UK, call Freephone 0500 004 033** or go to **www.granta.com**

Please quote the following promotion code when ordering online: **GBIUK108**

Bulletproof Vest

Maria Venegas

The Venegas family, Zacatecas, Mexico, *c.* 1965

Ambush (Zacatecas, Mexico, 2001)

Mexico's Rural 44 is the only road that leads from his ranch to the cantinas of Valparaiso. Unless he decides to spend the night in a bordello, eventually he will be on that road. But there he is, standing at the bar, one foot propped up on the chrome rail, the heel of his cowboy boot wedged against it, his hand wrapped around a beer, the *musicos* playing a *corrido* just for him.

He takes a cold one for the road, settles his tab. The tyres of his Chevy grip the concrete; the truck jerks with every shift of the gears. Through the rear-view mirror he can see the lights of Valparaiso growing dim as he disappears into the abyss of the desert night. He pushes a tape into the deck and cranks up the volume. Each note blasts through him as the drums and horns blare from the huge speaker he rigged behind the seat. One after another, he listens to the *corridos*, the stories of heroes, outlaws and bandits, men who took the gamble, took the law into their own hands. Some won, some lost – some lost it all.

The stars above and the occasional whiff of decomposing carcass are his only companions. The headlights slice through the pitch-dark. Bugs fly in and out of the beams and some hit the windshield, leaving streaks on the glass. The truck swerves freely from left to right; occasionally, he will veer so far that the tyres catch the gravel on the shoulder. Jagged rocks grind beneath the weight of the truck. He drives past the ditch where he and his buddy recently drove off the road – the truck rolled twice before hitting a mesquite, his arm pinned under the hood for two days before anyone found them. Best to take it nice and easy, he thinks as he slows to a crawl, take it right down the middle of the road, wouldn't want to end up kissing a tree again. The beams catch the tail lights of a blue car on the side of the road. *Pobre pendejo,* he thinks as he idles past the stalled car. There's no one inside.

The condensation from the beer can is already forming a small pool of water on the vinyl seat between his legs. He takes a swig, notices the headlights of an approaching truck through his rear-view mirror. Suddenly, it's upon him, practically pushing him out of the way, flashing its long beams. An arrow pointing at its target. Must be in a hurry, he thinks as he slows and pulls slightly on to the gravel. The truck flies by in a flurry of flashing beams. He grabs his beer but before the can reaches his lips, his truck is lit up in a hail of bullets. Every muscle in his body contracts, pulls him towards the steering wheel. Hot pressure pierces his body; bullets skid across his head. All around him glass shatters. The truck slows to a halt. The music has stopped, the speaker behind his seat pumped full of lead.

The sound of his breathing fills the cabin as a warm stream runs down his face and neck and collects in a puddle inside his shirt. Through his side mirror he sees the headlights of the blue car flick on. Two men with machine guns emerge from ditches on either side of the road and run through the beams, towards the car and jump in. Tyres screech as they do a U-turn and speed off in the opposite direction. Fucking cowards, he thinks as he watches their red tail lights vanish in the distance.

In his mind he prays to the Virgen de Guadalupe, to El Santo Niño de Atocha, to San Francisco de Asís, to any saint who will listen. It might be hours before another car comes down the road and his right arm is already going numb. He stares at the keys, still in the ignition, reaches for them, turns them slowly and, to his surprise, the truck lights right up. It's a goddamn miracle, he thinks as he reaches for the scorpion gear knob and, with both hands, manages to shift into neutral. The incline gives him a slight push and the truck rolls towards home.

The sounds of creaking metal and shattered glass fill the truck's cabin as he turns left on to the dirt road that leads to his ranch. The truck picks up momentum on the downward slope and wobbles violently as it rolls over gullies left behind by the flash floods of the rainy season. It flies past the shrine to the Virgen de Guadalupe and, in his mind, he makes the sign of the cross: up, down, left, right. It glides into the shallow creek, swims over smooth stones, crawls up the slight incline on the other side and goes through the entrance to the ranch. But he's lost speed on the climb and his focus is fading and the puddle collecting in his shirt keeps growing. The truck crawls past the small adobe church; the bell sits quietly in its tower above. Laundry flapping in the courtyard comes into view, clean sheets flying in the midnight breeze. Not that far away now, he thinks. His right arm slips off the steering wheel and the truck swerves off the dirt road, smacking into a limestone wall. The hood flies open; hot steam hisses into the cold air. He drifts off, comes to; pushes the door open and slips into unconsciousness.

He feels claws digging into his shoulder, warm breath in his ear, wet tongues on his face and neck. There is a distant barking, which grows louder and closer and then it's all around him. He opens his eyes. His dogs, El Lobe and El Capitan, are standing on their hind legs, wagging their tails and barking at him. He swings at them, tries to push them away and falls out of the truck; lands on the ground with a thud, a cloud of dust covers him. With his left hand, he pushes himself up and leans into the truck. The courtyard comes into focus in the distance. It takes all his might to drag the weight of his body towards home. He staggers past the encino woodpile he recently chopped, past the two alamo trees where the chickens sleep, reaches the blue metal gate, pushes it open and zigzags through the courtyard, leaving dirt and blood on clean laundry as he swats it out of the way, stumbling past the parakeet cage, the gas tank, the half-rubber tyre filled with drinking water for the dogs, the flowerpots arranged in large rusty tin cans along the cinder-block wall, until he reaches the green metal door of the house and collapses.

In the early hours, while the chickens are still tucked away in their trees and the chill of night lingers in the air, Doña Consuelo, one of the neighbours, goes out for her morning walk. She adjusts her headscarf and leans on her cane as she makes her way up the dirt road, her chihuahua prancing alongside her. She turns the corner and there it is. Pressed up against the limestone wall: the hood open, the windows shattered, the door ajar, the seat slick with blood. And the rumours start circulating. Jose is dead. His truck completely destroyed. By the time the news sweeps across the desert, crosses barbed-wire fences, travels north and makes it to the other side, my family hears conflicting stories.

'Hey, did you hear about Dad?' my sister Sonia asks when she calls from Chicago.

'No,' I say. I'm in my office in the garment district in New York City, filtering emails, reading my horoscope, checking out the special of the day at Guy & Gallard's, trying to decide between a salad and a burger. 'What happened?' I ask.

'He got ambushed,' she says. 'Apparently there were two guys with machine guns.'

'Oh.' I continue browsing through the menu. 'Well, is he dead?'

Bulletproof Vest (Chicago suburbs, 1987)

The first gunshot snaps me out of my sleep. I lie in bed and stare at the two blinking red dots of my alarm clock. 12.35 a.m. Thursday night and my father has been playing cards with the neighbours. I can almost see the eye of the gun following its target, locating it, and then the second and third shots ring out. Something is different. Whenever he drinks and fires his .45, it's in rapid succession, four or five bullets following each other into our front lawn or out at the night sky.

My older sister Sonia is the first out of bed. She hears someone coughing, as if choking, right beneath her bedroom window. When she goes on to the porch, there is a red streak running down the white aluminium siding. My father is sitting below it.

'*Escondela,*' he hands his gun to her. It is still hot to the touch. She takes it and helps him to his feet, helps him inside.

When I step out of my bedroom, he's standing in the middle of the living room, appears to be slightly swaying. He's looking right at me but his gaze feels distant, as if he's looking at me from a mountaintop.

'You're bleeding to death. You're bleeding to death. You're bleeding to death,' my mother presses a towel under his chin. Thin red streams run down her arm and on to her white slip. She pulls the towel away and readjusts it. There is a gash under his chin. Blood runs down his neck and chest, over his wife-beater and on to his jeans. On the hardwood floor beneath him, there is a dark pool forming, a dark pool that's creeping closer to my mother's bare feet. She presses the towel back under his chin. He's mumbling something about that *pinche pendejo*. How he knows someone put him up to this. Paid him. How, with him, all those *cabrones* go in circles, like dogs chasing their tails. How he's not going to rot in jail because of that son of a bitch.

'Salvador!' he yells for my brother as he pushes my mother's hand away and stumbles towards his bedroom shouting orders for Salvador to pull his car around the back. By the time he returns, red and blue lights are already flickering through the front-porch windows and dancing across his face. He goes out the back door, hops the chain-link fence and crouches through the neighbours' backyard. Salvador is waiting in the car, engine running, lights off. My father climbs into the back seat, lies down. Salvador drives to the end of the block.

We hear screeching car tyres all around the house.

'*Dios nos tenga de su santa mano*,' my mother prays out loud.

Five police cars have barricaded the end of the street. Officers squat behind open doors, guns drawn and pointing at Salvador. He hits reverse, but instantly there's another police car behind, shining a blinding light on him.

'Put your hands up and step out of the car, sir,' they instruct him through a megaphone.

He does as he's told. Four police officers close in on him.

'I'm driving my father to the hospital,' he tells them as they pat him down. 'He's lost a lot of blood.' They shine their flashlights into the back seat and there he is, semi-conscious and covered in blood. A police escort takes them to Good Shepherd Hospital.

About an hour later, my younger brother and sister and I are outside. Police cars with flashing red and blue lights snake from our driveway all the way up the street. It's so bright; it feels like the middle of the day. We're leaning against Rocky's doghouse and watching as eight police officers walk around our front yard pointing flashlights; looking beneath the wooden picnic table that sits under the mulberry tree, searching the bushes along the side of the house, scanning the chain-link fence that separates our driveway from the small wooden house where five little blonde girls live with their parents. They're all outside and lined up beside their mother, gripping the fence and staring at us. The Colombian woman who lives across the street stands on her stoop, hands resting on her daughter's shoulders, her son next to her. The old lady who lives alone in the three-storey white house next to them watches from behind her screen door with her arms tightly crossed around her waist. Javier and Cornelio, who live up the street and are in my class, stand on the other side of the yellow tape. Javier waves at me; I wave back. Salvador ducks under the yellow tape and is stopped in our driveway by a man with a huge camera strapped around his neck.

One of the police officers makes his way over to us, pointing his flashlight along my mother's zucchini and tomato garden, which separates our house from the small blue house next door where eight Mexican men live. We watch as they are questioned by police and re-enact the scene; how Thomas came at my father with a knife, was pushed away, came at him again, swinging from left to right, finally lodging the knife under his chin. How my father pulled out his gun and shot him, Thomas stumbled back, fell down, got up and lunged at him again. He was shot two more times.

'*Hola*,' the officer says as he gets down on one knee, points his black metal flashlight into Rocky's doghouse and peeks inside.

'What kind of a dog is it?' he asks as Rocky starts growling.

'A Dobermann,' Jorge tells him.

'Is he friendly?'

'Sometimes.'

'What's his name?' He turns off his flashlight and stands up.

'Rocky.'

'Is Jose your father?' he asks.

'Yeah,' we nod our heads.

He picks blades of grass off his pants, then looks up at us, presses his lips tight.

'Is he *nice* to you?'

'Yeah,' I shrug.

'Except when he's drunk,' my sister adds.

'Yeah,' my brother says. 'Then he can be kind of mean.'

He glances at him, then at my sister, then back at me.

'Does he ever *hit* you?'

'No…yeah…sometimes,' we overlap.

'Only when we're bad,' my sister tells him.

He looks at her and crosses his arms, inhales through his nose; nostrils flare.

'You wouldn't happen to know where his gun is, would you?'

He follows us into the house, where other officers are searching under the couch cushions, behind the television, inside the china cabinet, under the dining-room table.

'*Ni se les ocurra decirles donde esta la pistola,*' my mother tells us through clenched teeth.

'*Ama, ya saben,*' we tell her.

'*No digan nada de las otras pistolas,*' she mumbles under her breath.

'What did she say?' the officer asks us.

'Nothing,' we tell him as he follows us to Sonia's bedroom.

He looks through her closet, behind her dresser, under her bed, then picks up her pillow and there it is: my father's .45 resting on the paisley sheet.

'Murder weapon has been located,' he says, pressing down on an orange button on the walkie-talkie that's strapped to his shoulder.

Soon there are other officers in the room. One of them is wearing a white rubber glove. She picks up the gun and drops it into a clear plastic bag. We follow them back into the living room, where other officers are standing around, *murder weapon has been located* leaping between the static of their walkie-talkies.

'Does your father keep any other weapons in the house?' one of them asks us.

'Nope,' we tell him though the closet next to the dinning-room table, right behind him, is filled with rifles, handguns and machine guns.

The newspapers the next day read: *Argument over beer leaves one man dead, another critically wounded.* But we knew it had nothing to do with beer. My father had created a lot of enemies before leaving Mexico; had unsettled business that followed him from the dirt roads of Zacatecas to the quiet streets of the Chicago suburbs. Salvador is quoted in the article and is described as a neighbour, not related to Jose Venegas. I never trusted anything I read in the newspapers after that.

My father slips the heavy white vest over his undershirt and snaps the Velcro side straps in place. Then he throws on his cowboy shirt, buttons it up and tucks it into his jeans. He sucks in his gut and fastens his silver belt buckle: a horse's head inside a horseshoe.

'Can you tell I'm wearing a vest?' he asks us as he turns to one side, then the other.

'Sort of,' we tell him, pointing to his waistline, to the belt buckle, which appears to be pressing on the bottom edge of the vest.

By the time he was released from the hospital, Thomas's two brothers were already asking questions around town: Where did Jose live? How many kids did he have? How many sons? Daughters?

'Maybe you should pull your shirt out a bit,' we tell him.

He retucks his shirt, making it a bit looser, throws on a black leather waistcoat.

'Now can you tell?'

'Not really.'

He slips one of his guns into the back of his Wrangler's, grabs his black cowboy hat and goes out the door: Metal, leather, bulletproof – indestructible.

In early December, he begins preparing for his annual trip to Mexico. He packs boxes with towels and bathroom rugs from the factory where my mother works. Buys linens, pots, pans and a blender for his mother, men's shirts and a small television for his father. We go through our closets and throw anything we no longer wear into the growing pile in the corner of the dining room. He takes his guns from the closet and lays them out on the living-room floor. Wraps each one in several layers of tin foil, than swathes each with a towel; brand-new towels covered with yellow butterflies, purple flowers and pink flamingos. Finally, he wraps each contraption tightly with duct tape. They look like sloppily wrapped Christmas presents.

The night before he leaves, his two friends come over and help him load the car. They drive his maroon Cutlass on to two red metal ramps in the driveway, pop the hood, remove the spare from the back, split the doors open by pulling away the inside panel. Propped up on the ramps, the car looks like a giant metal bird with four wings, about to take flight. They load it up. Carlos, his Puerto Rican friend who is helping him drive down, shows up with a duffel bag and a big grin. He's excited; he's never been to Mexico. He also has no idea that – on paper – he's the legal owner of the maroon Cutlass. They pull out of the driveway before the sun comes up.

'Your father is never coming back,' my mother tells us a few days after he leaves.

'How do you know?' we ask.

'Because God showed me in a vision that He has taken him away for good,' she says. 'Plus he took all of his things.'

'He did?'

'Yes,' she says. 'He didn't leave a single thing, not in the closet or the dresser or anywhere. Nothing.'

After he leaves we begin noticing things, like the two men who park and sit in their black car across the street from our house in the morning. We go out the back door, hop the fence, cross the neighbours' yard and catch the bus on a different street. At night we start hearing noises. When I hear something outside my window, I roll out of bed, then drag myself by the elbows into the living room where, close to the hardwood floor, I bump into one of my sisters. They heard a noise too.

We crawl to the phone, reach up and pull it off its ledge and on to the floor, dial 911.

'911, what is your emergency?' the operator asks.

'Someone is trying to break into our house,' we whisper.

Soon we hear police cars whizzing on the back street, the front street, speeding all around the house with their lights off. We watch flashlights make their way from the kitchen windows to the living-room windows while we sit under the ledge, breathing into the receiver.

'Ma'am? Hello, ma'am, you there?' the operator asks.

'Yes,' we whisper.

'It appears the coast is clear,' she tells us. 'There is an officer at your front door, please let him in.'

My mother wakes when she hears the knock at the door.

'*Que andan haciendo?*' she calls out from her bedroom, then comes into the living room in her white slip, bra straps hanging halfway down her arms. 'You called the police again?' she asks, yawning. 'Hay, no, no, no. Next thing you know they're going to want to charge us,' she says.

'Mom, it's 911,' we tell her as we go to the front door. 'It's free,' we open the door and the officer comes in.

'Where exactly did you hear the noise?' he asks.

'Outside that window,' I tell him, pointing towards my bedroom.

'What did it sound like?' He takes a few steps towards my bedroom door. 'Did it sound like someone was trying to open the window?'

'Yeah,' I tell him. 'It was like a scratching noise.'

Other times there had been a shadow standing outside the living-room window, a gentle tapping at the back door, a strange noise on the front porch. He glances at my mother, then at us, then back at my mother.

'Where's Jose?' he asks her.

'In Mexico,' we tell him.

'When is he coming back?'

'He's not.'

'Doesn't he have a court date?' he asks.

We shrug.

'Can you guys park a police car in our driveway and leave it there?' I ask, though we've made this request before, have told them about Thomas's brothers, but since they haven't threatened us directly, since we don't even know their names, there's nothing the police can do to protect us.

'Maybe you should consider moving,' he says.

Shooting Guns (Zacatecas, Mexico, 2009)

Scattered stars begin to appear, one by one, glistening eyes against the cobalt sky. The sliver of moon doesn't illuminate enough of the darkness. Out there beyond the courtyard, on the dirt road where the dogs have fused into a ball of claws and teeth tearing through the night. Out there where dust is already clinging to fresh blood. One dog breaks from the pack, runs towards the small adobe church which sits under the single light post on the ranch. A cloud of dust rises towards the light as the pack pounces on the one that broke from them, on the one that tried to get away. A log collapses in the fire, red sparks fly into the cool air; mingle with the growling, then vanish.

'Should we do something?' I ask my father.

'About what?' he asks, leaning back in his white plastic chair, his legs extended in front of him and crossed one over the other so that the soles of his cowboy boots are almost in the fire.

'The dogs,' I say. 'Won't they kill each other?'

'Nah, they'll work it out,' he says, taking a swig of the rum and Coke in his nicked tin cup.

The battle continues out there where the distant mountains look like sleeping giants against the horizon. Out there where lights from other ranches are coming into focus. Where a pair of eyes could be watching the glow of the fire dance across our faces. I hook my index finger in the rubber band holding my ponytail and slide it off; my hair falls freely around my shoulders.

'Why are they fighting like that?' I ask my father who is now down on one knee, rearranging the logs in the fire. 'Maybe it's a sign,' I say.

'Yeah, maybe,' he says. 'Maybe *la huesona* is on the loose, desperate to take a few more souls before the year ends,' he rolls a thick log into the fire. 'Only a few hours left,' he grunts as he centres it in the burning pile. 'This log will last us all night,' he says, 'or at least until the New Year. Encino, great wood. I chopped it myself. It doesn't burn as fast as the others.'

He sits back down, glances at me and follows my gaze out to the rumbling that is now moving around the back of the house.

'I think one of those dogs is in heat,' he says. 'That's why they're all worked up.'

'Really?' I say and lean back into my chair, take a sip from my rum and Coke. The dry heat of the fire feels good on my bare arms.

'You see those three stars?' he asks pointing up. I look past the clothes line, past the electrical wires that hang above. 'When we were kids,' he says, 'we used to call those the three kings, *Los Reyes Magos.*'

'Over there,' I say, 'they call those the…' The word eludes me. It's like this sometimes. I can't find the right word in Spanish and hesitate, stutter. 'It's like the small pot or pan,' I say. 'Or like the big spoon. See how the three stars are in a row? How they seem to form a handle?'

'Uh-huh,' he says, and though his face is still turned towards the sky, he's giving me a sideways glance, a one-eyed squint.

The sky is filled with stars, thousands of stars sitting around the moon, waiting for the New Year to arrive. A small piece of raw meat clings to the clothes line above. A few days ago, a cow broke an ankle, had to be put down. Whatever didn't fit in the small fridge was hung on the clothes line to be dried by the sun, raw meat hanging like laundry in the courtyard. He reaches up, plucks meat off the clothes line and throws it into the fire.

'I made that rope when I was in jail,' he tells me, motioning towards the clothes line, a yellow rope tied to an extension cord that is then tied to the water-well post. 'That one and the pink one I tied to your saddle this morning,' he tells me.

'They teach you how to make rope in jail?' I ask.

'They teach you how to do lots of things in jail,' he says. 'If you pay attention, you come out knowing a lot more than when you went in,' he says. 'I gave those ropes to my father, when he came to visit me to tell me they had sold the house in the plaza and deposited the money in an account for the lawyer that was working on my case,' he says, his gaze drifting off.

'No, *mijita*,' he says. 'You've got no idea how much I've suffered.'

The dogs have worked their way around the corral and are now barrelling down the dirt road towards us, the snarling louder and louder as they approach.

'Maybe we should go inside,' I say.

'Nah. If we go inside, we'll fall asleep,' he says. 'It's nicer here by the fire; we can have a few drinks, a bit of a *platica*. After the New Year arrives we'll go inside, iron our ears out.' He looks at my arms, my ripped jeans. 'You want to borrow a jacket?' he asks.

'No, I'm fine,' I say then take a gulp from my drink.

'Do you really want to go inside?' he asks.

'Maybe,' I say.

'Well then, we should put out the fire,' he says.

We sit in silence for a while. I stare out past the two-room adobe house where he was born, the same house where I was born – then sit up and face him.

'What if someone shoots us?' I ask.

His whole body turns towards me.

'No, no, *mijita*,' he shakes his head. '*Que paso*, don't think like that.' He reaches into the fire, grabs one of the logs and flips it. 'No one is going to come bother us here, not at this hour, not just any *pendejo* would come near here,' he says. 'Besides, it's a holiday. Everyone is too busy celebrating.'

Everyone is celebrating, I think. Celebrating and drinking; drinking and celebrating. All day long men have been knocking them back at the rodeos, the cockfights, *las fiestas*, the horse races, the hot sun beating on their eyelids, visions blurring, old conflicts floating to the surface. It's during the holidays that tragedies seem to happen around these parts. It was on Christmas Eve, twenty years ago, on a ranch just up the road from here, that my brother was shot and left face down in the river to drown. Jose Manuel. The firstborn.

One gulp and I polish off my drink.

'Is there any more left?' he asks grinning at me, a glint of the fire in his eyes.

'Yeah,' I say taking his cup, 'I'll go make us two more.'

The minute I step away from the fire, the cold air grips me; night has fallen and so has the temperature. I make my way through the dark house, to the kitchen, hit the light switch; a single bulb covered with a layer of grease and dust dangles from a black cord that's slung over a pine beam. The fried chicken I made earlier sits in a large green plastic bowl on the table, a cheesecloth draped over it, grease already seeping through the fabric. Since the day I arrived, he kept mentioning how he had a taste for that fried chicken from the other side, how he hadn't had it in years, how he used to eat at the fried chicken place all the time, how even the side dishes weren't bad. I went into town, downloaded the KFC recipe off the Internet, bought two pounds of chicken, two bottles of Crisco, a few potatoes and some spinach: fried chicken with two sides.

I grab the bottle of rum from behind the white rusty metal cabinet where I'd stashed it earlier and mix two more drinks. This was the deal we'd made when he arrived slurring and glassy-eyed, pulling his red truck right into the courtyard as I was finishing frying the chicken. I agreed to have a few drinks with him, celebrate the New Year, as long as he gave me the bottle, let me be in charge, monitor how much more he drank, make sure he didn't have too much, black out, forget where he was – who he was with.

I finish mixing the drinks and make mine a double, his a bit weaker. I hear his truck door slam shut and expect a *corrido* to come blaring through the house, but that never happens. When I go back outside he is sitting in front of the fire, right where I left him, as if he never moved.

I hand him his tin cup and sit down; he takes a swig.

'Ouh, this doesn't taste like anything,' he glances at me, then takes another swig. 'It tastes like *pura* Coca-Cola,' he says. 'Did you put anything in here?'

'Yeah,' I say.

'*No parece*,' he grins at me, looks at the cup in my hand. '*A ver*,' he says, 'let me try yours.'

I hand him my cup.

'*A jijo!*' he coughs. 'Did you put the rest of the bottle in here?'

'There wasn't much left,' I say and watch as he takes another drink from my cup. 'Are you sure you don't have another bottle stashed somewhere?' I ask.

'No, that was it,' he says. 'And the only reason I had that bottle is because I ran into a buddy of mine in town and he gave it to me, wanted me to go with him to the cantina, but I told him one of my daughters was in town, that we were going to spend the New Year together.'

I take his cup and pour my drink into it, then pour it all into mine, mix the two together, then hand him his cup and sit down. Lobo comes up and nudges my elbow; I pet his head, run my hand down his neck; it's wet, sticky. I set my drink down and run both my hands down his neck, then hold them to the fire.

'He's bleeding,' I say, turning my hands for my father to see.

'*Se lo chingaron*,' he says looking at my hands. Then he gets up and walks over to his truck, which is parked right behind us, comes back with a flashlight, gets down on one knee and points it at Lobo. I hold his head still – there's a gash about two inches long on his neck, oozing with thick blood.

'They ripped his tumour off,' he says pointing at the spot, being careful not to touch it, not to get blood on his hands. 'Right there he used to have a bump and now it's gone. That's good,' he says, standing up. 'Now I don't have to cut it off.'

I press my finger gently against the gash. Lobo yelps.

'Should we take him to a dog doctor or something?' I ask. 'He's bleeding a lot.'

'He'll be fine,' he says grimacing at my hands, which are covered in blood. 'You should wash your hands; there's soap under there.' He points the light towards the grey stone sink, a giant bar of pink laundry soap, Zote, sits underneath.

I walk over to the sink, grab the soap and adjust the green rubber hose between my knees, bend into the ice-cold stream of water while he holds the light over me.

'This is the flashlight you gave me for Christmas last year,' he says.

It's a long black metal flashlight with adjustable beams. When we were kids he had one just like it, used to brag about how it was the same brand the cops used. I finish washing my hands, put the soap back and am still hunched over when we hear the first gunshots. Only a few scattered pops in the distance, then they seem to get louder and closer like an approaching thunderstorm, giant raindrops pounding the ground and soon they're all around us. My father drops the flashlight into the back of his truck, goes into the house and returns with two loaded guns, hands me the bigger one, a .357 Magnum.

'*Truenala,*' he tells me.

I look at the fire reflecting off the silver grooves in the revolver, the long slick barrel, the mother-of-pearl handle; I turn it over in my hands, taken by how beautiful it is.

'I don't know,' I say. 'I've never shot a gun before.'

'It doesn't matter,' he says, a huge smile flashing across his face. 'Just point it up and shoot it.'

I look at it again. Hesitate. If I shoot the gun, I feel as if I will have crossed some line, a transgression. All around us guns are going off. He points his at the sky and shoots it three times, one right after another, the way he used to do when we were kids in the Chicago suburbs, four or five bullets following each other into our front lawn, into the night sky, across the hardwood floor in the living room.

'See,' he tells me. 'Just point it up and shoot it.'

'*Bueno,*' I say. '*No puedo pensar en que otro lugar seria mejor, um, estaria mas bueno para truenar una pistola como...*' What I'm trying to say is that if I was ever going to shoot a gun, I can't think of a better time or place, but again my Spanish fails me and I'm slurring and now he is looking at me like maybe he's regretting having handed me a loaded gun.

'*Truenala*,' he says again, his smile fading.

I turn around and point the gun straight up, hold it over my head with both hands. Looking towards the small church in the distance, I press gently on the trigger. I'm surprised by how hard it is. It's as if gravity itself has reversed its course and is pushing back up against my finger. The pressure releases and a high-pitched ringing sound fills the air as red sparks rain down. I hear my father yelling something, but he sounds far, far away; it's as if I've slipped into a tunnel, or have fallen into a well, my ears slowly filling with water and muffling the world around me. The only thing I hear with utter clarity, inside this space I have cracked open, is the loud ringing. Its steady pitch sounds like an *om*.

Instinctively, my hands move to cover my ears, my elbows bend and for a split second I forget I'm still holding the gun.

'Do you hear that?' I yell to my father over my shoulder.

'*Que?*' he sounds like he's shouting at me from the top of a mountain.

'That ringing sound,' I yell back at him, 'do you hear that?' I turn around and he's ducking behind his truck.

'*Cuidado con la pistola*,' he says, looking at my swaying hand, the gun pointing slightly in his direction. 'Empty it out,' he says. 'Point it straight up and shoot it fast, one right after another; it sounds prettier that way.'

I turn around and hold the gun up with both hands, point it at a slight angle away from me, from him. There is nothing but the stars and the sliver of moon above and though there is no music playing, I swear I can hear the *tamboraso* coming down the mountainside, the drums and horns blaring all around me – his music, his drinking, his guns – they all go hand in hand. I aim at the moon, convinced I can put a hole in it. Fire shoots from my fingertips as four bullets follow each other into the night sky.

I hand him the gun and he hands me a heavy blue square-shaped glass bottle.

'What is it?' I ask.

'Tequila,' he says.

'Tequila?' I say. 'I thought you didn't have another bottle.'

I take a sip, hand it back to him. He takes a long pull.

'Are those the same guns you brought down from Chicago?' I ask.

'Ouh, no, I sold all of those,' he says. 'Except the rifle; you know the one that's hanging over my bed?'

'Yeah.'

'That's the only one I kept,' he says.

'What about your bulletproof vest, do you still have it?'

'Who knows what happened to that vest,' he takes another gulp, hands me the bottle. 'I think I sold it, or maybe I gave it away. I don't remember.'

I lean into his truck, prop my foot up on the tyre.

'How did you know Thomas wanted to kill you?'

'I don't know, I just did,' he says. 'There was something about him, he was a little too friendly,' he says and glances at me, then at the bottle in my hands. 'That night he had patted my back, acting like we were best buddies,' he says, 'but I knew he was checking to see if I had my gun. We were playing cards and I said I was running home to use the bathroom, and I did. I used the bathroom and then I grabbed my gun, the .45,' he says turning the revolver over in his hands, inspecting it.

I take another sip and hand him the bottle.

'Then when I went back outside, he proposed a toast, a *brindis*, and with one hand he held up his beer and with the other he buried a kitchen knife in my neck,' he says choking down another gulp. 'But the bullet turned on that son of a bitch.'

'You know the papers the next day said it was over an argument about who would drink the last beer,' I tell him.

'*Apoco?*' he asks. 'That's what the papers said?'

'Yes,' I say, 'you didn't know that?'

'No,' he says chuckling a bit. 'Imagine that, killing a man over a goddamn beer,' he says, laughing a bit harder.

'I know, but that's what the papers said,' I tell him and he's laughing so hard now that it makes me start laughing and soon we're both howling with laughter and leaning against his truck.

In the distance, three fireworks race into the sky, their tails trailing behind like comets, like shooting stars that crash-landed in the mountains years ago, metal carried down with the rains, washed into the rivers below and now returning to its home in the universe. ∎

W hen everyone was asleep, we put on our boots and waded out into the drifts of Glencoe – a suburban street remade into an eerie winter-scape. Humming the theme from *Lawrence of Arabia*, my friend Mark urged me to follow him on foolhardy adventures, saying, 'Aqaba by land.'

It was the beginning of the season of great storms, new fronts blowing in each week, dumping eight or ten inches of fresh snow. For me, it was an aggravating time, a time of comedy routines, as early Saturday mornings my father would throw open the door to my room in the attic and shout up the stairs, 'Are you gonna get your ass outta bed and shovel that walk?'

I would mumble in a sleepy reply: 'For the love of God, let me sleep for one more hour.'

Ten minutes later, he was back at the foot of the stairs, shouting, 'What about that goddamn walk?'

'In the name of all that is holy, let me sleep for twenty more minutes.'

The door would slam, then, a moment later, I would be rattled by the sound of steel on ice. I opened the window, looked out. And there he was, the old man in a cloth coat, a cigar in his mouth, swinging the shovel and muttering like Patton. Before I could think, my door flew open and my mother shouted, 'Heart attack! I hope you are well rested when your father has a heart attack!' I pulled on a coat and ran outside, where the real battle began. Same script every time. He would not hand over the shovel, wanted to do it himself, would show me how it was done, etc. At last, he would give in, settling for the role of coach, standing in the door, chewing his cigar and saying, 'Not like that, schmucko!'

Fed up with such indolence, my father came up with a strategy, a psychological tactic as counterproductive as the late-in-the-war bombing of Hanoi. For what seemed like an outrageous sum – twenty dollars an hour – he hired Mark to work on weekend mornings as I slept. Waking at eleven, I would see the following picture through every window: Mark bundled up and nodding as my father, in cowboy hat and gloves, gave orders and stole glances at my window. Meanwhile, I would have a leisurely breakfast, then wander outside with two mugs of hot chocolate, exchange the news of the day and go back in to watch the football game – the Bears won the Superbowl that year! For my father, the tactic was a failure. I felt not a moment of shame. For Mark, it was a success: not only did he earn a bunch of money, he got to spend hours with the old man, whom he admired.

There are no longer winters like that in Chicago, or there haven't been for a long time, but when I was growing up the city was as cold as people say it is. It snowed for days at a time, blizzards that swallowed up the world. My mother would step out of the house, vanish into the storm, be gone for hours, then, without warning, reappear with a bag of groceries. 'It's madness out there,' she would say. 'Madness.' When the storm let up, Mark and I would go to the lake and stand on the frozen shore, or venture on to the ice, which, in cold winters, ran to the horizon. It was my dream to tie on my blades, pack a lunch and skate to Michigan, houses drifting off behind me, ice spreading before, reaching the bluffs of Benton Harbor in the dusk – a suburban Lindbergh, carried on the shoulders of the people.

At night, we would sneak out of the house and meet our friend Dan, who waited down the street in his car. He would shift into low and go fishtailing down the road, off to sled hills west of Chicago. On the way, we would stop before a tiny house with a single light burning in a low-slung garage. Dan flashed his headlights and Blake Renn came loping out, a sleepy kid with a sappy saloon-singer face. Blake had grown up a short walk from the lake, and he had developed, over the years, a love for the habits of the waters. Before school, he would hang around the fisherman, listening to their shop talk. We wondered if Blake was a genius or a fool, a happy, slow-talking idiot. Not long ago, an old friend told me Blake is now a pilot, flying commercial props out of a small

Midwestern airport, which my friend described as the 'O'Hare of northern Wisconsin'. I imagined Blake in the cockpit, surrounded by spinning dials and flashing meters, his voice low and confident over the PA – Off to the left of the plane, you can see the lights of Waukesha – or showing a kid around the cockpit, pulling him on to his lap –That is the altimeter, son – or in a bar out by the airfield, throwing back a few with the boys, talking about the mysteries of wind shear.

In those days, we most admired Blake for his sleds, which he built in his garage, nailing together parts he scavenged in the junkyards and along the expressway – old skis, cast-off car seats, broken side mirrors. Each sled was a work of art, an expression of Blake's personality. Leaning into the window of Dan's car, he would say, 'I built a big one this time; someone's got to help me carry it.' We would lash it to the roof, a crazy monstrosity, two bucket seats (from a Honda) welded on top of six skis. 'I call it the A6 Tomcat,' Blake would say. 'I hope to God she flies.'

We drove to a hill that rose like a pimple from the flats, two hundred feet of sled run made from landfill and trash, mount garbage, with an orange flame burning at its summit. It was ghostly in the moonlight, with stairs cut into the ice. We dragged Blake's sled to the top. From here we could see dark cornfields, yellow stars and streets lined with blue lamps. I climbed on the sled, Dan next to me, Mark in the back seat Blake made from a floor mat. Mark put his hiking boots on my legs and said, 'When I shout, "Pull!" everyone lean left. It's the only way to turn this boat.'

I asked why Mark did not simply shout 'Left'.

He said, 'Because pull sounds cooler.'

He then said, 'Now!'

Blake gave us a hard shove and then stood back on his heels, his face closed in thought, a nuclear scientist observing a blast in the Nevada desert from a distance. As we picked up speed, my stomach fell away and I could see only the dark hill and the lights of Glenview. Blood rose in my cheeks. A great happiness roared inside me. Mark gripped my shoulder and I could hear him breathing and he shouted,

'Pull!' I was never good at telling my left from my right, so as Dan and Mark leaned one way, I leaned the other. The sled split and the skis went flying. For a moment, I was looking at the world upside down, right side up, upside down. I saw Mark describing the same suicidal arc down the hill. I landed in a heap. An instant later, Mark landed next to me; then Dan. We gathered the debris, hiked back up the hill, kept on. By the end of the night, there was snow in my boots, slush in my underwear and my pants were soaked. It's the best way to break in a pair of jeans. ■

An *Ofrenda* for my Mother

Sandra Cisneros

Sandra Cisneros's
parents, Elvira and
Alfredo, 1940s

I became a writer thanks to a mother who was unhappy being a mother. She was a prisoner-of-war mother, banging on the bars of her cell all her life. Unhappy women do this. She searched for escape routes from her prison and found them in museums, public concerts and the public library.

As a child she lived in the parish of Saint Francis of Assisi in Chicago, off Roosevelt Road and South Halsted Street, close enough to downtown that she could walk there. I have a photo of her as a very young girl on the steps of the Field Museum with her girlfriend. I know my mother often ran off all day with her friends and paid her younger sisters to do her chores. She did not know what awaited her in life, and if she had she might've run farther than the museum.

Because my mother needed to fortify her spirit, every weekend she herded us to museums, concerts in Grant Park and the library. I used to think this was for our sake, but now I realize it was for hers. She loved opera, Pearl Buck novels, and the movie *A Tree Grows in Brooklyn*. Later she would ditch Pearl Buck for Noam Chomsky, but in the beginning she read novels. I know she dreamed of becoming some sort of artist – she could sing and draw – but I'm sure she never dreamed of mothering seven kids.

I think she married my father because he rescued her from a house with peeling paint and beds crowded with sisters and bedbugs. At least this is what my father reminded her when they argued. He came from Mexico City and spoke an impeccable Spanish as stiff and formal as the beautiful suits he wore. He was a gentleman, and I think my mother saw him as cosmopolitan and sophisticated. She did not know he was a dreamer and would give her seven kids and an unimaginative life.

My mother was the beauty of the family, used to being spoiled by her eldest sister. If there was one thing my father knew how to do, it was how to spoil a woman. He believed women wanted words more than anything, and he had a lot of them. *Mi cielo. Mi vida. Mi amor.* So for a little while she must have been happy. I have a photo of them dancing and kissing. It's obvious they're in love, but it didn't last very long and was replaced with a more durable, daily love, and the words were replaced with more durable, daily words too.

'*Vieja, donde estás?*' [Where's my old lady?]

'*No me llamas vieja, yo no soy vieja.*' [Don't call me 'old lady', I'm not old.]

Because she couldn't drive, Mother insisted Father take us downtown on Sundays, to the museums. Father waited for us in Grant Park under a tree, or, in the winter, on a bench by the coatroom.

'My feet hurt,' Father said.

He had corns from dancing all week around the sofas and chairs he upholstered, so we knew better than to ask him to come inside with us.

On Saturdays we walked with Mother to the library. For me, the library was a wonderful house. A house of ideas, a house of silence. Our own house was like that of the cook's in *Alice in Wonderland*, a lot of shouting and banging of pots. Would someone hand me a baby and would the baby turn into a pig? Anything could happen in this kitchen. It was a nightmare, and I was condemned to the lowest job of scullery maid because I was too daydreamy to learn how to cook. The rice burned on me – too expensive a mistake – so I was ordered to cut potatoes into little squares, or scrub pots, or set the table, or anything else my mother thought of while she was busy banging pots and yelling.

Hell was a kitchen. Hell was having to go to the supermarket every Friday with her. Sometimes Father drove us. Usually we walked there and back with a collapsible shopping cart and a red wagon. It was a cross, buying groceries for our army. Neither Mother nor I enjoyed it.

Sometimes my father and mother went to the Randolph Street market to buy eggs and vegetables wholesale for the nine of us. Occasionally my mother walked down North Avenue, beyond Humboldt Park, to the bakery to buy us day-old sweet bread. On Sundays after scavenging the flea market at Maxwell Street, we stopped for Mexican groceries on Eighteenth Street; *carnitas* and *chicharón* served on hot tortillas with dollops of sour cream and sprigs of cilantro. These Sunday dinners were one of the few times Father 'cooked'. He stood over the cutting board and chopped like a Japanese chef, humming while he worked, until the *carnitas* were diced to his liking.

Father was meticulous. He liked to remind everyone that he was from a good family, the son of a Mexican military man and the grandson of a pianist who was also an educator, but Father's appreciation of the finer things in life did not extend beyond nightclubs. He loved the big bands of Xavier Cugat, Perez Prado and Benny Goodman, the sultry voice of Peggy Lee singing 'Why Don't You Do Right?' – whose lyrics always made him laugh – and the dance halls and cabarets of Mexico City. He was a good dancer and a sharp dresser. And then he got married.

Like everybody we knew, we took road trips from Chicago to Mexico to visit family. We witnessed paper Judases exploding on Holy Week, saw Aztec pyramids sprouting in the middle of downtown, watched dancers swing from a giant pole planted in front of the cathedral, listened to ancient music played on drums and conch shells in the central plaza. Art was in the paper flags fluttering above us at a fiesta, in the mangoes sliced like roses and served on a stick, in the cheap trinkets we bought with our Sunday allowance at the market, in the pastel wafer candies studded with pumpkin seeds. We didn't have to ask anyone to drive us to a museum. Art was everywhere around us.

On these vacations, Father caught up on his reading. His library consisted of Mexican comic books and pocketsize *fotonovelas* printed in a dark chocolate ink on paper so cheap it was used as toilet paper by the poor. When father was done with his little books, he'd turn them over to me, and I'd paint over the ladies' chocolate-tinted mouths with a red-lead pencil dipped in spit. This is how I learned to read in Spanish.

Father also had a private library, a secret stash of *¡Alarma!* magazines, whose covers were so savage, Mother forced him to keep them under the mattress in paper bags. *¡Alarma!* featured sensational stories about everyday Mexican events – yet another bus drives off a cliff, yet another quake swallows a village, yet another machete murder.

All with detailed photos. Mexicans love staring at death. I wasn't allowed to read these magazines but once in a while I did catch a headline when Father was reading in bed. WIFE KILLS HUSBAND AND SERVES HIS HEAD IN TACOS.

Back in Chicago, Mother painted geishas in paint-by-number sets in the kitchen after her housework was done. She made fake flowers with crêpe paper until she grew real flowers from seeds she sent away for. She sewed stuffed toys and doll clothes, designed theatre sets and created puppets. But it wasn't enough. Mother felt duped by life and sighed for the life that wasn't hers. Father watched television in bed, content, chuckling, calling out for pancakes.

'There's no intelligent life around here,' Mother said out loud to no one in particular.

When she was in a bad mood, which was often, she threw sharp words like knives, wounding and maiming the guilty and the innocent.

'Your mother,' Father complained to me, near tears.

Sick and tired, miserable, Mother raged and paced her cell. We tiptoed around her feeling gloomy and guilty.

I understood Father. He understood me. Neither of us understood her, and she never understood us. But that didn't matter. A stack of pancakes. A pay cheque. A bouquet of dandelions. A ride to the Garfield Park Conservatory. A box of popcorn from the Sears. A language for the things we couldn't say. ■

GRANTA
THE MAGAZINE OF NEW WRITING

If you enjoy good writing, you'll love Granta – fiction, reportage, memoir, biography and photography five times a year

Subscribe to *Granta* or buy a subscription for a friend and receive, with our compliments, a *Granta* special-edition **MOLESKINE**® notebook

Subscribe online at **www.granta.com** or call **toll-free 1-866-438-6150** or fill in the **back of this card** and send to us

'Provides enough to satisfy the most rabid appetite for good writing and hard thinking'
WASHINGTON POST
BOOK WORLD

Yes, I would like to take out an annual subscription to *Granta*.

PERSONAL SUBSCRIPTION

Your address:

FIRST NAME: LAST NAME:

COMPANY: ADDRESS:

CITY: STATE: ZIP CODE:

COUNTRY: TELEPHONE: EMAIL:

GIFT SUBSCRIPTION

Gift address:

FIRST NAME: LAST NAME:

COMPANY: ADDRESS:

CITY: STATE: ZIP CODE:

COUNTRY: TELEPHONE: EMAIL:

Billing address:

FIRST NAME: LAST NAME:

COMPANY: ADDRESS:

CITY: STATE: ZIP CODE:

COUNTRY: TELEPHONE: EMAIL:

NUMBER OF SUBSCRIPTIONS	DELIVERY REGION	PRICE	SAVINGS	
	USA	$45.99	32%	All prices include delivery
	Canada	$57.99	32%	YOUR TWELVE-MONTH SUBSCRIPTION
	Rest of World	$65.99	32%	WILL INCLUDE FOUR ISSUES

I would like my subscription to start from:

☐ the current issue   ☐ the next issue

PAYMENT DETAILS

☐ I enclose a check payable to '*Granta*' for $_____ for ____ subscriptions to *Granta*

☐ Please charge my ☐ MASTERCARD ☐ VISA ☐ AMEX for $_____ for ____ subscriptions

NUMBER ☐☐☐☐ ☐☐☐☐ ☐☐☐☐ ☐☐☐☐   EXPIRATION ☐☐ / ☐☐

SIGNED _____ DATE _____

☐ Charge my card automatically annually

☐ Please tick this box if you would like to receive special offers from *Granta*

☐ Please tick this box if you would like to receive offers from organizations selected by *Granta*

Please return this form to: **Granta Subscriptions, PO Box 359, Congers, NY 10920-0359, Call toll-free 1-866-438-6150** or go to **www.granta.com**

Please quote the following promotion code when ordering online: **BUS107PM**

Easter Island
Noodles Almondine

Thom Jones

7-20-49

The General Mills factory, Chicago, 1949

I grew up in a factory town, Aurora, Illinois, some forty miles west of Chicago. There were so many factories in Aurora that you could get fired from one in the morning and be spot-welding or running a punch press in another by early afternoon. When I landed a production line job at General Mills in West Chicago, the work was go, go, go, but the bosses were okay. They drove around the plant in two-seater white golf carts wearing white coveralls. None of them growled or yelled or threatened to kill you. If something went wrong they would say, 'How can I help you out here?'

I worked the cake-mix line. Machines did most of the packaging. They shaped and folded spring-fed cardboard, forming it into boxes, inserted wax-paper envelopes, then passed them on to a conveyer belt that dropped eighteen ounces of cake mix from gleaming chutes, weighing the boxes – shunting the partially filled ones along a dead-end rail – as the filled and fitted boxes were sealed and sent rolling along on the express line at breakneck speed. At the end of the line production workers such as myself stood at the ready grabbing six boxes at a time (heavy little mothers) that seemed especially dense on days when you showed up sick or hungover, or on shifts when your back might be sore and all that repetitive weight cantilevered away from your spine. Six at a time they came at you, a blizzard of flour when boxes of lemon poppy-seed cake mix emerged from machines like clowns from a Volkswagen, pi squared only more so. Pi squared to infinity.

The next worker taped the boxes shut and stacked them on pallets. There was lemon poppy-seed flour in the air; it got in your eyes and nose. I imagine that you breathed it in and swallowed it, too. If you let something like that throw you, there was a pile of cake boxes on the floor and the whole line had to be shut down. If you wanted your days to go by at a slower clip you could go to the heavy industry factories of Aurora where school lockers, earth-moving equipment, vending machines and power tools were made. A day could last a century.

A week, a millennium. A year could start in the Jurassic Age and go backwards rather than forwards in time. A year was forever.

At GM, time could actually fly and space could move into new dimensions. It was utterly fantastic, everywhere except on the New Country Corn Flakes line. It was not a punishment or a disciplinary assignment, but packing monstrous boxes of cornflakes required unnatural strength and stamina. They hit you harder than the defensive line of the Chicago Bears. Corn Flakes could break the human spirit. I was witness to dazed men staggering from the back of the plant drenched in sweat who, if they could speak at all, said things like, 'Who the fuck needs this goddamn motherfucking shit, anyhow? I am gone!'

As I saw it, New Country Corn Flakes was the maker of men. An Olympic event. Neck, shoulders and arms turned to steel. Backs, obliques and abdomens moulded to flexible iron. Hearts developed the sleek splendour of racing steeds. And lastly, it was mind over matter, as is the case with life's most difficult challenges. If you could make it back there, nothing in the everyday world was impossible.

In truth, when a manager pulled over to the cake line and politely requested my services back in Corn Flakes, my knees tended to buckle, my throat became dry, my palms moist but, like a soldier in the mob, I went into the belly of the beast without complaint. The workers made all this easier, and if not easy, at least fun. Many of them were college students who could earn enough in a summer to get them through a year at undemanding state schools like Northern Illinois U in DeKalb, or Southern Illinois U, where you partied, got drunk on your ass and laid every weekend.

The Betty Crocker Noodles Almondine line was a beauty. Two production workers dropped small packets of cracked almonds into the colourful boxes that shuttled past on their way into a machine that filled them with light crispy noodles. A pal, Bobby, handled them like a card shark. He could backhand them in and juggle with them. ('Four in the air, can he do five? Oh *yeah!*') Bobby coordinated doo-wop songfests with the 'B'-operator running the machine. It was a lot of fun but things spun out of control.

Bobby took me aside with alarm on his face. 'Some woman wrote executive management about a handwritten note in a box of Almondine. HELP! SLAVE CHAINED TO THE CORNFLAKES LINE. CALL THE NATIONAL GUARD. She said someone carved almonds into little Easter Island heads!' You would think they'd found a dead mouse in a bottle of Coke. What was the big deal over a few carved almonds?

Word spread around. Any moment the hammer would come down, hard and fast. The plant worked three shifts: days, swing and graveyard. Every two weeks day-shift workers moved to swing and so on. No one on my shift had any notion of who was writing the notes. And the men on the adjoining shifts, whom we knew peripherally, sorely lacked imagination.

Our guys looked at one another inquisitively. They lay in bed at night and pondered. When you were with a buddy working a line together, eating lunch together, taking breaks side by side in the naivety of youth, you trusted them. And now, suddenly, there was a sociopath among us with the steel-trap mind of an East German spy. I was the guy jabbering on about writing a great novel. I could just see it: *Novel my ass! Jones hasn't penned a line other than those Typhoid Mary fucking notes he stuffs in the Noodles Almondine.*

But it wasn't me. I was being framed!

When I found myself back out in cornflakes I knew it was only a matter of time. It's hard to box New Country Corn Flakes when you keep looking over your shoulder. You sweat extra.

It was no better the next week when I was head-to-toe in Strawberry Swirl cake mix. Since people were assigned here or there, I realized it could have been anyone. Trusted friends, well, you just had to wonder. None of my pals were talking to me. The plant buzzed along as always. It remained fastidiously clean as always. Anything that hit the floor went into offal containers. There were times when the cornflakes oven overflowed and it would snow cornflakes from three storeys on high. The 'B'-operator on the line would immediately shut down the machine and run pell-mell to various portals to prevent jams in a notoriously difficult machine. The cornflakes were an inch-and-a-half deep.

One night during a corn storm a relief team was on level one shovelling New Country Corn Flakes into huge waste barrels. In 1965 cornflakes cost a half-cent per box and printed cardboard boxes, a quarter. The plant facilities, overhead, payroll, etc. Take this into account the next time you buy a nine-dollar box of breakfast cereal. The storm grew worse and I went upstairs to investigate. Throughout the plant were vertical escalators. A worker could place a foot on a step, grab the pole and ride up. You would pass through a hole on the second level and step off there, or continue your ride to level three. You could also reverse the procedure and come down meeting people in either direction, firing off a Beetle Bailey salute, anything, just so you didn't fall off.

That night I saw the ovens backing up and extra help dashing forth to control the problem on level three while I just watched in a detached fashion and rode up and down. What great evil had befallen us? On level two an oven was baking a new snack product, Bugles corn chips. They were made of the same corn that was snowing. Things were going like clockwork. The workers moved methodically with neutral expressions. It reminded me of the pod-loading scene in *The Invasion of the Body Snatchers*. Oh, my God! I knew this was going to happen. Are there any *actual* people left or is it just me?

There was an enormous thunderstorm going on outside. The lights flared on and off. Thunder boomed. On and off and then it was just off. Bobby and I were handed flashlights and sent to dispose of discarded barrels of cornflakes.

'With all this flavourful nutritious food,' Bobby said as he scooped up flakes, 'you could feed half of Africa.'

The plant had a huge furnace and its flames provided light. Throughout the plant, workers began to revel in the darkness. They sat in small groups and talked Cubs and White Sox.

'Hey, now, kick back, brother. We are getting paid for this shit. Paid overtime!'

'Yeah, man. Paid in spades.'

Bobby and I passed a group of layabouts who handed us a large sack of Bugles, still warm from the oven. They were delicious. Bobby and I sat on a pallet of flattened cardboard boxes in the furnace room eating Bugles.

Billy Pierce, Sherman Lollar, Luis Aparicio, Nellie Fox, Ernie Banks... *Note writer.*

Bobby started laughing. His body was jiggling as he fought to restrain it. His merriment overflowed in waves.

'What's so funny?' I said. 'I'm the one headed for Pelican Bay. They think I did it.'

He laughed all the more.

'Tell me, what in the fuck is so goddamn funny; what in the fuck is the matter with you?'

Bobby straightened up, twisting his neck side to side, making loud cracks. He said, 'There was no note.'

'What?'

'How many times do I have explain *no*? What is it about *no* that you don't get? There was *no* note, all right? It's all a big hoax. A joke. Nobody wrote a note. Noodles Almondine are germ-free. Every box is cleaner than an operating room.'

'Well, okay, but who tossed the miniature Easter Island heads in the Noodles Almondine?'

'No one! Nobody! It was all a joke, dipstick.'

It took me a few seconds to drink this information in. I said, 'You fucker! It was you! You did this to me! I'll kill you!'

Bobby leaped from the cardboard and ran off into the dark night, baying like a hound: '*Bah rah hahaha ha.*'

I saw his flashlight beam cut through the darkness. It was Bobby's last night. He was driving down to Carbondale the next morning in his MG Midget. Registration for fall-semester classes began early Monday morning. The last fleeting words from his mouth were, 'Suck-*ah!*'

I was too stuffed with Bugles to give chase. In fact, I had to laugh. What a clever motherfucker, Bobby.

They still make Bugles, but forty-four years and counting I have touched nary a one. Too much of a good thing. For all I care you can toss in a box of Noodles Almondine and send them all to Somalia. ∎

Knight with Lady

It was this way: my sister changed
rooms with my father; I forgot, and opened
the door. Fronting me, he stood,
torso twisted in *contrapposto*, nude,
reaching into her closet. My head (I was small)

was at the level of his genital.
How could I, from my own,
my tucked, my tactful, my smooth-
peeled – how could I have known?
Long dun-colored *unaware*

Dodona bough it seemed to me,
– pale hornbeam suckering and sprawled.
Indifferent, it had the quality
of Fact; of old, seamed, Entity:
I was called to a lifetime of study.

Two prints on the wall, my child and Master E's *Knight
with Lady*: his limber, net-metaled foot
crosses to fix her skirt-hem; she flings her head back
to enforce the masterful X-composition, and put
his lance by with her left hand, his helm with her right...

Sprawled nude in my study's sunk armchair
like a hare in its form, inked fingers, hair in a maze,
I don't think to stop work to gaze down
at Pindar's *grayed mother-groin* – my lair's
silvering Hera-mound, crayon-shadings, silk paws,

ringlets of vervain and elver-otter hairs –
Nascitur, it's forgotten how not to be there.
Mater, materia prima, it's everywhere –
Withindoors, my globes and strewn papers; without,
my garden of green cones, green spheres.

AGATE *Fine Print.*

BEFORE I FORGET
by Leonard Pitts • $16.00

"A powerful novel about regrets, second chances, forgiveness and responsibility....This is a beautiful, tragic and riveting work. A compelling, moving novel about fathers and sons and what it means to be a man."—Marilyn Dahl, *Shelf Awareness*

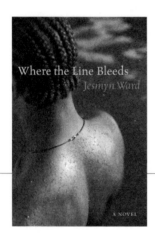

WHERE THE LINE BLEEDS
by Jesmyn Ward • $15.00

"A fresh new voice in American literature, Ward unflinchingly describes a world full of despair but not devoid of hope."—*Publishers Weekly*

LOOPED
by Andrew Winston • $14.95

"Great cities deserve great literature. *Looped* is as intricately woven and real as the modern, diverse Chicago it describes. Well done."—Po Bronson

Independent publishing, Chicago-style
DISTRIBUTED BY PGW
agatepublishing.com

Domp-Domp

Ben Ratliff

Bo Diddley with the Bo-ettes, and the Duchess (right) on rhythm guitar, Los Angeles, 1965

There's Bo Diddley. Big hips, pointy shoes, glasses. A gap between his teeth, and a bow tie, in 1965. He's performing on *The Big T.N.T. Show*, a rock-and-roll variety movie. A stage set, a studio audience in LA. It's spectacular.

He's playing his tail-fin guitar, strumming in a figure-eight shape. The drummer is beating Diddley's signature rhythm: roughly, domp-a-domp-a-domp/a-domp-domp. The groove volts through Diddley's body. On the one the rhythm comes through his legs and up his torso. On the two it reaches his top, which shudders in a shoulder shrug. He looks like he's spouting.

He's singing 'Bo Diddley', a schoolyard-rhyme song with one repeated chord. Rhythm makes the song. He's on the left, his bass player Chester Lindsey on the right. Between them, his two beehived backup singers, the Bo-ettes, Gloria Morgan and Bee Bee Jamieson; and his rhythm guitarist, Norma-Jean Wofford, known as the Duchess: a woman with a guitar, a rare sight in a man's band. Behind them all, on a pedestal, sits his drummer, Clifton James, who's got three cymbals but isn't using them; he's focusing his rumble on tom-toms and bass drum. With his hi-hat he lines out the underlying pulse.

'Bo Diddley' is all gestural scratchety-scratch, hi-hat clicks, steady thumps, moaning and hollering: toms, rhythm guitar, call-and-response chants. Led by the Duchess, the women advance in tight white satin dresses. The Duchess rabbit-hops. The Bo-ettes shuffle.

Then the Bo-ettes begin this movement: knees slightly crooked, arms slightly crooked, palms out, come-here gesture with all fingers together in quarter-note beats with a slight hip-thrust. They're also panning left and right, not completely in sync, shy smiles. They're new to this: performing, crowds. They might even be embarrassed. They're saving something for themselves. Diddley advertised the Duchess as his sister. She wasn't. She must have been the Bo-ettes' supervisor, beneath Diddley's executive control.

After Bo Diddley sings the fourth line, about a private eye, all three women retreat, repeating his line, moving their hips and their arms carefully, elbows out from torsos, swinging their hips in modified mambo. White girls in the audience: clapping on the two and four. They're making the rhythm theirs. The screaming grows louder. The Bo-ettes resume the come-here gesture. They look so encouraging, as if to say to the girls in the crowd (where are the boys?), that's it, keep going. Just before the end, the camera cuts to five black girls sitting in a row. They're hand-jiving to it, bowing on every other beat, working together.

Bo Diddley controlled this mongrel ritual. He looks imperious, sometimes professionally sanguine. He wasn't as bumptious as he'd first been. Commercially he was cold. He'd been on fire ten years before, in rock's infancy. But the weathervane kids were on to Motown and Bob Dylan, not this home-made street-corner stuff, no matter how potent it was. He'd had two careers already. At the beginning of rock and roll he had real success. He made Chuck Berry look wanting. ('Registered nicely,' wrote Jack Schiffman, the owner of the Apollo Theatre, in his notebook, on November 18, 1955, about Berry's first gig there. 'Though not as exciting as Bo Diddley.') Later he experienced the demi-success of authenticity. He got his second chance through British rock bands that adored him, especially the Rolling Stones and the Pretty Things, and influentially toured the United Kingdom, from September to November of 1963, with the Everly Brothers, Little Richard and the Rolling Stones.

By 1965, he was watching the new rock and roll advance on him and push him underwater. In New York he was gigging at the Cafe au Go Go, downtown; up at the Apollo they had forgotten him and moved on to the Supremes. Three years later at Madison Square Garden, Janis Joplin sang 'Bo Diddley' and a critic in *The New York Times* described it as 'an old rock song'. In context it was. But it was only as old then as TLC's 'Waterfalls' is to us now. Bo Diddley songs sounded like they were from the public domain. Which had been the point.

Great pop stars can look like liars or actors or pretenders, but usually they know what they're up to: they keep raising the heat on a paradox. They make bitter rise from sweet, or femininity from masculinity, or clarity from clutter. Even Michael Jackson – especially Michael Jackson. But he lost control of his paradoxes. He became inflicted with ludicrous helpers. He lost his sense of making something. Even worse, he came to seem naive.

Bo Diddley never had that problem. The opposite of the tortured artist is the cheery mechanic. They existed in early rock. He had big hands and felt they were clumsy. Some of his paradoxes were country and city, intuition and technique, ancient and future, white and black, adult and child. Not adult and teenager: adult and child.

He was born Ellas Otha Bates in 1928, and grew up first in McComb, Mississippi, raised by his mother's cousin, Gussie McDaniel; thus his name changed to Ellas Otha McDaniel. In 1934 the family moved to the South Side of Chicago, settling in a house on South Langley Avenue, near East Forty-seventh Street. He sang and played violin in church. He went to Foster Vocational School, in a part of the South Side very close to the Maxwell Street open-air market, where he and his classmate the guitarist Earl Hooker sang for tips. At Foster he was a woodworker, making a violin and a double bass. He learned basic plumbing, too: he became a Fixit. He must have understood that he was going to have to fend for himself. 'I was the kid in the neighbourhood that didn't sit around and twiddle my thumbs,' he told his biographer, George R. White. He went further:

> It didn't look like I was learning anything at school, so I said the best thing for me to do was to get out and start buildin' my survival kit now. In other words, to secure myself for old age – because I didn't want to be in the predicament that my mom had fallen into: she didn't have nothing, and it was too late to get anything.

He quit school at fifteen and formed a band, the Hipsters, later renamed the Langley Avenue Jive Cats. Two guitars, washtub bass, and Samuel Daniel, known as Sandman, who poured sand on a board and swished it with a broom. Underage and bluffing their way into joints, they played neighbourhood places not far from Diddley's house, like the Indiana Theater, at East Forty-third and Indiana, where they won amateur shows. (Bo Diddley was curiously proud of winning amateur shows. When the *Chicago Defender* wrote its first big story on him, in 1955, you can almost hear the subject whispering into the reporter's ear: 'In fact he was a winner so frequently that many shows barred him from competition.') Finally, around 1951, he got a regular gig at the 708 Club, across East Forty-seventh Street near Halsted, a club important in the transformation of country blues into electric Chicago blues. He worked as a blacktop spreader and a dump-truck driver during the day, making a little extra on nights and weekends with his music. He wasn't playing deep blues, like Muddy Waters, whom he loved. He was playing Louis Jordan-style rhythm and blues with funny lyrics, and he had gotten used to the performance rhetoric of amateur shows: make them laugh, show them something new.

His name, like his beat, had been in the air. It was a semi-obscure American comic persona: the rootless misfit entertainer, the figure so ignored for his haplessness that he's free to reinvent himself. Through different tellings of the story, various people may have brought up the name Bo Diddley around Ellas McDaniel, or suggested that he use it professionally: schoolmates at Foster Vocational, his Jive Cats bassist Roosevelt Jackson, his harmonica player Billy Boy Arnold, his label boss Leonard Chess. There is an African-derived one-string instrument played around the South called the diddley bow, but he said he'd never heard of it until later. He is part of the story of Southern blacks moving north. But his art was more than that story.

He wasn't as refined a guitar player as Muddy Waters. He wasn't as expressive a singer as Howlin' Wolf. (He couldn't hold a smoulder or a menace like either of them.) But he saw his little angle and worked his way in. By 1953 or so he had set himself up in Chicago's firmament as a singer-songwriter in blues and jump music, and a few years later in a music of his own construction: a kind of Antillean-American fun-house rock and roll. He was a man with a contingency plan: if all else failed, he had his songs and his guitars and could set up on the corner and play by himself. If that failed, presumably, there was plumbing. Starting in 1955, he wrote nearly everything he recorded for Chess, the Chicago record company that had him under contract until 1973. The songs were simple but the concepts were radical. His first single, 'Bo Diddley', rose to number two on the R & B charts. The first version, about farmers' daughters, was too dirty for Chess. No problem: he made up another version, clean, with his name inserted. 'Bo Diddley' was both a first-person and a third-person narrative, and a call-and-response schoolyard chant. On its other side was 'I'm a Man', a stop-time electric blues.

Look at the picture of him on *Bo Diddley is a Gunslinger*, his fifth album, from 1960, a quasi-concept record with some western-themed songs. He's in a cowboy costume with fake pistols, posing in a horse corral. White writes that he'd just seen *The Magnificent Seven*, but I can't believe he's interested in cowboys per se. Surely the reason for the cowboy costume is to look good while standing in dirt. The dirt is there to off set his new red guitar, his design, with sharp angles, modelled after the tail fins of a 1959 Cadillac. Tech and dirt: Bo Diddley. He'd recorded the album in his basement. He was living in Washington, DC, with his white wife, Kay Reynolds. She'd helped him nail in the acoustical tiles.

He sang about machines: 'Cadillac', 'Road Runner', 'Heart-o-Matic Love'. He also sang about horses and mules and dogs, like other blues and rock-and-roll singers, but less as metaphors than as the real quadrupeds: in 'Bo Diddley's Dog', on the great live record *Bo Diddley's Beach Party*, he makes dog wails, for about fifteen seconds, over the tom-toms, while crowd noises fade in and out. He didn't seem interested in songs that defined him geographically – songs about Chicago or about the South. Too restrictive. He wasn't of one place only. He sang about doing rather than being. He was selling his brand, but giving away his materials, which anyway weren't his to save. He had a fat guitar sound and a lovely airhorn voice: what was the point of being a rock star if you weren't going to sing really, really loud? He had a name and a beat you thought you'd heard before. Then he made them recognizably his, along with his guitar. The point of Bo Diddley was so that anyone could encounter him and say, that's Bo Diddley! I know that guy in particular: I've seen him in a magazine. But I know what he does from somewhere else.

Bo Diddley drives musicologists crazy. He made two comments about his beat: that he 'stumbled upon it' when he was trying to play a version of Gene Autry's '(I've Got Spurs That) Jingle Jangle Jingle', and that he heard it in a Chicago church as a boy. None of this helps much. Erasing his tracks, he denied hotly that the Bo Diddley beat had anything to do with Hambone, the rhyming hand-patting game evolved from plantation dances. But his beat was definitely related to it. Hambone is related to the clapping-and-patting game called Patting Juba. The word 'juba' comes from Djouba, the Haitian voodoo dance. And Diddley's beat – or at least the beat of his early drummers, Clifton James and Frank Kirkland – was Afro-Cuban in that it expresses the clave, the basic rhythm of Cuban music: three beats in one bar, the middle one syncopated, followed by two in the next (ONE-and-two-AND-three-and-FOUR-and/one-and-TWO-and-THREE-and four-and).

There was the rest of the Antilles, too. In 1959, he made a record called 'Limbo'. In 1960, during the beginning period of his home-studio sessions – when he fed his voice, not just his guitar, through the tremolo box – he made a song called 'Merengue (Limbo)'. Both use a version of the habanera beat, the one he used most famously in 'Crackin' Up'. The habanera rhythm is related to various calypso rhythms. The merengue is the national dance of the Dominican Republic. The limbo is the dance popular from various West Indian carnivals. Rhythmically, there's not much relation between Diddley's 'Merengue' and what we now know as Dominican merengue. But there is a traditional Haitian song form called the *méringue*, and there is a closer relation there. It uses shakers, it's heavily syncopated and swinging; it sometimes uses clave and suggests the habanera.

But beyond the origins we can tease out of songs and beats was black music's natural vernacular drift, a force much greater than copyright. The reason the Bo Diddley beat connects with Cuban music, calypso, and ultimately Kongo culture is because it's just another moving part of the black new world. It's the same reason that the hip-hop dance called top-rocking resembles the battle dance of the Mardi Gras Indians. Popular songs and beats breed like viruses in bars, parades, schoolyards, beach cookouts, park jams.

And for a while – during the best years of Bo Diddley's career – that family of Afro-Latin songs and rhythms made white pop delirious. The limbo and the watusi and the shimmy and hully-gully, cutting across race. The habanera beat in Del Shannon's 'Runaway'. White America looked for motion and modifications and flexibility; it went in hard for beach culture and hot-rods at the same time that it started absorbing, unknowingly, the music of the black Atlantic.

In Bo Diddley's records there was a one-man-band in his riffs and his feel: a single force making melody, bass line and rhythm. (For the first three years of his records, until 1958, there was no bass player.) 'Mama Keep Your Big Mouth Shut', from 1964, has a beautiful two-bar question-and-answer guitar riff. I heard a rock band play it in London in 1981, outside a pub, with the riff shifted entirely to bass. I didn't know the song. I thought it was some kind of white reggae.

Bo Diddley ran his guitar through a tremolo effect-box, making the guitar sound surge and retreat at a regular pulse, *whupawhupawhupa*. The pulse varied – and sometimes the pulsations were so light that you felt it but couldn't quite hear its rhythm – but in the song 'Bo Diddley', it implied a triplet. So you had a three-beat pulsation over a four-beat strumming groove. (Once he called it an 'offset rhythm'.) If you listen to the song's two alternate takes, you can hear that he didn't quite have it yet: his strumming feels too mechanical. But the correct one got released. The guitar rhythm jabs and weaves. It's mystery, rhythm on rhythm. You hear it in four, in three, in six.

You can over-think Bo Diddley. I suspect he liked it if you did. He was an opportunist, a scavenger, a parts maven. He was loud and novel and strange and heavy with mother-wit. By his reckoning, his black audience abandoned him in the first few years. Five or seven years on, the Stones and the Pretty Things loved his rhythm and the strength of his sound. But the rock bands who idolized him ten and fifteen and thirty years later still – like the Clash, who took him on tour, the New York Dolls, who covered one of his songs, and the Fall, whose Mark E. Smith has often talked about him and pointed towards him in lyrics – surely they admired him in part because his importance would forever outweigh his fame. They knew about that. They liked that he was street and wily and plain-looking and dedicated to his hustle. They liked how much style and gamesmanship and improvisation he could use without being mistaken for a master musician. And certainly they all liked Bo Diddley because he took an interest in them: he liked them back.

He created his own authority and authenticity, through to his last days as a performer in 2007. The rock-and-roll oldies circuit has always been boring. It's the exaltation of copyright. It's an advertisement for the royalty system, a promoter's racket, and a kind of opium den for nostalgic spectators: for ninety minutes they can gorge on a younger version of themselves. But Bo Diddley, who worked on these circuits from the 1970s onward, wasn't boring. His shows were a little anarchic. He was too fond of variations and random sass. He kept a database in his head of what sounded like very old insults and rhyming couplets. (He knew how to deliver them without speaking: in 'Mumblin' Guitar', he played two-line taunts on his guitar strings.) At a gig once, I saw him single out a man in the audience and rain antique scorn on him: 'He ain't gonna get no pancakes in the morning. He'll get a bowl of scorched water.'

He sang songs slightly differently than how they were known, as forcefully as the first time. He was playing: not re-enacting, but playing. Nothing was fixed; nothing had got frozen by ownership. 'Nursery Rhyme' was one of his best songs, and in it he sang lines about Puudin' Tame and Little Jack Horner with great feeling and even a little melancholy. When you're entertaining a child, you tell him a story. When you finish, he says, 'Again.' You don't want to lose his attention, so you tell it in a different way, and he says, 'Again.' And so on. It's a form of respect towards the child. I think this is what Bo Diddley was doing: treating his listeners like children, without condescension. ∎

GRANTA

Parrot
Peter Carey

ILLUSTRATIONS BY GEORGE BUTLER

I

You might think, who is this, and I might say, this is God, and what are you to do? Or I might say, a bird! Or I could tell you, Madame, Monsieur, Sir, Madam, how this name was given to me – I was christened Parrot because my hair was coloured carrot, because my skin was burned to feathers, and when I tumbled down into the whaler, the coxswain yelled, here's a parrot, Captain. So it seems you have your answer, but you don't.

I had been named Parrot as a child, when my skin was still pale and tender as a maiden's breast, and I was still Parrot in 1793. In 1793 the French were chopping off each other's heads and I was already twelve years of age and my *endodermis naturalus* had become scrubbed and hardened by the wind and mists of Dartmoor from whose vastness my da and I never strayed too far. I had tramped behind my darling da down muddy lanes and I was still called Parrot when he, Jack Larrit, carried me on his shoulder through the Northgate at Totnes. My daddy loved his Parrot. He would sit me on the bar of the Kingsbridge Inn, to let the punters hear what wonders came from my amazing mouth. *Man is born free and is everywhere in chains.*

If that ain't worth sixpence what is?

My daddy was a journeyman printer, a lanky man with big knees and knubbly knuckled hands with which he would ruff up his red hair when looking for First Principles. Inside this bird's nest it was a surprise to find his small white noggin, the precious engine of his bright grey eyes.

Children remain tied to their father by nature only so long as they need him for their preservation. As soon as this ends, so wrote the great Rousseau, *the natural bond is dissolved. Once the children are freed from the obedience they owe their father and the father is freed from his responsibilities towards them, both parties equally regain their independence. If they continue to remain united, it is no longer nature but their own choice, which unites them; and the family as such is kept together only by agreement.*

More or less that's it.

My daddy and I were two peas in a pod. The acquisition of knowledge was our occupation but of my ma I knew nothing but that she had a tiny waist which would fit inside her husband's hands. I missed her all my life.

I knew Adam Smith before I reached fractions. Then I was put to Latin which my father liked no more than I did, and this caused us considerable upset, both with ourselves and with each other. It was due to Latin that my father got in a state and clipped my lughole and I grabbed a half-burnt bit of kindling and set to drawing on the floor. I had never seen a drawing in my life, and when I saw what I was doing – Dear God, I thought I had invented it. And what rage, what fury, what a delicious humming wickedness I felt. All over the floor and who will clean it? I had seen my daddy's hand reach for his belt buckle and I was, ipso facto, ready for the slap. Yet at this moment I entered a foreign jungle of the soul. I drew a man with a dirty long nose. A leaping trout. A donkey falling upside down.

But my daddy's belt stayed on his buckle.

He stared at me. His hair stood up like taffy. He cocked his head and my ears began buzzing. I permitted him to take my charcoal stick and kiss me on the head. Not a cross word, nor a kind one. He led the Parrot downstairs where he ordered the landlord pour me a ginger beer. Then he sat and watched me drink, and what was he pondering, do you reckon?

Why, the benefits of having an engraver in the family.

Thereafter I was a mighty protégé and we forgot about our upsets and our Latin and our fractions, and even though my drawings were not always wanted where I placed them, he encouraged me at every turn, always on the lookout for a quiet church porch on account of the quality of slate. As to subjects, he was not fussy, although once he gave me a pound note to see what I could make of it.

On another occasion he was compelled to scrub clean the

Dartmouth footpath on which I had drawn the great bloody head of Louis XVI. My father said he didn't mind the scrubbing, it being a pleasure to make any tyrant vanish from the earth. It was suggested we might leave the town. There was no work in Dartmouth anyway. But up in Dittisham, Dit'sum as they called it, we found a strangely isolated printery, situated just at the place where the estuary became the river proper and there we found members of that better-educated class. I mean Printers. There is nothing like them. Having spent all their day with words and proofs, they are monstrously well read and disputatious beasts, always – whilst setting up the type, tapping in the furniture, rolling out the ink – arguing. If it was not that they spoke varying types of English, you might think yourself in France. It was the drunken height of revolution and all was Girondins or Cordeliers. Hume or Paine.

The printers at Dit'sum were family genus species *Textus miraculus*. They would shut up only at the long deal table which they shared with their master, Mr Piggott, and his wife, them both being Catholics of a put-upon variety, and very sarcastic about Tom Paine in particular. Mrs Piggott was a young Frenchwoman easily made tearful by events in her country, which left the men with nothing they could safely say at table, but I am ahead of myself. I did not say our single aim was to find shelter and a decent meal.

We arrived from Dartmouth at dinner time. My father knocked and hallooed, until we discovered seven full-grown humans, all supping at a table, quiet as Lent.

We finally sat down at the end with big bowls of stew and lumps of rough bread and a cup of rainwater and about twenty cats mewling about our legs. No sooner did my daddy have a mouthful than the master wished to know who he was. He replied he was a press or case man, whatever was needed worst. In fact Piggott required a case man, that is, a compositor who would lift types for sixpence a thousand, but at first he said nothing of it, for he was staring hard at me. No matter how girlish his wife, Mr Piggott himself was all of sixty. He was almost bald, with a little lump of a nose.

'The devil, are you?' he demanded.

'Me Sir?'

'You lad.'

He had a very short neck and colossal shoulders that seemed as wide as the table and when he stood to see me better he began to butt his big head against the ceiling, like a goat.

I would have run but my father clamped my thigh.

I said that I was twelve years old and, being too young to be apprenticed, I was accustomed to taking the job of devil.

My father was occupied cleaning the tines of his fork with his shirt tail.

Many is the dirty job I did, I told old Piggott. I would rather work than play. I could clean the proofing press, I said. I was a dab hand at 'dissing' which is what they call putting the type back in its right case.

'See him draw a racehorse,' said my father.

This comment caused some puzzlement but finally I was given pencil and paper. The result was then passed around the table. No one made a comment until the horse arrived in front of Mrs Piggott; she rose up from her chair.

The mistress could not yet have been twenty, but I saw a small old person, camouflaged like a lizard, and she came around the table at me flicking out a measuring tape like some enormous tongue.

My face and neck burned bright red while I stood in front of all these men and Mrs Piggott, with no word of explanation, having completely ignored my racehorse, measured me, not only my height but around my chest, from armpit to extremity.

'Ah, ain't that lovely?' said my da who would say anything to get a nice hot feed. 'See that Parrot – you are to be measured. What a treat,' he said to Mr Piggott.

Mrs Piggott slipped her tape measure in the pocket of her pinny. Mr Piggott thumped his fist twice against the ceiling which was even more alarming than the butting. At this signal each printer bowed his atheistic head.

'*Benedictus, Benedicat per Jesum Christum Dominum Nostrum*,' then moving from Latin to English without a cough, Mr Piggott formally employed my father, passing down to him, from hand to hand, a copy of Miss Parsons's *The Castle of Wolfenbach* which, just published in London for ten shillings he would soon have on the roads at six shillings and sixpence.

My father said, 'Good-oh,' and did not seem to worry about what might happen to me on account of the measuring. My racehorse was left with all the breadcrumbs. I never had so little praise before.

Even when we went out after dinner my dad said not a word about what had happened. Instead he lit his pipe and told me this was certainly the River Dart. It was a place where cattle crossed so the bank was bad-smelling from their droppings mixed with earth. 'Lovely night,' my father said, turning with one arm behind his back, to survey the printery which occupied what might have once been a grand house but had long been encroached upon by woods, tangled in wild creeper, guarded by thistles on the riverbank, surrounded by carts and wheels in such a style you would think it the graveyard for old carriages.

Piggott's was what was called a *black house*, not because of the grimy slate tiles that wrapped themselves around the soft contours of the roof, but on account of printing what was *on the cross*. To make this cheap edition of *The Castle of Wolfenbach* was an offence against the Crown.

Soon Mrs Piggott gave us each a bundle of bedlinen and when my father paid her a florin, she silently showed him to a bed by the dormitory door. Me she led to the far end and left in what was once a kind of scullery. My da said it was a fine accommodation but this was like him, to become most enthusiastic when most oppressed by life. He showed me how I could lie in bed and watch the cattle go home for milking. His bright eyes were a fright to see.

On this first night, I was sitting on my bed, wondering if I dare walk outside to do my business, when something attacked my shoulder. I thought a bird or bat, but discovered a pile of quarto proofs wrapped in string.

My da was always at me with a book and I was not displeased. When I had unwrapped the bundle I was excited to find engravings for a picture book. Alas these were depictions of human congress too disturbing for a child. I could chop the head off a king, but I was not strong enough for this.

I never told my father what I had seen, or why I abandoned my own place and walked the length of the dormitory in my nightshirt and squeezed into his narrow crib.

'Oh this is a grand place,' he said, and I agreed it was and got ready to protect myself from his nightmares and his bruising knees.

II

That first morning our bathing in the river provided amusement for the printers whose yawning faces appeared in a line of windows like noggins at a fair. One of them asked us were we mermaids – it was not what he said, but he was a Londoner with all his lovely London sounds and I did adore the voices of mankind.

'Mer-mayds,' said the Parrot to his da.

My dad tried to wad the washcloth in my mouth. If I was a good boy I should have let him, but I squirmed away as wicked as a slippery eel.

'Mer-mayd,' I called.

'Shush,' he said. And ran away, my da, sausage bouncing, splashing nudey through the water, lurching towards the riverbank with the idea, I suppose, that I would have no one left to talk to if he was not there.

'Oh lor,' I shouted from the middle of the stream. 'Blow me down. It must be a mer-mayd.'

Came my father's voice, faintly, from the shore. 'Shush.'

'Mermaids,' I cried, making a funnel with my hands. 'Mermaids.' I had the lovely vowels, I was a pearly king.

My daddy dressed and walked back to the printery, head down, combing at his wet hair in such a way I knew he was trying to hide his grin. He had a soft sweet heart, it was a burden to him. 'How *do* you do that?' he would often say. He could not whistle either although he often tried.

When breaking fast the cockney fellow winked at me and I knew I had made a friend not the enemy my father must have feared.

After breakfast we were taken to the printery. The cockney announced he was known as Gunner and he proceeded to show my da his frame. Piggott watched suspiciously, it seemed to me, as my dad set up the implements of his trade and mounted a pair of cases full of shining type in readiness for *The Castle of Wolfenbach*. Then I was set to clean the proofing press.

It was not only Gunner who had a nickname. There was also Weasel, Bunter, Chooka, Chanker, to name a few. Gunner was a press man who operated his machine with the darting little Weasel. Bunter was tall and gone to fat, a slovenly worker, scrambling and shovelling his types together without any regard to the exact mechanical neatness which is an instinct with the good compositor. All this I observed as I cleaned the ink slab. When that dirty task was done I was set to work humping heavy bundles of the Dit'sum newspaper from the back door to a trolley. After this, with my hands already harrowed and scarified from binding twine, I was ordered by Bunter to clean myself with spirit and printer's soap, and this hurt a great deal as it had the texture of coarse sand. Then I was ordered to drag this four-wheeled monster up a rutted road and then along a maze of lanes and footpaths which – being always unsure if I could find my way home again – I did not like at all.

Dit'sum being a decent size and the people of a secretive disposition, it took the best part of the day to get the newspapers to their subscribers. I was relieved to find my way back to the old printery, grey and lumpy, like a turtle in the mud.

After supper my father and I bathed again. He had the hands of a drowned man, my dear daddy, blanched to death by endless washing. When we were dry and decent we found the men gathered by the broad dormitory steps pursuing what was clearly an ongoing argument about the utility of kings in a republic. My father was excitable by temperament but cautious by habit, and he smoked his pipe, nodded his head but offered no opinions.

In the night he was alarmed by some bad turn his dream was taking and nearly took my eye out.

The second day involved washing in the river and then getting dirty and then delivering a job lot of docket books to the Swan. This was formally received by an older girl who looked me up and down like I was the living filth. She took me into a dark parlour where some old ladies sat wetting their hairy chins with stout. Thus it was at a table in a pub I first saw the quality of Piggott's engraving which was what you might call *cack-handed*.

She said, 'What happened to Sniffy?'

I said I did not know.

She said, 'Did Sniffy die?'

'I don't know, Miss.' I thought I could draw a swan much better. I was bursting to show her what I could have done.

The third day began just the same. I washed. I got dirty. Mr Piggott himself came to give me my instructions.

'Get the trolley, lad,' he said. 'Today it is a pick up.'

I set off at a great speed in order to get the heavy trolley up on to the road, but he snatched the machine from my care, and shoved it underneath a pussy willow. He then led me through some stinging nettles arriving hard against the backside of the house, at a place where there was a stink of moss and lichens, also a peeling grey door, which I was told to open. I found myself in an empty dark stale-smelling room which had once been a kitchen. From here I was shooed like a hen into another room which held nothing but a big fireplace of grey carved stone.

'Now,' said Piggott, 'come in the fireplace and I'll show you.'

I said I was not allowed in fireplaces.

For answer Mr Piggott threw his head back against his wide shoulders. Then he folded himself up, all shoulder, head and knees and – maintaining this strange arrangement of his limbs – edged himself inside the fireplace.

'Come here with me,' he said, taking off his spectacles and sliding them inside his apron.

'I'm going to fetch the trolley,' I said.

'Forget the blessed trolley. We need no trolley.' He came crabbing out to snatch at me, his naked eyes gone wet and fishy. He twisted up my shirt front in his fist. I tore away and broke my buttons and rushed out into the dappled woody light of morning, bawling in fright, but I wanted a sleep and a feed and so fetched the stupid trolley from its hiding place and brought it back to the main door of the printery where I met my father rushing the other way, a stick of type grasped in his hand.

Mr Piggott rounded on us, arms swinging, head nodding.

'What's he done now?' my father said.

Mr Piggott removed the stick from my father's hand, assessed the type composed there, before laying it carefully on a windowsill. Then he led my da away from me, down towards the stream. I saw the water sparkling behind their dark figures, light shining like a halo through Mr Piggott's ring of hair. The master stroked my da on his long back then watched as he returned to his son.

'What?' I asked.

He attempted to mimic me but he did not have the ear. He was hangdog, red neck, and could not look at me. 'Come on, my Parrot,' said he at last. 'Master needs your help.'

'No,' I said, slipping from his grabby hand.

My daddy permitted himself to be led into the stinging nettles, through the empty kitchen, to the empty fireplace. I followed.

This time I noted Piggott took the trouble to explain, and when he did this his voice became both whispery and loud.

Said he, 'I have a very good press man working in a very hard-to-get-to place.'

My father squatted and peered towards the chimney.

'That's right,' said Mr Piggott, jerking his head at my father. 'That's it, John.'

My father winked at me.

'Nothing's going to hurt the nipper,' said Mr Piggott. 'All he has to do is—'

I took a step back but my da had already locked his arm around my shoulder.

'That's it,' whispered Mr Piggott. 'All he has to do.'

He got down on his hands and knees and crawled into the fireplace where he grunted and then lit a match. 'Come on, young'un,' he whispered, and I smelled an airy rush of peppermint.

'See up there,' my da pointed, squeezing in. 'See that?'

I allowed myself to be pulled in beside my da and Mr Piggott who had a tussock of white hair growing out of his wattly ear.

'See that!'

'No,' I said, but I did see: a little metal door inside the chimney.

'Yes, it looks all dark, don't it, but once inside, young'un, why there's matches and a lantern, see. You light the lantern, it's like bloody Christmas.'

'Well, so to speak,' my daddy cautioned.

'Yes, so to speak,' said Mr Piggott. 'In a way of speaking. Not Christmas, of course, but plenty of surprises. You see, young'un,' he said, plucking at my open shirt, 'once you've got your lantern going, you'll see there's a passage tailor-made for you, and even though it goes this way and that, it keeps on going just the same, and you come to a bit of a step which you climb up, and then there is another door. Doesn't look like a door at all, even when your nose is hard against it, but you give it a good hard knock. You will, I know you will. Because what's inside but a printer like your father, not so tall, or so handsome. Mr Watkins is his name. And he's going to give you something.'

'What?' I asked.

'See,' said Mr Piggott, 'it's not hard.'

'What will he get given?' my father asked.

'Well it's a funny thing when you say it, but it's as regular as your daily bread.'

'What is it,' I asked.

'It's his chamber pot I suppose,' said Mr Piggott, 'and the printer fellow would be very grateful if you could bring it back out here so we can nicely deal with it.'

I was tremendously relieved to hear all this, and I was ready to set off immediately, but my father was now edging me back out into the room and Mr Piggott had no choice but to follow, although the three of us continued bunched together as if packed into a box.

'How was this job done previous?' my daddy asked.

'We had a lad, of course. It requires no training,' said Mr Piggott, who must have seen which way my father's mind was working.

'Ah, there you are,' my daddy said. 'Then he's better than an apprentice.'

'How's that?' said Piggott.

'No training. Less eaten. Less laundered. Less found,' my father said. 'And why was he measured, well it's obvious. It was an act of employment. Speaking legally.'

'A penny,' said Mr Piggott.

'Threepence each way,' my father said, 'and another threepence for each time he's needed. '

'I could get anyone to do this,' Piggott said. 'Threepence in and out this first time. And a penny each way thereafter.'

By now my father had his hair combed up into a big mess and he was scratching at his neck in an attempt to hide his happiness, but I had been there long enough to decide that the previous boy had been Sniffy, and although I allowed my father to lift me to the dark door, the tiny red hairs on my boy arms were standing up on end.

It was a tight fit in there, but passing clean, and the so-called passage bent and twisted and arrived at a wall that I did not understand. This was what Mr Piggott had called a step.

Then I was over this and soon I came to another deadend and, just as my throat was closing up with terror, I knocked. A hidden door swung open. And there it was – the printer's chamber pot, filled to overflowing, thrust right in my face.

'Take it,' the press man said.

He was a fright, I won't pretend he wasn't. For although he was a young man and had therefore often walked the earth and seen the sun, he seemed, at that moment, like one of those transparent creatures they say live in rivers far below the earth. His hair was fine as silk, and long and white, not like the English, but the Swedes. His forehead was very tall, and so white and smooth it seemed as if it must be carved from ivory. He had pale projecting eyebrows, and eyes like water.

'Now put it down,' he said.

'What?' I asked, having heard him perfectly.

'Put down the filthy pot,' he pleaded. 'On the stinking floor.'

I saw no reason to be afraid of such a nervous creature, but when I obeyed he gave me an awful cuff across the head and took me by the ear and twisted it.

'If you ever leave me waiting again,' he hissed, 'I will come out "the hard way"' – that was how he put it – 'and Piggott don't want that. Smell it,' he cried, his voice cracking. 'Smell.'

He meant his room. I looked above his shoulder and saw he was like all men who work with black ink and white paper. That is, his printed sheets were as clean as sawn timber and his narrow bed was tightly made. He shared his tight space with a guillotine and the first iron hand press I ever saw. He was all hunched over, his arms were long and thin and he held them across his chest in a way that made me think of the roots of a pot-bound tree. I could not make out how tall he was.

It would be many years, on the other side of the world, before I understood that Piggott's house had been designed by Nicholas Owen, a clever fellow who had devised the many hiding places for priests in the reign of Elizabeth I. Whether Piggott had inherited or purchased the property, I still don't know. At the time, of course, I did not care, for while it had been easy enough to crawl along the tiny passageway, it was quite another matter to return, nudging and sliding the sloshing chamber pot. Gently, gently catchee monkey. This was now my job, penny both ways, a fortune, to bring Mr Algernon Watkins his sandwiches and take away his slops three times a day and if I was ever to breathe so much as a word to anyone, then I would be murdered and my body bricked up inside the house. 'That's an exaggeration,' my father said.

III

I had never set eyes on a silkworm and I dare say young Watkins was in no way like one. Yet it is a silk worm that I think of when I recall him in 1793, a poor pale secret thing at the service of a Chinese emperor, sitting on his heels before his press, playing it like a dice box, and with all the papery essentials within the reach of his long arms. It will be no surprise, I reckon, that I got to know Algernon Watkins well enough, although the path will be curly, and not as you expect.

Piggott was as sly as a fox, as clever as a poacher. So well did he cover my tracks (and his own) that not even Weasel, the socialist, or Chanker, the Benthamite, had any idea what was taking place above their heads. As for my revolutionary father, it is a sad fact that you could kill his famous curiosity with less than threepence. So when I slipped away after tea he knew better than to ask me why.

It took a good many nasty trips to Watkins's dark door before I crossed the threshold, and only then did I really comprehend his terror of the chamber pot. As anyone who has served at His Majesty's Pleasure will tell you the smells that make your guts first heave soon become your home sweet home. But Watkins was, put plainly, a more fastidious and secretive young fellow than all your sisters put together.

There was ventilation of a sort which we will come to, but because he must clean his press, the air always contained white spirits – which he feared would blow him to kingdom come. This sensible concern had him pulling on the ventilator pulley with one hand even while he worked the press, so he was – as he said himself – like one of the Jack Puddings you see outside the George and Dragon with twenty instruments, the left foot beating drums, the right one cracking walnuts, this not being a bad picture of Watkins for he also – apart from being both press man and ventilator – kept vials of aromatics – oil of cloves, sweet geranium – in a row before his knees and was constantly dabbing these on to the silk scarf he wore across his nose and mouth.

But it was not only the straight thin nose he covered. He had white cloth draped everywhere, across the chamber pot, the press, the guillotine, his paper stock, brush-box blocks, and the burins which were to play so painful a part in my life I have sometimes wished to God I never saw them. You do not know what a burin is, and nor did I, mistaking it for a shiv, a murdering steel shaft with a hemispherical handle. It was very tight inside Watkins's 'shop' as he called it, but he offered a place for Parrot to sit, jammed in a corner just inside the door. His place was also just inside the door, but on the other side, and there he remained, with his pot-bound arms around his knees and his high head bowed beneath the ceiling so we were like a pair of ill-matched firedogs.

Although he could have been no more than twenty, he had clearly forgotten what it was like to be a boy. He conversed by means of questions, answers, commentary, as if I was there to learn my catechism.

He would ask me what I had seen that day. This was mostly birds and animals, and his commentaries, particularly about the birds, were very queer and very personal and often of surprising length.

When my da was in his cups, we had some strange conversations, but none like this. For Watkins's memories could turn him so suddenly and wildly happy, and he would make a picture of stomping on the moor and all the colours of the birds and gorse he could count off on his fingers. You would think he was a saint with the light of heaven on him. In this condition he could make you share his wonder at plain old tomtit, for instance, and it was by catching this intoxication that I drew a field mouse for him, showing off, right on his floor.

I had done this trick so often, I knew I was a prodigal. So when Watkins peered at my mouse and twisted himself around and I saw his hand burrowing under a cotton cover, then why, I thought it was my just reward. I was in no way surprised to see a big square of chocolate.

I put it in my mouth and saw him laugh at me. It was hard and brown, would break your teeth.

'What is it?' I asked. I was used to beer for my daddy or taffy for myself. Not this, this cold hard thing inside my palm.

'You are not an artist's bootlace,' said he.

'What is it?'

'It is a brush box,' said he, 'and if you are an artist it is butter beneath your knife.'

I asked him was he an artist.

For answer he would only smile and I thought how large his eyes were when they hid behind his purplish lids. He retrieved the square of steel-hard wood like a card sharp on the Strand, not letting me touch it but allowing me to glimpse the very artful drawing of a quail he had made upon one side. I hated it and was angry that he would not praise me. At the same time he was a mystery like none I ever knew. He was uncanny, pot-bound, excitable. He was watchful and ugly but graceful too. He was close as a tomb but on that same day I drew the mouse he revealed to me, a boy, his great ambition and the reason why he had sold his services to Piggott. He planned to amass sufficient geld to produce and print the best book of birds the world had ever seen.

Saying this, his watery eyes were very bright and everything in that dreadful little tomb seemed illuminated by his joy.

'What are you smiling at?'

I said I was thinking how nice it would be to see a book like that.

'You can't imagine boy.'

I supposed I couldn't.

'You don't know what I am,' he said.

'I am just a boy.'

He looked at me very close as if sizing up my utility and, without shifting his gaze, reached out for the shiv, that lethal-looking object we had been waiting for. I bolted for the door but he stuck his leg out so it would not open and then, picking up the brush box he began to work. I understood he would not murder me, but he did not look up at me or speak to me for a very long time, and even then he had not finished his work but I saw how he wielded that burin.

When he had done all he planned to do he let me touch it very briefly. I was not his bootlace. He sent me out so he could do his business in the pot.

IV

A fortnight previous the precocious Parrot was Leonardo, Cicero and the perfect future of the working man. Now he was plucked and naked, a printer's devil, the silkworm's fag. There were more suitable skills to be acquired – for instance, holding the piss pot off the floor with my elbows and pushing through the darkness on my knees, a painful business.

The first pot I dispatched into the hydrangeas and for this I got my ears boxed and would have got my bum whacked except Jack be nimble Jack be quick. It was a case of dig hole, bury shit, return empty pot. No time for drawing on the Church of England's slate. Collect empty water pail. Fill pail in stream. Other matters besides – ink, trolley – don't get lost. At the end of each long day I received from Watkins some ten parcels the size of four house bricks, sealed with red wax and wrapped tight with brown paper. These I pushed along the burrow one at a time, as instructed to by Piggot, leaving them hidden inside the trapdoor to be taken in the night.

What happened to these parcels was a mystery I would not solve for many years. They disappeared leaving no clue but a mess of broken sealing wax like the remains of something eaten by a dog. The wax was hard as broken glass and I was mostly concerned about the pain it caused my skin. But whether I was torturing my knees or strapped in the harness of the dog cart, I thought about not much else except how to make Mr Watkins teach me to engrave. The deep green oaks arched above my head but I was blind to all their splendour. I imagined the burin in my hand, carving with a flick and a push, feeling the steel moving through the hard wood like a knife through butter. I arrived in Mr Watkins's presence like a beggar on my knees.

I could hardly look at him, nor did he deign to glance at me.

If I had asked him to teach me he would have been haughty as a goose. So I sat in my place beside the door. On sufferance, I observed his long fair hair falling like a curtain across the mystery of his hands. I dared not ask to touch that unforgiving steel. I saw how his four long fingers were drawn back and curved and how he pressed the tool against the ball of the thumb. It looked so easy, but on the fetid night when – at last – without warning he pressed the tool into my warty hands, I found it completely resistant to my passion.

'You see,' he said to me, 'it is a gift.'

And took his burin back.

I was not worthy, but I would not go away and something in my wilfulness must have stirred him for he finally allowed me to ruin one of his brush-box blocks. How many nights was this for? Three? I sat cross-legged in the stinky hole, trying to engrave – not the rural scenes I had imagined, but ten straight lines close together. That was all he would let me do.

I was tired. I was very angry. I would not quit.

'You'll never be an engraver's bootlace,' he said. I will not say this did not hurt my feelings.

'Yes Sir, I know.'

'Then go.'

With his long spidery arms he opened the door for me and was nice enough, on this occasion, to personally hand out the wrapped parcels of his day's production. Then the door closed as usual, and I was outside in the blackness. No skerrick of light snuck around his door and I knew he had put out his lamps and set to clean his equipment in the dark, his long hands fluttering across blade and type bed like a blind watchmaker. When his labour was done, he had earlier informed me, he lay in bed pulling the rope of his ventilator, removing the flammable white spirit in time for work. Lighting the first lantern each morning, he feared he would be blown to bits.

One overcast dawn I arrived inside the fireplace to find an entire red wax seal broken as a biscuit. Then, deep in the dark of the crawling space, I came upon an item that must have spilled from the parcel – a sample of Mr Watkins's labour, a job so fine, I decided when I brought it into the light, that he would have found employment anywhere on earth. The strange pale silk spinner was an artist and although I already knew this from watching him work the burin, this single *assignat* confirmed him as the highest of the high. Of course you, Monsieur, know that an *assignat* was, at that time, the paper currency of the revolutionary government of France. Although the Parrot was only an ignorant printer's devil who had no clue about the *assignat*, the hair on my neck prickled. I recognized the power and danger of this ornate and clever forgery. I had only seen one British banknote in my life, and it was pale and ordinary as a cabbage moth, requiring the endorsement of Lord Hobnob or I knew not who. The *assignat* was a power unto itself, a goldish colour, one part butter yellow, the remainder mustard, printed on pearly linen paper. Across the upper part was printed *Domaines Nationaux* and although I was no lawyer I believed that a man could be hanged for printing what was in my inky hands. A wise boy would have destroyed it, but was a wise boy ever born? I could not kill such a lovely thing. Nor could I bury it, for it was too beautiful. So I folded it until it would fold no more and then I thrust it in my britches and kept it like you keep a treasure you can worship under the bedclothes in the early light of morning.

I was always tired, always busy, falling asleep when my head hit the bed, being awoken by my father to get myself washed. The printers had long given up finding our *ablutions*, as they called them, amusing. So we were left alone to clean ourselves and, on Sunday mornings, to wash our clothes as well.

The Sunday I will now recall was hot and overcast, and we found ourselves in company, not only with a hatch of mayfly, but with a gentleman I had observed the night before at dinner, a tall Frenchman with a broad chest and a rich man's manner who was noteworthy on account of the glint in his small grey eyes, the mass of curling red hair around his big head – this latter making him look like a Scots laird – but all of these distinctions were trumped by his left arm which was *completely missing*.

At dinner he had mostly engaged with Mrs Piggott who I saw was tremendously excited, and although she was a little bantam with fretful eyes, she now began to bat them like a girl. She was suddenly so talkative she hardly touched her food. Back and forwards they went – *parlez-vous* and so on.

We were told to call our visitor Monsieur but he did not seem so ordinary to me, and all the while he talked with Mrs Piggott, sugaring her with *d'accord*s and *Madames*, he had his eyes on the men around the table, engaging each of them, even me, letting us know he was very fine and fancy and that we would be unwise to cross him or betray him or even dream of such a thing.

We were at war with France yet we were in Devon very near the coast, and at Piggott's it was always ask no questions and you'll be told no lies. We never knew where the fruits of our labours would come to rest, in Louvres or Auxerre, or Oxford Street. The Piggotts were always feeding up their customers, plying them with brandy and Madeira, and after they had slept off their dinner they were on their way.

I expected the Frenchman to be gone by morning. But there he was nudey in midstream, and all I could see was the shocking violet skin shining in the place where his arm had been, and nothing left of it but a kind of flap, or turtle fin. Elsewhere his body had been pierced more times than St Sebastian and each site of injury was like a patch of angry silk.

My father was a terrible talker who wanted to know everything at once, but here he had a powerful wish to know not a bloody thing.

'*Bonjour*,' the Frenchman called to us.

My father's eyes went dead and milky.

'*Bonjour*,' he called again, but my father was taken by the sights downstream.

It was I who called back, not from wickedness, but because I could. Perhaps I might never draw a proper mouse, but I was a perfect mimic. That was a talent. Vowel for vowel, a parrot on the wing.

Says I: '*Bonjour*'

Says he: '*Parles-tu Français, Monsieur?*'

Says I: '*Parles-tu Français, Monsieur?*'

He had a face like stone. I squeezed a grin out of it. '*Vous*,' said he. '*Ah, vous?*' said I.

I wish you could hear me now because you would understand the unholy jumble – that rough little English boy falling over his *vous*s and *tu*s in the perfect accent of the Faubourg Saint-Germain. I dived into the stream in triumph, scraping my bare boy chest along a gravel bed as lightly as an old brown trout. Surfacing I saw my father had retreated from me, scrambling to the bank to fetch our laundry.

'*Où habites-tu?*' the Frenchman asked me. You could hear the money in his voice.

'*Où habites-tu?*' I replied

The Frenchman was not sure what was being done to him, whether he should be offended or amused.

My father came splashing towards me, the clothes clutched to his chest. It was rocky and difficult but he never once looked down.

'Wash-oh,' he cried to me. 'Wash-oh.'

Monsieur was a great wide bear, the hair on his chest pale and tight and curly. He sent a splash to me, a kind of kiss. I splashed him back again, like a mad creature, in a frenzy of happiness.

Then I joined my daddy in the middle of the stream where, in the midst of a shallow run, he was already beating my britches against the river rocks. He turned the left pocket out and left it hanging empty as a spaniel's ears. I arrived at his side as he turned his attention to the other where I had hidden the *assignat*.

I dared not say a word but set to rubbing at my collar while my father, not inches from me, coughed and passed his hand across his mouth. All the while he scrubbed my britches I knew he had the forgery inside his mouth.

At last the Frenchman left the river and, once on the cattle path, shook himself like a great wild dog. My father watched him as he returned to that great grey lumpy printery with its dragon's-back roof giving up its dew, mist rising, bleeding into the grey sky, and all its windows dark and secret, declaring its business was not for you to know.

When the Frenchman went inside my father finally spoke.

'That's the job then.'

He stared at me, pointing with his big burnt nose, like some fierce ostrich.

'What job?'

'Shut your mouth,' he said.

My father was a plucky man. But now I knew him seriously afraid, and his fear made him hard and unkind towards me.

'Tell no one,' he said. 'Here,' he said, throwing my britches at me like they were the skin of a dead beast. 'Here,' he handed me a bar of soap. And so we occupied ourselves as usual for a Sunday but I had never, on any day, in all my life, felt my heart so heavy or seen my father's eyes so dull and far away.

At last, we brought our clothes ashore and spread them on the gorse, hoping some breeze would come before the thunderstorm, to put it mildly.

V

It was a Sunday and the revolutionary factions of English printers dispersed themselves around the woods and riverbank in endless arguments about the rights of man. There, amidst Piggott's graveyard of wheels and broken axles my father and the Weasel conferred together. I fancy I can make an honest sketch of this – the single iron ring springing free of a rotting wheel, the humpbacked printery, the elder bushes, the oaks and poplars, the fuzz of hatch above the shallow stream, the Piggotts' cat rubbing around the Weasel's bandy legs, my lanky daddy with his hands pushing violently into the pants, and there, in Jack Larrit's white scrubbed hand, an *assignat*, all golden in the sun.

You, Sir, doubtless know that thousands of these *assignats* were forged in France and Britain and the Netherlands. Their purpose was to devalue the currency and thereby, by dint of ink and paper, destroy the beloved revolution. All I knew was that forgery was a capital offence. Witnessing the two printers examine Mr Watkins's work I understood I had betrayed the poor queer creature, trapped inside his cage.

Of course I should have confessed to Mr Watkins, but I wished him to like me and I was so ashamed that, on that Sunday night, I would not take my burin lessons. I said I was needed by my father.

'Indeed,' he said. His eyes were as frail as plover eggs, the prey of raging boys.

VI

Next morning the Weasel slung his misbegotten bedroll across his narrow shoulder and headed off into the woods without, it seemed, a word to anyone. Concerning this departure the printers – arguers and complainers to a man – made not a boo, although the absence of our best press man would make more work for everyone.

So it was – my father, a compositor of the first water, was removed from his tray of type and ordered to take the Weasel's place at the press. Da would now work with Chooka, five foot tall, a proud pernickety press man with chin and nose like Punch. My da's poor work would have Chooka in a rage, I knew it. But it was worse than that, for Piggott had contracted to produce a fancy chapbook on expensive linen paper, and the press men would be fined for spoilage.

Yet after the third sheet was thrown away, I witnessed little Chooka, who had a famous temper, reach up and pat my father's back while he, my da, grinned and shrugged in shame.

And still no one blamed the Weasel. Which meant – there was a Higher Cause. And although I was only a printer's devil – I understood that every one of these men was sworn to this cause in secret. They were comrades, solid as a wall.

Piggott ordered me to perform a hundred dirty chores including a message to the Dit'sum Swan which meant running across the stubbled fields with the beery harvesters calling me to them *cootchum cootchum coo*. I returned alive, with a fierce stitch in my side. I was late for Mr Watkins who was so kind to me I almost cried. I mean, he offered me the burin but how could I touch it after my betrayal.

'Sorry Mr Watkins.'

'You won't sit, boy?'

'No time Sir,' I said. I was certain the Weasel has gone to report Watkins to what you might call The Authorities. I thought, this fellow will never make his book of birds.

'What is it, boy? What happened?'

I thought, I have destroyed you. 'Nothing Sir,' I said.

He brushed his fine white hair back from his high forehead and considered me directly, long and slow until I felt my ears burn red.

'Sorry Sir,' I said and carefully manoeuvred his doings through the doorway.

'No time for Mr Watkins, boy?' he called.

I snaked away from him holding his piss pot high, pulling myself forward on my elbows.

That afternoon, when the men took their *tea-oh* on the steps, I drew my da away amongst the rotting wheels.

'Where did Mr Stokes go?' I asked, for I was not permitted to call him Weasel.

My father looked directly at my face which I imagine thus – dry lips parted, brow furrowed, heat showing on the cheeks and mottling down the smudgy neck. He reached a hand towards me and I went to hold it tight, but he ducked inside my cover and got his fingers in my ribs and when he had me wailing and shrieking without breath he grabbed me by my ankles and held me upside down so that my penny and two favourite stones fell to the ground.

I was upside down, blood filling my head like a bucket, crying loud – 'Where is he?'

'Good old Weasel is a journeyman,' my father said, setting me back the right way and helping me pick up my treasure. 'He's journeying. It's his nature,' he said, and gave me back my penny and another one besides, but even this did not persuade me. If the Weasel had been a French printer, that would be his nature sure enough – always on the road, travelling to jobs as far away as Switzerland. The French printers get paid for the time they are on the road, but the English printer has no such excitements and don't argue if you please, for this is true.

I knew my father was lying to me about the Weasel's nature, but if I was worried about the *assignat* and worried about Mr Watkins, I was worried about my daddy even more. If you were ever a boy you will remember the worries of a boy and how they swarm around you, and if I have had no reason to name mine for you until now, it does not mean they were not my constant companions. A boy's life, like a bird's life, is not what is generally assumed. For bird examples, watch the whitethroat gorging in the bramble patches, the warblers gluttoning amongst the blackberries, the blackcaps swinging off the rosehips, all in a panic to get fat before the summer ends. I, for my part, was forever in a fret lest my daddy die like my mother and leave me with no one to care for me, no one to save me from my cheeky nature, my mimicking, my fear of strangers on the road or in the woods at night, tramps, scamps, hermits, men who put paper noses on their face to frighten boys.

He was a dear tender man, and if he lied to me it was only because he loved me, and his eyes were moist when he gave me the penny and I put my hand inside his and walked back to the printery and worked very conscientious until tea.

Only two days later I was on the lanes with my cart of newspapers, and all around me bindweed, bluebell, chamomile and coltsfoot, ferns uncurling like a thought, white butterflies around my shoulders. All these things I could name, and draw, although not so well as I imagined, but they were my deep familiars and they must have given me that comfort a boy does not know he has until it is lost to him and he finds himself robbed of names by providence. There was heather, wild primrose, and around the corner of the rutted lane there came a man, walking, duck-footed, bandy-legged, a new white straw hat upon his head.

It was the Weasel and I saw him lift his staff and was afraid.

But of course – you guessed already – he greeted me with a punch to the arm and a sticky dust-covered humbug from his pocket. I sucked on my lolly and he picked a paper from my cart and read through Bunter's setting, finding fifteen faults in as many column inches. 'Home sweet home,' said he.

And after that, everything was calm, and I was able to visit Mr Watkins and take up his burin once again. It was still summer. My da and I saw glow-worms in the night. Then it was almost autumn. I found hazelnuts, hawthorn berries, and sycamore seeds amongst the leaves. The harvest was ending and as I cut across the paths to Dit'sum I would see the drunken workers at their games, throwing their reap hooks at a sheaf.

Now I had worn the sharp edges off my guilty conscience Mr Watkins became cooler to me once again. Just the same, he instructed me in what is called the crosshatch. After that I was finally permitted to attempt a creature. I chose a butterfly and he was very fierce about it but I knew I did it well enough because he recognized it as a silver-washed fritillary and taught me how to spell its name.

Then I was sent to deliver a box of wedding invitations to the next village after Dit'sum, I forget its name, and I cut across the commons towards its spire only to find myself set upon by a mob of harvesters who came rushing out of the deep shade of an oak and chased me across a ridge and down towards a sluggish stream and by the time I emerged on to a road through a hedgerow I was cut and bleeding and had lost my invitations and my courage. I set off crying, having no idea of where I was.

I passed a group of men with scythes who did not speak to me, although I suspected them of being the ones who chased me so I would not ask them the way. The hedgerows were high and it was impossible to get any bearing and when a carriage came along I had to press myself back into the blackthorn. It was a very large and black affair, doubtless with some fancy name I did not know, and I can remember no more than the single line of gold along its trim. When its gleaming back wheel was almost past me it stopped, leaving me imprisoned, so to speak, behind its bars. I would have ducked beneath the axle, but feared being squashed and so I remained, black-faced, slashed with red, pinned like a butterfly. I was thus easily identified by the gentleman inside the coach, who poked his smooth-shaven face out the window to consider me.

'Printer's devil,' called he. His voice was very Windsor arsehole and he had a hat like an admiral's.

I pulled my forelock although my father would have wished I did not. 'Yes Sir.'

'And where is your printery, devil?'

'Near Dit'sum, Sir.'

'Is it old Piggott who is your master?'

'Yes Sir.'

'Isn't it a little late in the year for bird nesting?'

'I was on a message Sir. I was chased Sir.'

'By whom were you chased?'

'Farmers Sir.'

He lowered his spectacles on his nose. It was a good-sized nose at that, not fat, but long and bossy. I could smell the wheat starch powder of his wig.

'Well Piggott's boy,' he said at last, 'let me give you a ride home.'

'I'm lost Sir. I don't know where to go.'

'Then you're an exceptionally fortunate devil,' said the gentleman who was – as he told me when I was sitting in his coach together with two gents whom I took to be his gamekeepers or something of that nature – Lord Devon himself. His men were Mr Benjamin and Mr Poole and they also told me I was a lucky little devil and please not to put my filthy hands on His Lordship's seats. I had never travelled in such style before and I sat up very straight with my bleeding legs held away from where they might touch anything and, with my hands clasped in my lap, I was left alone to enjoy the privilege of being able to see, above the hedgerows, a peregrine falcon sailing high up in the pale sky.

'That's a hawk, that is,' Mr Poole said. So he was not a gamekeeper, even if he did have leather patches on his jacket elbows. I looked to His Lordship to see what he would say it was.

'What do you say devil,' he asked me, smiling so his beaky face became suddenly very kind. 'Is it a hawk?'

'It's a peregrine falcon, Sir.'

'And what does a peregrine falcon eat, devil.'

'Birds, Sir. Although I heard it will eat a fish,' I said. 'My father saw one take an asp.'

'In fact, 'Mr Benjamin said, 'almost everything.'

'Including printers,' said Mr Poole.

His Lordship said nothing to that, but took an urgent and violent interest in what was outside his window – a great flock of birds, as it happened, about fifty of them, attacking the fruit inside the hedge. This seemed to engage his attention for a very long time.

'You are an enormous fool, Poole,' he said at last.

Waxwings, I thought, but did not say.

VII

Mrs Piggott held her locks back from her appley face.

Then Lord Devon clamped my upper arm, and together we marched to her doorway. She must have been astonished to see the Parrot in the company of a lord.

'Madame?' Devon asked. *'Je suppose que votre nom est Marie Piggott?'*

Mrs Piggott curtsied as if very pleased. *'Mais oui Monsieur,'* she said. 'That's me.'

'Did you know, Madame.' And here he used his cane to flick a dead oil beetle from her steps. 'Did you know Mrs Marie Piggott, that the Aliens Act of 1793 requires all foreigners to register with customs officials of the police office?'

'What?' she said.

But His Lordship was not waiting for an answer or an invitation, and he charged on up the steps with the Parrot still attached.

A small girlish cry from Mrs Piggott. A fast retreat.

Benjamin and Poole were hard behind us. Their hats were small black dinghies beached upon their wigless heads. All four of us pursued the fleeing mistress through the hall and into the dining room where she awaited us, standing alongside Mr Piggott, the pair of them in check against the panelled wall.

For a moment both residents and intruders paused to consider their positions. Then Piggott thrust himself one square forward, all eighteen stone, rubbing his hands together. What larks, he seemed to say.

'Bert Piggott at your service, Sir.' He would not tug his forelock. He gave his head a little bob instead.

His Lordship did not so much as lift an eyebrow. He removed his top coat, revealing himself in his waistcoat like some dangerous red-chested bird with gold embroidery around its buttonholes and pockets. An older boy would know to be afraid of all this Tory needlework, but I was thrilled to see Piggott in a state of terror.

His Lordship threw his coat across a chair. So peaceful did he seem that it was a wonder he did not call to have his slippers fetched.

'Have you registered your wife, Sir?'

Piggott lifted up his thirty-pound bucket of head and thrust out his chin. 'As you say, Sir, she is my wife.'

'Then you understand your legal position, Mr Piggott. You must take her to Exeter tomorrow. You will register her, do you understand?'

'She is as good as English, Sir, please.'

His Lordship must have been a funny fellow when with his mates, for he bugged his eyes up very big. 'She is *what* exactly?'

'In a manner of speaking, Sir.'

Devon turned to Poole and Benjamin. 'Mr Poole,' he said, 'you are the wicketkeeper. Mr Benjamin – you are silly mid-on.'

They are playing cricket now, I thought. His Lordship retrieved his coat, a silky thing as light as butterfly wings, and tossed it to Poole. 'Bees sting,' he said. 'Ants bite. Do keep an eye out.'

This was not cricket or any other game I ever heard of and the hidden language was very frightening. I knew it was time to see my father. However, His Lordship, as if reading my mind, lifted a finger and raised his eyebrows and I understood I was under his orders.

'So I shall take her to Exeter,' said Mr Piggott, shoving his hands into his apron pockets. 'I do business in Exeter so it is quite convenient.'

'So, this is your property, Piggott. *En avez-vous hérité? Ou avez-vous volé une banque?*'

'I'm afraid I don't parler the lingo, Sir.'

'Your house. A lovely old place,' said His Lordship, running his hand admiringly over the tight curling grain of the panels. 'Nicholas Owen,' he said.

'Sir?'

'Are you a Catholic yourself, perhaps?'

'I am Sir, yes.'

'Poor old Owen was a Jesuit, I think. They were bad times for Catholics, when he designed this place.'

'Could I fetch you some refreshment, Sir. A brandy?'

'Brandy?' Devon raised his cane, and smashed it down upon the panelling. Mrs Piggott was not the only one to flinch. 'No one told you your house was famous?' he asked, not looking at Piggott but tapping on the wall with his knuckles.

'Famous Sir. Ha ha.'

'Famous Sir,' said Lord Devon, who was now caressing the house as if it were a horse, casting an extraordinary smile across his shoulder at the Piggotts. You would think he loved them half to death.

There was a sharp clear click.

'There you are, Madame,' he said, sliding a small panel sideways. 'Here's a nice place for your prayer book.'

'Monsieur?'

'*Un endroit parfait pour cacher un livre de prières* if you were here two hundred years ago.'

'Good Lord,' cried Piggott, stepping forward urgently. 'Good heavens, Sir. Who would credit it?' He was so set on inspecting the secret cubbyhole that he would have jammed his big booby head inside, but his majesty detained him.

'Ha ha, Sir. Nice place to hide a bottle, Your Lordship.' He wiped himself with a rag, leaving printer's ink upon his neck.

His Lordship smiled so sweet, he might have been the printer's mother. 'Oh there is plenty more than this, Piggott,' he cried. 'All manner of holes and chapels contrived within no less skill and industry. They've hidden traitors in this house, Mr Piggott. Can you imagine?'

'Good grief.'

'Oh yes, Mr Piggott, in chimneys.'

'Chimneys Sir,' said Piggott. 'I have a lovely brandy. Let me fetch it now.'

The fireplace was set and ready as it always was and it was certainly the talk of chimneys that drew Lord Devon to inspect it. Piggott hovered at his back, a white fat presence which His Lordship seemed at first put out by, but then.

'Ah yes, Sir,' he beamed. 'A brandy would do the trick.'

Piggott bobbed his head and winked his eye and tapped his nose and soon I heard him on the stairway, an unexpected direction for the brandy bottle.

His Lordship nodded amiably at Mrs Piggott. She tucked her curls inside her hat as if she might, in doing this, make herself more English.

'Printer's devil,' he said to me. 'Fetch back your master. Have him bring the brandy now.'

I used the door through which Piggott had departed and immediately found him on the staircase. He had lifted up a set of three steps, all fitted to together like a zigzag lid, and in the dark space there revealed I saw the back of the one-armed Frenchman who had reappeared last night at dinner.

Said I, to no one, 'He wants his brandy, Sir.'

The man with one arm pushed Piggott violently. And as the stair returned to its rightful place, Piggott took me by my neck. I thought he meant to finish me, but he opened a door and forced me down stone steps into the dark. Never once lightening the grip, which I took to be both a punishment and a warning for the future, he pushed me very cruelly up the stairs and I barked my shins and cut my hands upon the stone.

On my return I found Lord Devon kneeling before the fireplace. Behind him Mrs Piggott wrung her hands and silently beseeched her husband please to save her from what I did not know.

'Do you mind?' His Lordship asked politely, holding up his flint to indicate he wished to start the fire.

'Oh no Sir, please Sir,' cried Piggott in alarm.

'No Sir?' queried His Lordship who now seemed in a very jolly frame of mind. 'Please Sir, no Sir, is it?'

'It's a summer's day, Sir.'

'Oh I do like getting warm,' Lord Devon said. He struck his flint to the tinder which ignited fast as gunpowder and the kindling – which had lived a lifetime in the house – fairly leapt to its own destruction.

His Lordship stood, brushing down his stockinged knees.

'Now,' he said, 'that drink you promised.'

Piggott, you will remember, was a big man with a big head and he was, even when malicious, slow as a cow in his manners. By now, however, both of the Piggotts were in a state they no longer could disguise. Mrs Piggott left for the scullery, Mr Piggott ran after her. They returned by different doors, each holding a different-shaped glass.

'Here's a riddle,' said Lord Devon, considering the choice. 'Bless me, if I won't have them both.' He clasped his hands behind his back where the fire was crackling fiercely, exploding in the way of dry pine logs showering tiny grenades into the room.

Piggott filled the glasses with clearly trembling hands.

'Thirsty weather,' said His Lordship, raising both in a toast. He sipped. He giggled. Then, in sheer delight at his own wickedness, he threw the brandy on the fire which now leaped at him, licking with its yellow tongue, leaving a glowing bite upon his wig which Piggott, in his panic, attempted to pat out.

For this he was poked right in the belly.

Lord Devon removed his burning wig, astonishing me with the hard bony brightness he revealed. He patted out the damage, keeping his eye on me as if I had some news to give. But it was only the genius forger Watkins I was thinking of and I would not betray him now.

It was hot inside the dining room and no one would move away from the fire. To admit the heat, I saw, would be to confess to something worse. Lord Devon rested his gloved hand on my shoulder and carelessly poked his stick into the fire. The stick was handsome black oak with a silver top to it, but he used it like a common poker, jabbing it and banging it, until it was charred and glowing on the tip which he showed to the Piggotts with no nice meaning, I was sure.

'Your stick is burning.'

'So is your hearth, Sir.' And with this he gave a good hard jab into the heart of the fire and Piggott watched dumbly as the burning logs were knocked on to his dining-room floor and the charred walking stick was stabbed again and again into the hearth as if it were a spear to kill a dragon.

'You see, Piggott,' His Lordship said. He was having a great old time – careless of the choking smoke, the soot on both his face and hands. As for his silver stick, he now reversed it so he could use it like a navvy's crowbar.

'You see,' he said, and – completely indifferent to the heat and burning wood – thrust in his hand like a farmer at a calving, and drew into the light a fist full of smouldering currency, not *assignats*.

The dreadful Lord Devon, who was later paid a bung by Mr Pitt for services to King and country, held up his treasure – pale white English notes, five pounds every one.

Behind my back I heard a noise, and turned to see both Piggotts on the floor, poor devils, him kneeling, her curled up in a ball, her stockings showing.

VIII

As a lizard drops its tail to save its life, so must the Parrot sacrifice his sleeve to escape Lord Devon's grip. Out the door I fled into a green and inky evening, not a living soul in sight except the house martins scything across the sky. I stumbled coughing, spitting, down the dark side of the mansion, flushing a quail from beneath the pussy willow. The bird was much more wily than the boy, for while I was heading straight for Watkins's secret hole, she pretended a broken wing and hobbled and fluttered towards the river, intending to lead me away from her nest.

I had reached the stinging nettles, just before the door, when the designated wicketkeeper caught me.

Mr Benjamin dropped on me like a spider, wrapping his huge hands around my chest, binding me to him, so close I could smell the inside of his nose.

'Got you,' he cried.

The Parrot slid right through his nasty knot, surrendering the

remainder of his shirt. I feinted towards the house, cut back towards the river, crashed through the pussy willow where Mr Poole was waiting for me.

'Got you.'

He had fair hair and blue eyes and a red blush to his cheeks like a toy soldier. He was slight but as hard and stitched together as a leather casing of a ball, and though I kicked and spat and scratched at him, there was no escape from the bony shackle around my wrist.

'I'll break your frigging arm,' he said.

'Where is he?' That was Lord Devon, hollering from the steps.

'Here Sir,' called Poole, dragging me brutally, skidding me on my knees, a half-skun hare.

'Not him, you fool!' Lord Devon had a captive of his own – Mrs Piggott, tripping and stumbling after him.

'Not him, not him!'

'Who Sir? '

'Try to remember,' cried Lord Devon. 'Lord Jesus save me, who did we come to get?'

'Piggott Sir? Where is he?'

'I do not *know*,' His Lordship cried, advancing with his still-burning stick. Poole jerked me backwards and away. The red-waistcoated dervish continued closing and was only halted by an awful bang. *Deus ex machina*, as they say. And what a *machina* – a hot wash of light bathed His Lordship's upturned face and there, for all to see, his cold gleaming rage was caught and held by a writhing rope of fire running along the ridge line of the house.

'Shit,' cried the member of the House of Lords, and I had time to be astonished he would speak like that.

The printers came running down their stairs, tumbling into the evening, walking backwards, faces illuminated, necks craned, their gazes on the smoking humpback ridge. The first line of flame had died, but what was left behind were three conflagrations, flames bursting from three beds of tiles.

Mr Benjamin clipped me across the ears. The show continued –

exploding squibs now bloomed like wild flowers in the gloom. These also whacked my eardrum, five times, as hard as anvils. Then came bursts of fire, broken tiles erupting from hips and valleys and places not in my view.

The sky was now a cloudless shade of green and as Benjamin dragged me from the hail of heavy tiles, I feared for Mr Watkins's life. Poor Watkins – he had dreaded fire amongst all things, and now there were at least eight separate fires all erupting from his roof. Then – from where I do not know – a great flock of bats burst forth, and in amongst the bats, at first almost indistinguishable from them, a thousand sheets of paper tipped with Pentecostal tongues. It was as if Piggott's brain had exploded through its bony casing and all its greed and argumentative confusion, its secrets and whispers and smugglers' boats, had burst in smithereens and scattered through the darkening air, landing like stinging wasps upon our arms and faces, and through all of this my captor was transfixed, as if he had seen the assumption of the Virgin Mary in the Devon sky.

All nature was disturbed. The nightjars, who would have normally stayed quiet till dark, came diving and flapping around their territories, swooping down above Lord Devon's smoking wig. In flight they made a soft 'coohwick' and a dreadful hand-clapping with their panicked wings. The printers were equally disturbed, shouting, running to the stream with buckets.

I politely asked to be let go.

Poole knew not what to do. He watched Lord Devon who, like someone drunk or dreaming, stared at the men carrying water into the house.

Then came a great soft thump like a chaff bag thrown out of a loft.

'Good God,' cried Poole.

On the ground beside the steps I saw the broken body of a man. It was Piggott. When Benjamin dragged me to his side I saw the printer's big white carcass twisted like a doll, his eyes wide open, the most horrific look of triumph on his face. This expression was not diminished one iota by the wailing of his wife to whom he spoke impatiently. '*Marie, il n'y a plus ici aucune preuve. Tout est brûlé.*'

Lord Devon quickly decided Mrs Piggott was worth not a damn to him. He set her free to moan.

'Fool,' he cried to Piggott, as burning five-pound notes fell to the dark ground like cherry blossom. 'Fool, it is *raining* evidence.' Then: 'Let the house burn,' he ordered the printers, but they were Jacobins and they hated him and all his kind.

Understanding his position, Devon rushed to his carriage from which he produced a heavy tangle of chain and threw it hard against the ground.

'That's one lesson for you,' he shouted at the men.

He disappeared a moment and emerged waving two pistols. 'And here's another.' One of these pistols was quickly taken by Benjamin whilst Devon confronted the bucket brigade with the other.

'What's that you say?' he cried. 'What's that?'

He struck Bunter on the shoulder and by dint of a great deal of barrel-poking 'persuaded' the bucket brigade to stand in line while he walked up and down, reviewing them like Grenadiers.

Not once taking his eyes off his captives, he ordered Benjamin to pass Poole his pistol so the latter's hands were free to fetter these good men's ankles with the chain.

While Devon snatched evidence from the sky, my flame-licked father smiled at me. He shrugged, dear man, dear father.

'Come,' called Devon to Poole. 'You can help as well. You're not a bloody nursemaid.'

'But I have the boy,' said Poole.

'Yes, yes, yes,' cried Devon.

My daddy was tossing his head at me, as if he had a flea in his ear.

'I have the boy, Sir,' said Poole.

'Devil,' Lord Devon said, 'I will blow your brains out if you move.'

'Yes Sir,' I said.

Chooka tossed his head. He meant that I should flee.

'Run,' my father cried.

Devon swung around. But now Poole shrieked. He pointed, and

who – even Lord Devon – could not follow his gaze? A fiery angel had appeared upon the roof, its hair ablaze and streaming upwards, fire right down its spine. It ran along the ridge and flew into the air, smashing into an old oak through whose ancient branches it crashed noisily before passing out of sight. Three others followed, forgers rising like hatchlings in the night, their cries beyond the edge of nightmare.

'Run,' my father cried. 'Parrot, run.'

I heard the shot go past my ear and Devon screaming. I ran like a rabbit, through the smoke and haze, through the gloom, through the field of broken wheels. The men were cheering me, a pistol roared. I ran, shirtless, into the open woods, through the broken bracken, into dark, so many years ago. ■

From Peter Carey's forthcoming novel, Parrot & Olivier in America.

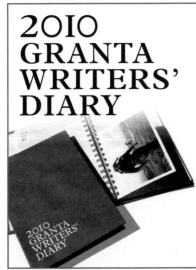

CONTRIBUTORS

Nelson Algren's 'The Lightless Room' is taken from *Entrapment and Other Writings*, a collection of previously unseen work to be published in 2009 by Seven Stories Press to celebrate the centenary of Algren's birth. 'The Lightless Room' was first performed at the Steppenwolf Theater in Chicago on April 6, 2009, in *Nelson Algren Live* with Willem Dafoe in the lead role. Nelson Algren died in 1981.

Peter Carey's 'Parrot' is taken from his new novel, *Parrot & Olivier in America,* published by Hamish Hamilton in Australia in November 2009, Faber and Faber in the UK, Knopf in the US and Random House Canada in 2010.

Sandra Cisneros is the founder of the Alfredo Cisneros del Moral Foundation, the Elvira Cisneros Award and the Macondo Foundation, all of which work on behalf of creative writers. She is currently at work on a collection of essays, *Writing in My Pajamas,* and a short-story collection, *Infinito.*

Rich Cohen's books include *Tough Jews, Sweet and Low* and his latest, *Israel Is Real* (Jonathan Cape/Farrar, Straus and Giroux). He lives in rural splendour in Connecticut.

Bei Dao is currently Professor of Humanities at the Chinese University in Hong Kong. In winter 2009 New Directions will publish his forthcoming poetry collection, *The Rose of Time: New & Selected Poems.*

Don DeLillo has published fourteen novels and three stage plays. 'Remembrance' was written for *Nelson Algren Live* at the Steppenwolf Theater and appeared in the evening's printed programme (Seven Stories Institute). DeLillo's fifteenth novel, *Point Omega,* will be published in 2010 by Picador in the UK and Scribner in the US.

Tony D'Souza grew up on Chicago's North Side, the setting of many of his short stories, as well as scenes in his novels *Whiteman* and *The Konkans* (Portobello Books/ Mariner Books).

Stuart Dybek is Distinguished Writer in Residence at Northwestern University. He was born and raised on Chicago's South Side and has published two collections of poetry and three short-story collections, including *I Sailed with the Magellen* and *The Coast of Chicago* (Picador).

Aleksandar Hemon was born in Sarajevo in 1964 and has lived in Chicago since 1992. He is the author, most recently, of *Love & Obstacles* (Picador/Riverhead).

Thom Jones is the author of the short-story collections *The Pugilist At Rest*, *The Cold Snap* and *Sonny Liston was a Friend of Mine* (Faber/Little, Brown).

Alex Kotlowitz's books include *There Are No Children Here* and, most recently, *Chicago: Never a City So Real* (Crown). He teaches writing at Northwestern University.

Dinaw Mengestu was born in Ethiopia and raised in Chicago. He is the author of *The Beautiful Things*

that Heaven Bears (Riverhead), published in the UK as *Children of the Revolution* (Jonathan Cape).

Richard Powers's tenth novel, *Generosity*, will be published by Atlantic in the UK in early 2010 and Farrar, Straus and Giroux in the US in late 2009.

Ben Ratliff has been a pop and jazz critic at the *New York Times* since 1996. His most recent book is *The Jazz Ear: Conversations over Music* (Times Books).

George Saunders grew up in Oak Forest, a suburb of Chicago. His books include the short-story collection *In Persuasion Nation* and a collection of essays, *The Braindead Megaphone* (Bloomsbury/Riverhead). He teaches at Syracuse University.

James Schuyler was born in Chicago in 1923. He received the 1981 Pulitzer Prize for poetry for *The Morning of the Poem* (Farrar, Straus and Giroux). He died in Manhattan in 1991.

Elaine Showalter is Professor Emeritus of English and Avalon Professor of the Humanities at Princeton University. Her new book is *A Jury of Her Peers: American Women Writers from Anne Bradstreet to Annie Proulx* (Virago/Knopf).

Wole Soyinka was imprisoned in Nigeria in 1967 for his opposition to the dictatorship. His books include *Aké: The Years of Childhood* and, most recently, *You Must Set Forth at Dawn* (Methuen/Random House). In 1986 he became the first African to receive the Nobel Prize in Literature.

Neil Steinberg is a columnist at the *Chicago Sun-Times*, where he has been on staff since 1987. His memoir, *Drunkard*, was published by Dutton in 2008.

Maria Venegas was born in Mexico and emigrated to the United States when she was four years old. She grew up in Chicago and currently lives in New York where she is at work on her first book.

Camilo José Vergara was born in Chile and moved to the United States in 1965. After becoming a photographer in New York, he began to focus on urban architecture, developing a methodical approach to photographing inner cities. His most recent book is *How the Other Half Worships* (Rutgers University Press). He is now completing *Harlem: The Unmaking of a Ghetto.*

Anne Winters's most recent poetry collection is *The Displaced of Capital* (University of Chicago Press). She currently lives in Chicago.

Jeffrey Yang is the author of the poetry collection, *An Aquarium* (Graywolf Press), and has translated Su Shi's *East Slope* (Ugly Duckling Presse). He works as an editor for New Directions.

Contributing Editors
Diana Athill, Peter Carey, Sophie Harrison, Isabel Hilton, Blake Morrison, John Ryle, Lucretia Stewart, Edmund White.